AF394641

the theatre of apparitions

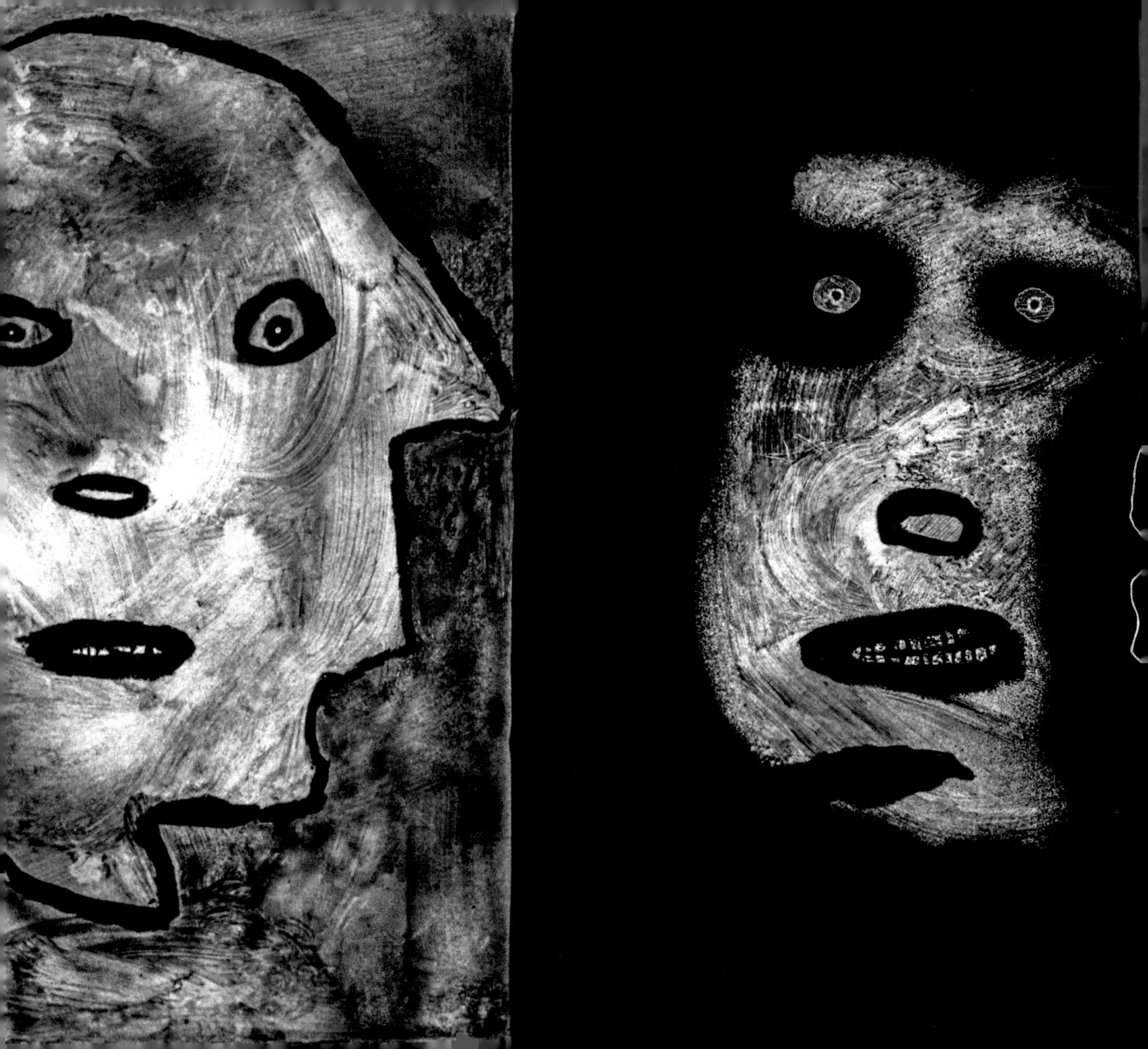

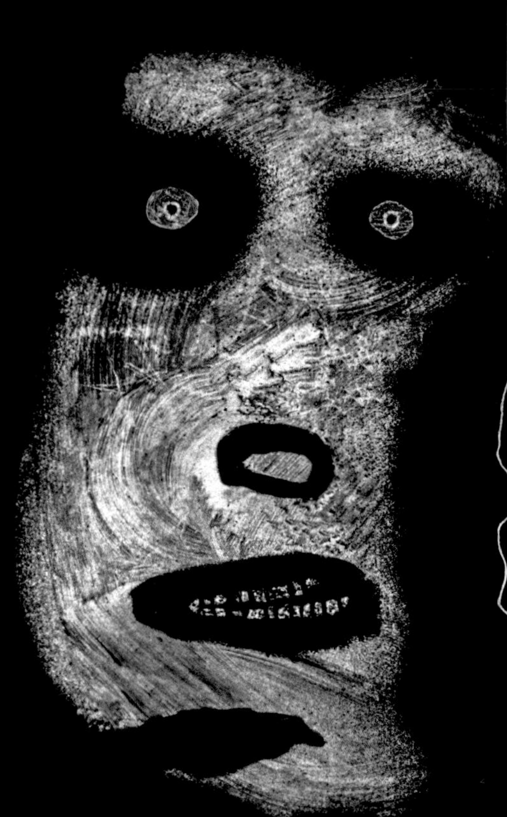

the theatre of apparitions

ROGER BALLEN

in collaboration with Marguerite Rossouw

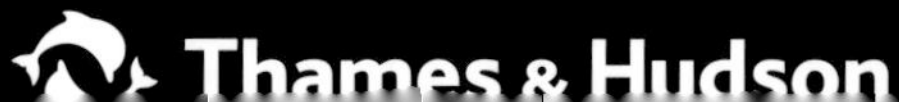
Thames & Hudson

*It has become apparent to me that all forms of life have
a unique spirit. If we become a spirit after our short stint
on Earth, then it is not inconceivable that everything that
has ever lived will become an apparition. The Universe
is a very big place, so there should be room for all.*

ROGER BALLEN

preface

ROGER BALLEN

Traditionally speaking, photography documents and validates our perception of physical reality. For me, throughout my career, the camera has always been by definition the *camera obscura,* a kind of opening into the dark chamber of my murky interior.

The images that make up the photographs in this book, which I have titled *The Theatre of Apparitions*, are a combination of our inner and outer worlds.

The first of these kinds of images was taken in an abandoned women's prison during shooting of my film *Memento Mori* in 2004. A former prisoner had painted over the windowpanes of one of the cells and had then drawn figures into the black paint, leaving herself completely isolated with only the barren cement walls and dim light to comfort her (*fig. 1*).

Shortly after this discovery, I began to recreate images similar to those in the prison using glass windows. These initial images typically featured objects placed in front of windowpanes that had been painted white (*figs. 2, 3* and *4*).

Early in 2007, Marguerite Rossouw began working with me as my photographic assistant and took a great interest in this project. She had extensive experience in painting techniques, as well as a profound understanding of my aesthetic. Consequently, the creation of these images

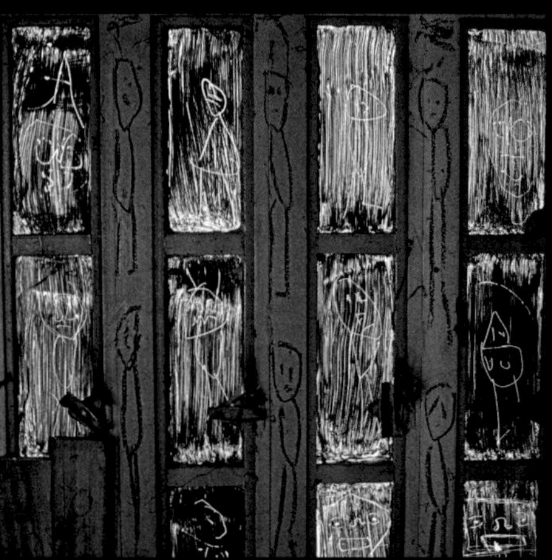

fig. 1 · *Prison Windows*, 2004

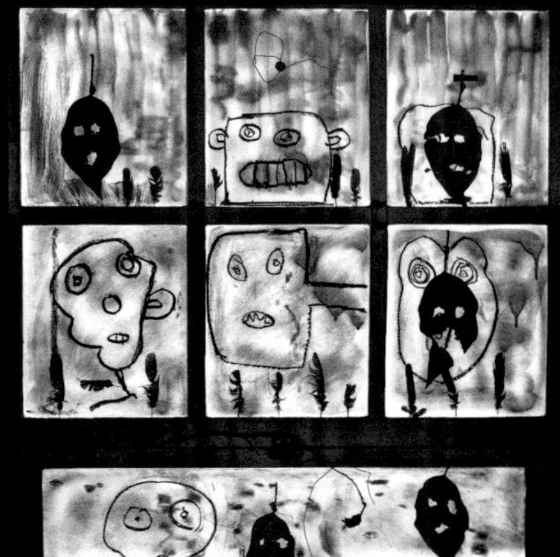

fig. 2 · *Dream Drawings*, 2006

was a combined effort. Through trial and error using various techniques – some more successful than others – we were eventually able to establish methods that culminated in imagery of a new dimension.

We experimented with numerous paints, epoxies, emulsions, brushes, etc. to allow us to achieve the otherworldliness that we desired. As we wanted to produce images that could be photographed immediately, we were not concerned about preserving the works, which allowed us to reuse the same glass windows over and over again. Therefore, I had a very short period of time to photograph the finished image before it would disintegrate. Like most other photographs, these ones preserve the transient.

The images were rarely planned and were instead the results of a spontaneous process in which the choice of material sometimes created magical and inconceivable outcomes. I often compare the process to the one in a darkroom where an image emerges mysteriously in the liquid developer.

As all of these photographs were taken without flash, it was crucial that there was sufficient light from behind the camera. If the light in the room was not sufficient, the images would lose their luminosity. These photographs had to capture, in one five-hundredth of a second, an image with lasting value. Every piece of information had to be brought together in that single moment.

Initially I took the photographs with my Rolleiflex 6cm x 6cm film camera, which I have used since 1982 to the present day. However, as the windows were rectangular and not square, it became apparent that I had to resort to another

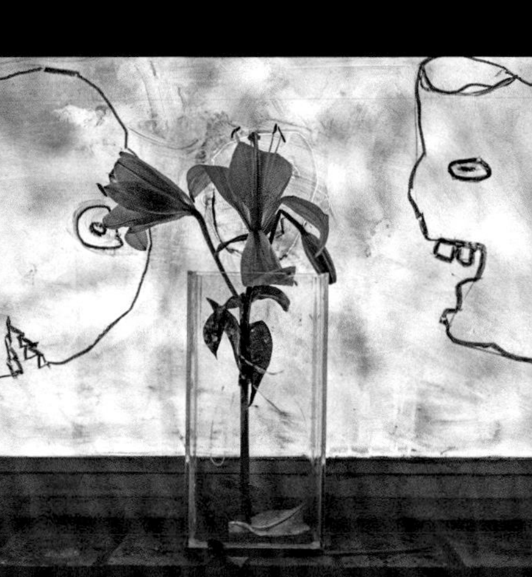

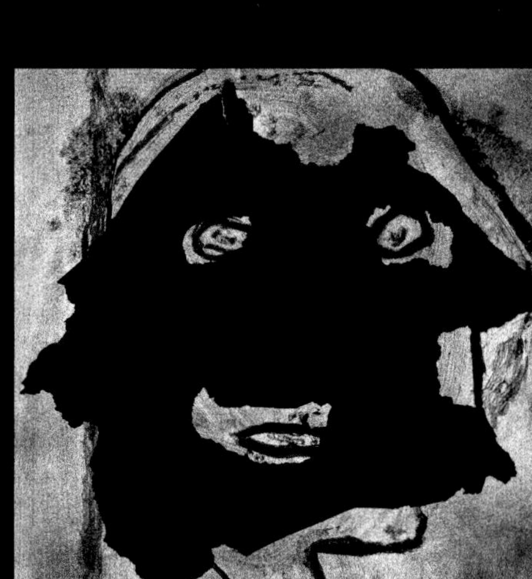

fig 3 · Giggles, 2004

fig 4 · Effigy, 2007

format: a Mamiya 4.5cm x 6cm film camera. As I wanted to produce sharp, non-grainy images, I used T-Max 100 film.

Although this style of work might be viewed as purely drawing, it is crucial to realize that, without my decades of experience in black-and-white art photography, these images would not have been possible. My deep understanding of the essential ability of the camera to integrate form and content was pivotal in creating this unique imagery.

During this same period 2005–2013, I also produced my books *Boarding House* and *Asylum of the Birds*, in which drawing and painting began to dominate my photographs (*fig 5*). As a result of the inherently innovative nature of *The Theatre of Apparitions* and the fact that we were constantly improving and transforming our technique, the project took much longer than was anticipated.

The world within these pages, and the images that arise out of them, are old. Inhabiting a kind of amniotic darkness of the womb, the images occupy a perceptual realm – a fragmented world of part-objects where fears of annihilation and chaotic perceptions merge reality and fantasy, self and other. These silhouettes are flickering archetypes originating from the collective unconscious of humankind. They call to mind weathered, Palaeolithic cave paintings: some of the recurring relationships within this book – that of

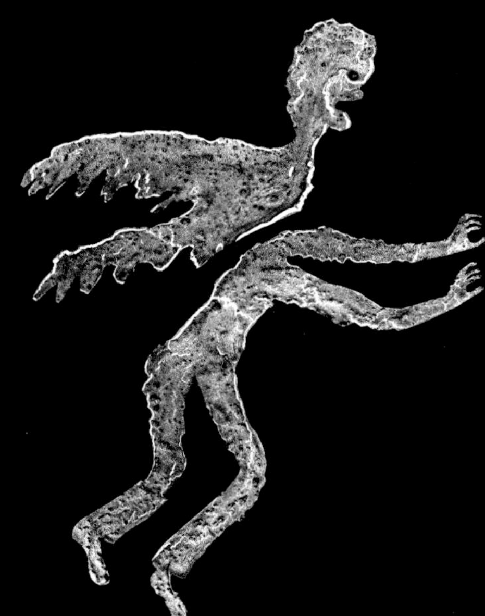

human and canine, bird and beast – invoke familiar, primordial bonds in the viewer. They operate as a kind of mythological 'memory fossil'; they hark back to ancient shamanistic visions and sacred symbols that we have inherited and embedded within ourselves through the process of evolution.

These images share a complete absence of conscious awareness. They are all, in some way or another, pictographs made into photographs: they are born out of the unbearable, the unacceptable and even the unthinkable. They depict characters that live in the depths or peripheries of consciousness where they have been repressed, extruded or exiled. At times they may escape and visit us, projecting themselves onto the screen of our mind's eye. We may ignore them, watch with intrigue or dispel them as nightmares entering as a curse from afar or as signs of psychosis. But the apparitions are in fact answers to a calling of absence; a comforting gift from deep within ourselves or from a more spiritual realm elsewhere. They are hallucinations making up for that which is lost, and they offer contact with that which we desire but do not possess.

I have entitled this book *The Theatre of Apparitions* because I wish to convey the theatrical mechanics in this introspective experience: the way in which mental forms of life – dreams, the imagination, memories or meditation – act out on stage for the psyche. Often, especially when we allow our mind to bubble up and 'dance' in its free-flowing stream, we find ourselves watching these performances. It is as if our psyche is no longer felt to be our own, and we become audience members sitting in on the wondrous entertainment provided by the diverse expressions of our internal world.

The visions presented are glimpses of parts otherwise invisible to the eye; the stuff of dreams made perceptible to us through the power of the photographic lens. Now embodied as living artworks, they are reminiscent of cave paintings and, like the unconscious itself, they are timeless. In keeping with my profession as a geologist, these works deem me an excavator of the mental. This is a journey deep into the psyche, like the journey of the Aborigines who penetrated the remotest parts of the Australian outback, not to find dreams themselves, but the origin of dreams instead.

It is my hope that the images in this book will connect viewers to their core selves, to crack their defence mechanisms, to unite one part of their mind to the other, to find the spirits that live inside us and to realize that what we refer to as reality is essentially delusionary.

Ladies and gentlemen, I invite you into my theatre, where adventure awaits for the eyes.

introduction

COLIN RHODES

These are spirit drawings.

In a way.

They are the permanent record of a bubbling up of deeper, more primal psychological realms made manifest on a surface through the interaction between a particular individual and fluid, physical materials.

Or, rather, they are photographs of visual reports from some psychic elsewhere. Each image is tied to a particular time, place and experience that has now been superseded. And the accumulation of textures, smells, smears, scratches, caresses and thoughts that were once part of the fabric of the original artefact are no more. However, they linger ghost-like in the photographic image. With the pressing of the shutter release, an apparition was created and fixed in an instant. Until that act of reification, everything had existed only in the world of the artist Roger Ballen. These residual apparitions, though, work on all of us, insinuating their realities into each of our psyches. From this moment, a series of new encounters is made possible.

There is something of theatre in all of this. Not the regular dramatic theatre of proscenium and auditorium in which a codified dramatic performance is witnessed by a detached audience, but the theatre of encounter and participation. Perhaps it is similar to the operating theatre or the theatre of war? Or maybe it is something more akin to the so-called 'Theatre of Cruelty' theorized by the French writer and artist Antonin Artaud, which is also connected to a more primal kind of performance. Believing that Western theatre had become ossified and enervated, Artaud spoke of the need to regain a 'naked theatre language' that would 'allow us to transgress the ordinary limits of art and words actively – that is to say, magically – to produce a kind of total creation *in real terms*, where man must reassume his position between dreams and events.'[1] In such a theatre, the boundaries between actor and audience would be blurred and experience would be active, not passive. Each performance would begin anew and be unrepeatable, since it would always exist only in the moment and in the specific context created by the particular human presences. This is the way in which Ballen's apparitions are made and remade, both individually and as series (or acts). Their agency resides in the participatory encounter they demand and the psychological depths they evince.

As to technique, Ballen's apparitions seem to mirror Artaud's desire
to pursue in his theatre both outer and inner worlds, created not through
description but rather by the introduction of 'temptations' and 'vacuums'.[2]
Ballen's apparitions exist in indeterminate spaces, at once claustrophobically
shallow and infinite voids. His characters interact – with each other and with
us, the viewers – meaningfully, authentically, but without hope of closure or
reassurance: this is also reminiscent of the theatre of Samuel Beckett. Ballen
blends absurdism, sexuality, violence, cruelty and humour. This mixture is
important, since it is the stuff of both lived experience and dreams, and via
these methods Ballen prods our hopes, our desires and our fears. All of this
reflects cruelty in the way Artaud conceived it, as 'the sense of hungering
after life, cosmic strictness, relentless necessity.'[3] And Artaud could just
as well have been referring to the seven acts of Ballen's theatre of apparitions
when he said, 'Neither Humour, Poetry nor Imagination mean anything
unless they re-examine man organically through anarchic destruction.'[4]

Ballen's theatre belongs emphatically to the carnivalesque, as described
in the writings of the Russian theorist Mikhail Bakhtin. In his critique of the
work of Rabelais, Bakhtin reaches back to the Medieval European practice
of carnival, in which for a brief moment each year the strict feudal social
order was fractured and the world turned upside down, so to speak. Carnival
is a kind of communal performance that exists at the borders of life and art.
It is characterized by excess, grotesqueness and the suspension of (social)
order. In Ballen's apparitions, as in carnival, bodies are always immanent,
mutable. They exist in states of constant becoming, without resolution and
as often as not in fluid processes of intermingling. Living, thinking skulls
are fractured and their invisible contents are scooped out by a disembodied
hand. A breathing figure breathes fearful existence into face upon face, or
spews ectoplasmic lightning into the very brains of a rank of giants. The
insides and outsides of bodies become impossibly confused. Even the laws
of speciation are laid waste as hybrid animals form, reform and conjugate.
Are these devotional or blasphemous scenes? Are they simple reports of
otherness or transgressive provocations? Moreover, how do we, as viewers,
measure our interior lives, our motives and actions against these tangible
apparitions? Ballen says simply, 'the work actually makes people generally
uneasy because it affects their concepts of normality and order.'[5]

The co-extensiveness of bodies and their parts is a key signifier in the
created worlds of Ballen's apparitions. Their grotesqueness causes viewers
to compare them with and to confront their own selves, which are also in
a constant state of becoming in the worlds they inhabit. As Bakhtin argues:

'Contrary to modern canons, the grotesque body is not separated
from the rest of the world. It is not a closed, completed unit; it is
unfinished, outgrows itself, and transgresses its own limits. The
stress is laid on those parts of the body that are open to the outside
world, that is, the parts through which the world enters the body
or emerges from it, or through which the body itself goes out to
meet the world. This means that the emphasis is on the apertures
or convexities, or on various ramifications and offshoots: the open
mouth, the genital organs, the breasts, the phallus, the potbelly,
the nose. The body discloses its essence as a principle of growth
which exceeds its own limits only in copulation, pregnancy,
childbirth, the throes of death, eating, drinking, or defecation.
This is the ever unfinished, ever creating body.'[6]

We see all of this at work in Ballen's theatre of apparitions.

Ballen's figures are primitively rendered. In spite of the nature of his
primary medium, photography, in his drawings he never reaches for
mimetic representation, preferring instead the directness of the more
or less unmediated image from within. In this he is a fellow traveller with
the French painter Jean Dubuffet, with whom he also shares an interest in
what Dubuffet calls *Art brut* and what has come to be known in English as
'outsider art'. A contemporary of Artaud, Dubuffet argues that 'art is another
means of cognition' that traverses the boundaries between dream and
reality: 'its ways are clairvoyance'.[7] Painting, he says (and this also holds
for the drawing process that lies behind Ballen's apparitions), is also
a language, and furthermore one that is 'far more immediate' than words.
But it is a primal language, closer to things themselves and almost
incantatory in its operations. He claims that painting and drawing
'can more or less evoke things at will, that is, with more or less presence.
At any degree between being and non-being'. Moreover, he says, painting
'opens wider gates to the inner dancing of the painter's mind.'[8]

According to Dubuffet, compliance with social dictates and norms
dims and ultimately extinguishes this power, so people who might produce
such works in anything approaching a pure form would only be found in
places situated outside or in the margins of the dominant culture. Dubuffet
found his examples of outsider art primarily in the psychiatric hospitals
and spiritualist salons of Europe in the 1940s. Ballen encountered his in
the rural *dorps* (small towns) and inner city 'boarding houses' and squats

of South Africa in the 1980s and 1990s. This discovery resulted first in
Ballen's increased interest in incorporating these drawings and constructions
in photographs that maintained something of a documentary impulse.
Then, he says, 'around 1999, drawing started to come into the pictures
with a vengeance. It was round about this time that I started to let the
people make drawings; I asked people to make drawings on the wall.
And then I made these photographs. In a way the issue of *Art brut* in the
pictures wasn't necessarily a conceptual one but an experiential one.'[9]
The encounter also reawakened Ballen's own urge to make marks, to draw;
a practice he pursues intensively and with immediacy so that his images
might carry more or less unmediated messages from psychic depths.

Ballen says his work 'is about the human condition in a place. It's
a place in my mind. Reflecting the human condition in Roger Ballen's
condition.'[10] His drawings are perhaps the purest, most direct expressions
of this. However, in spite of the immediacy of their construction and unlike
Dubuffet's paintings, the drawings which constitute Ballen's apparitions
are accessible only in their spectral form – indeed they now only exist in that
form – placing a further layer of separation between viewer and thing in itself.
Yet, as spectral images, these things are somehow doubly tantalizing and
immediate in their effect. Humans, after all, tend to be drawn irresistibly
to ghosts.

1   Antonin Artaud, *The Theatre and Its Double*, London: Alma Classics, 2013, p.65
(emphasis in the original)
2   *Ibid.*, p.64
3   *Ibid.*, p.73
4   *Ibid.*
5   C. Rhodes, interview with Roger Ballen, 14 January 2016
6   Mikhail Bakhtin, *Rabelais and His World*. Trans. by Helene Iswolsky. Bloomington:
Indiana University Press, 1984, p.26
7   Jean Dubuffet, 'Art Brut Preferred to the Cultural Arts' (1949), in Mildred Glimcher and
Jean Dubuffet, *Jean Dubuffet: Towards an Alternative Reality*, New York: Abbeville Press, 1987,p.102
8   Jean Dubuffet, 'Anticultural Positions' (1951), *Ibid.*, p.131
9   C. Rhodes, interview with Roger Ballen, 14 January 2016
10   *Ibid.*

ACT ONE

persona

Super Ego, 2010

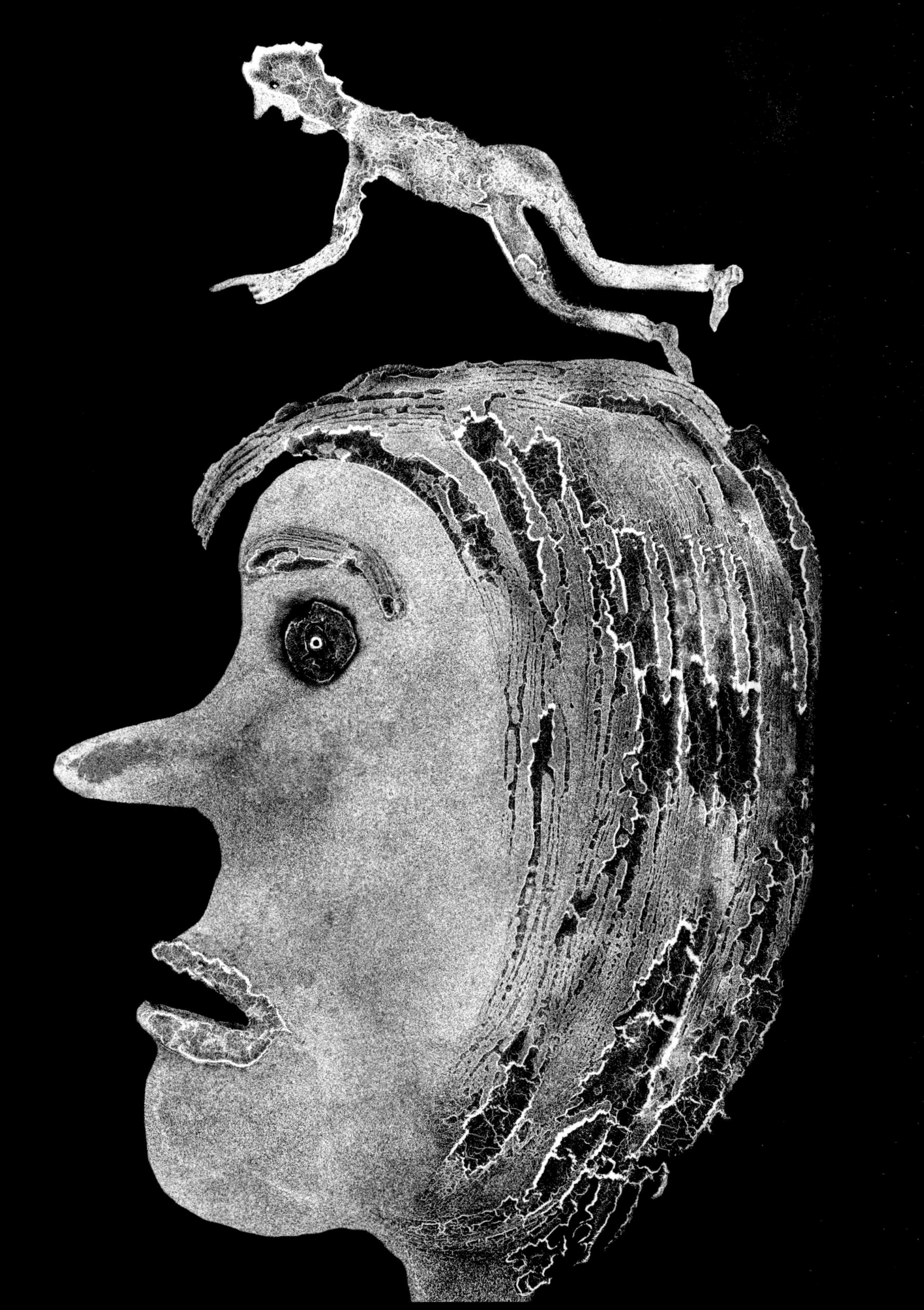

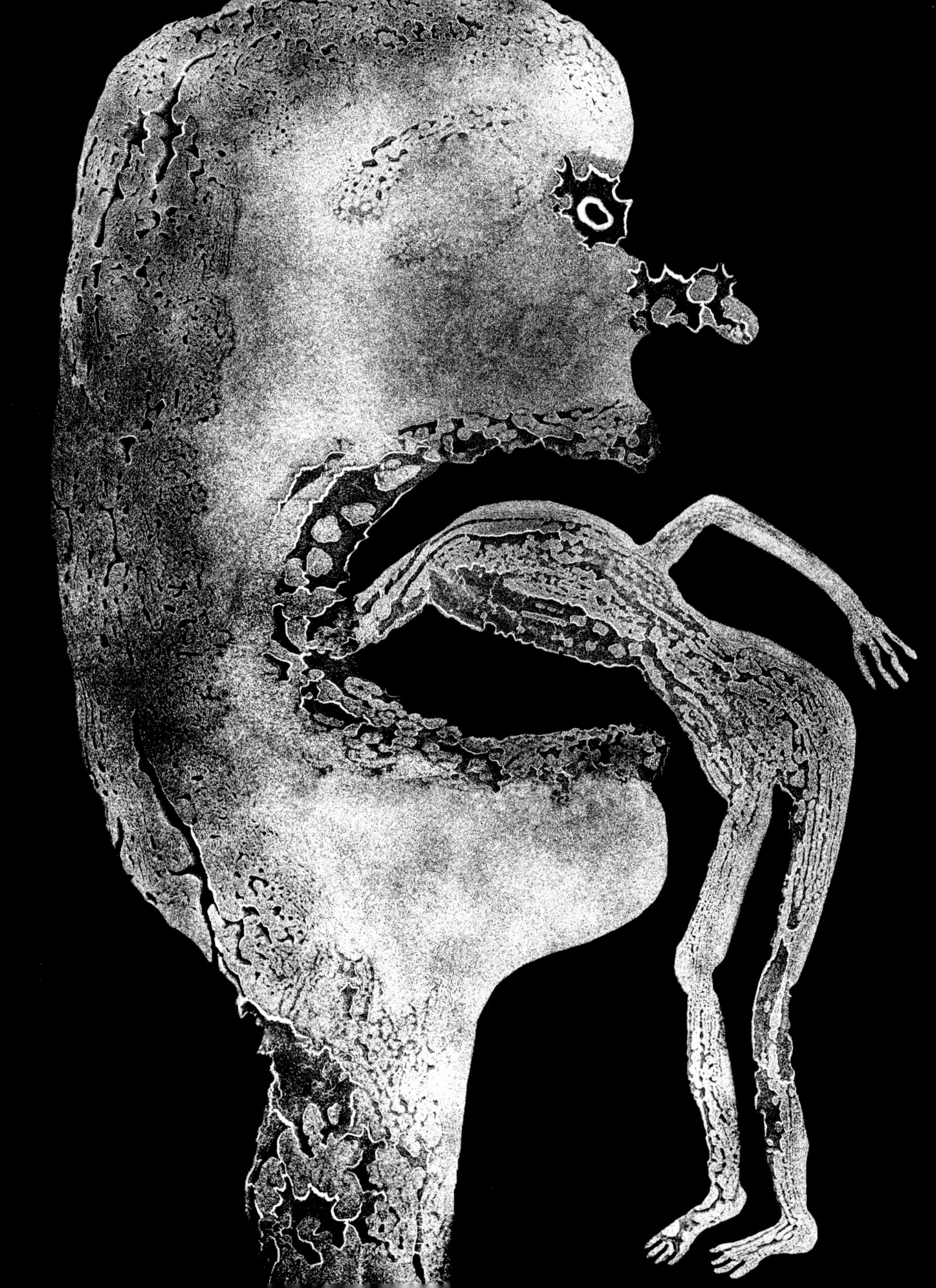

Fucked, 2010

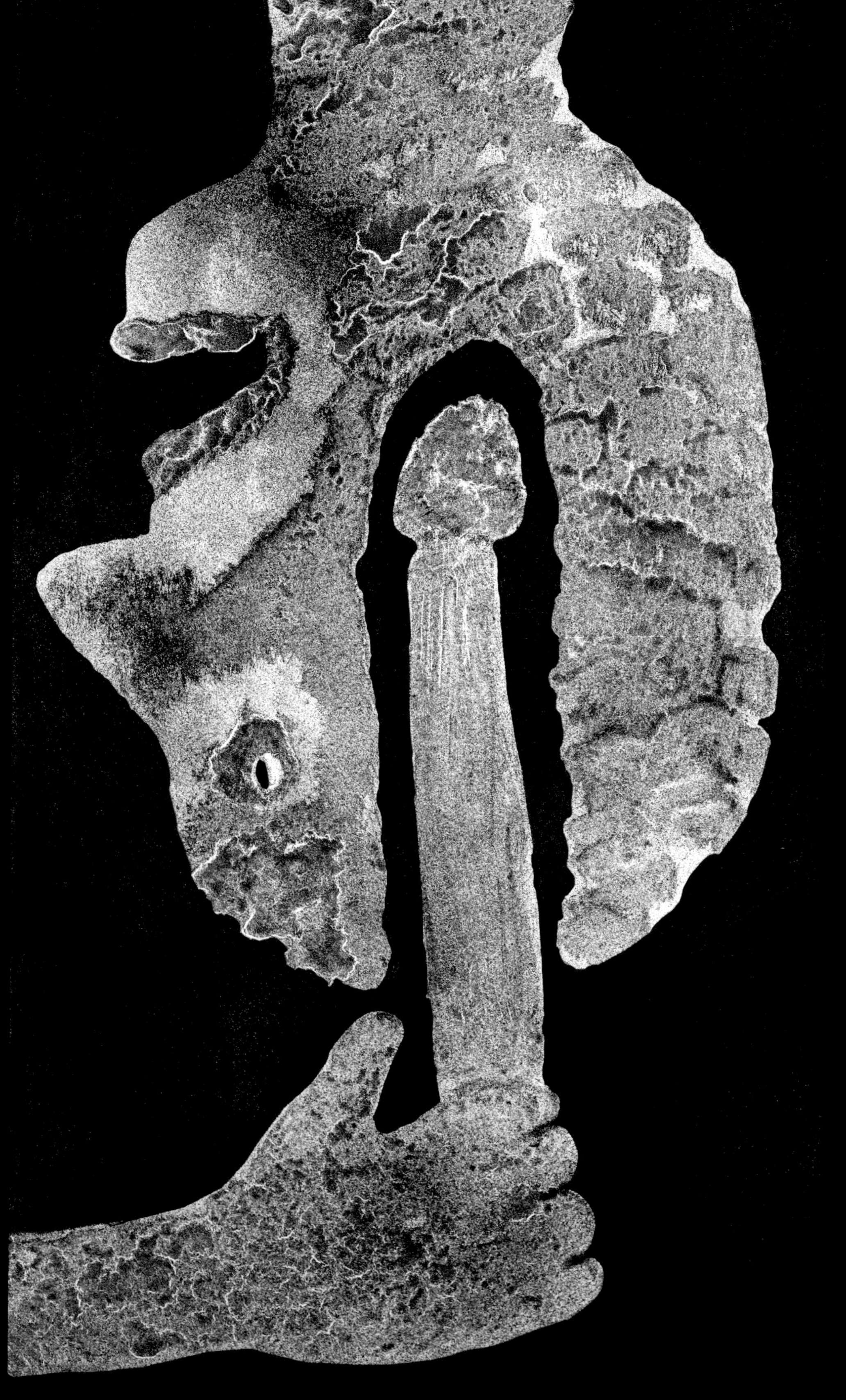

Black Hole, 2013

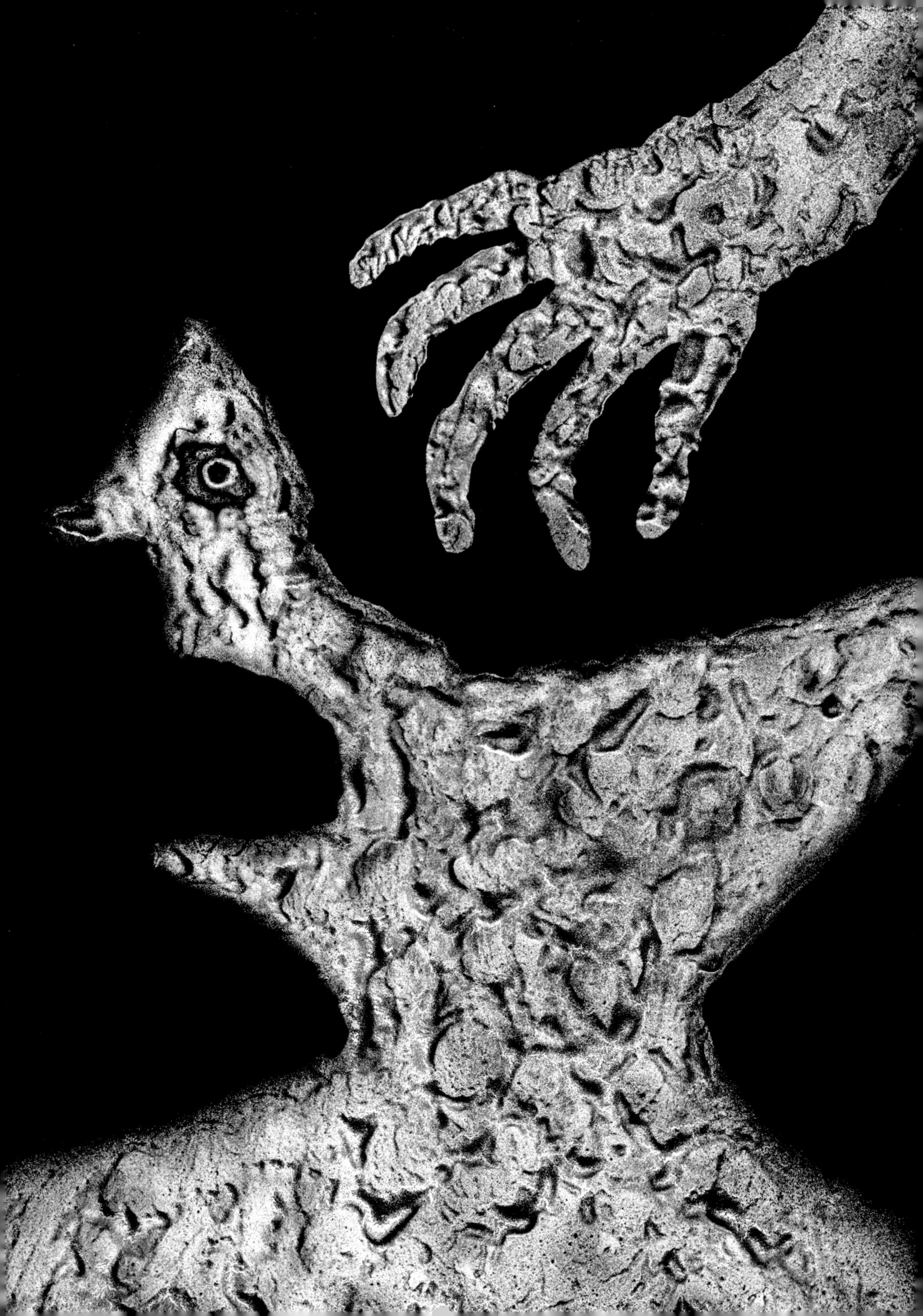

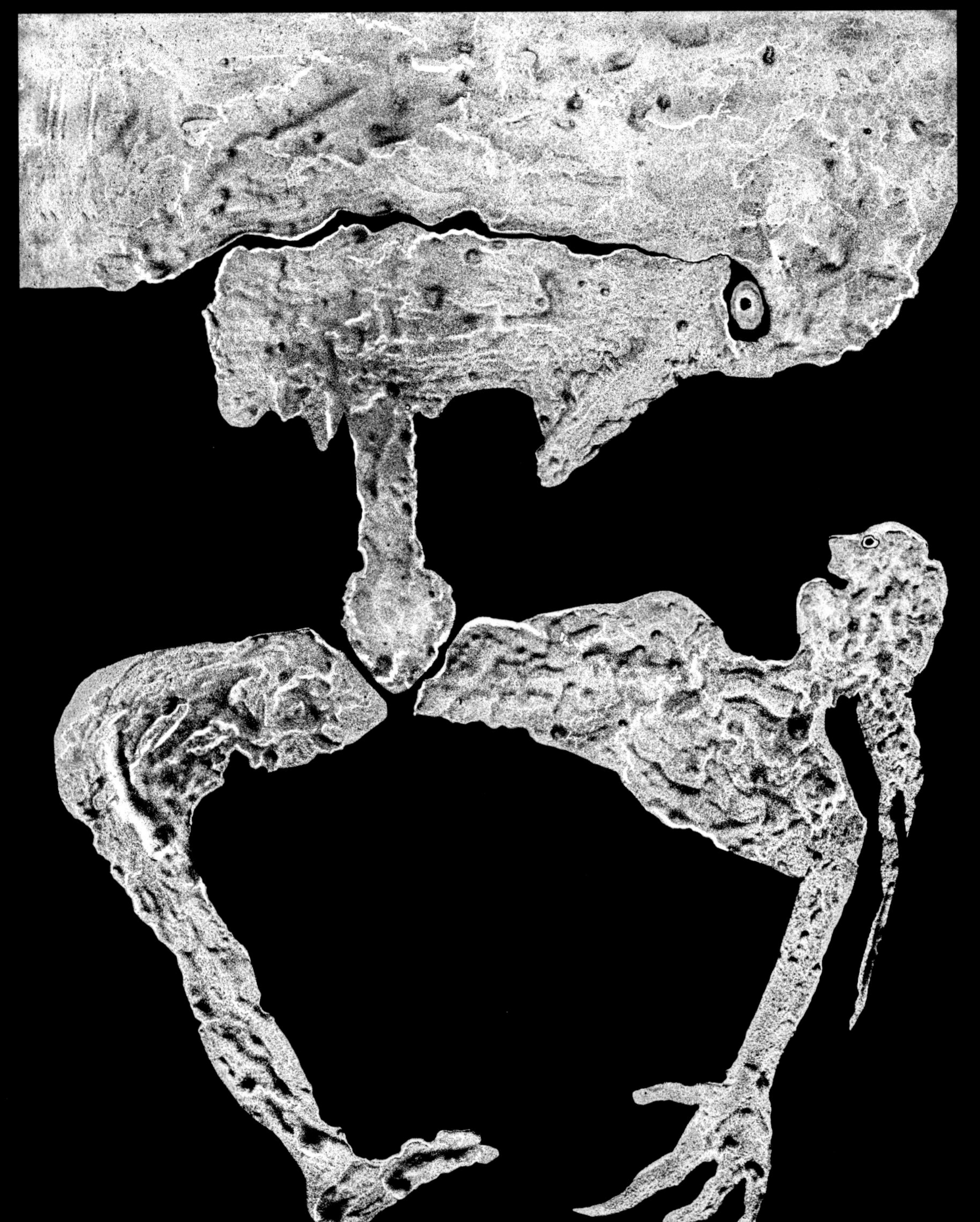

Split, 2011

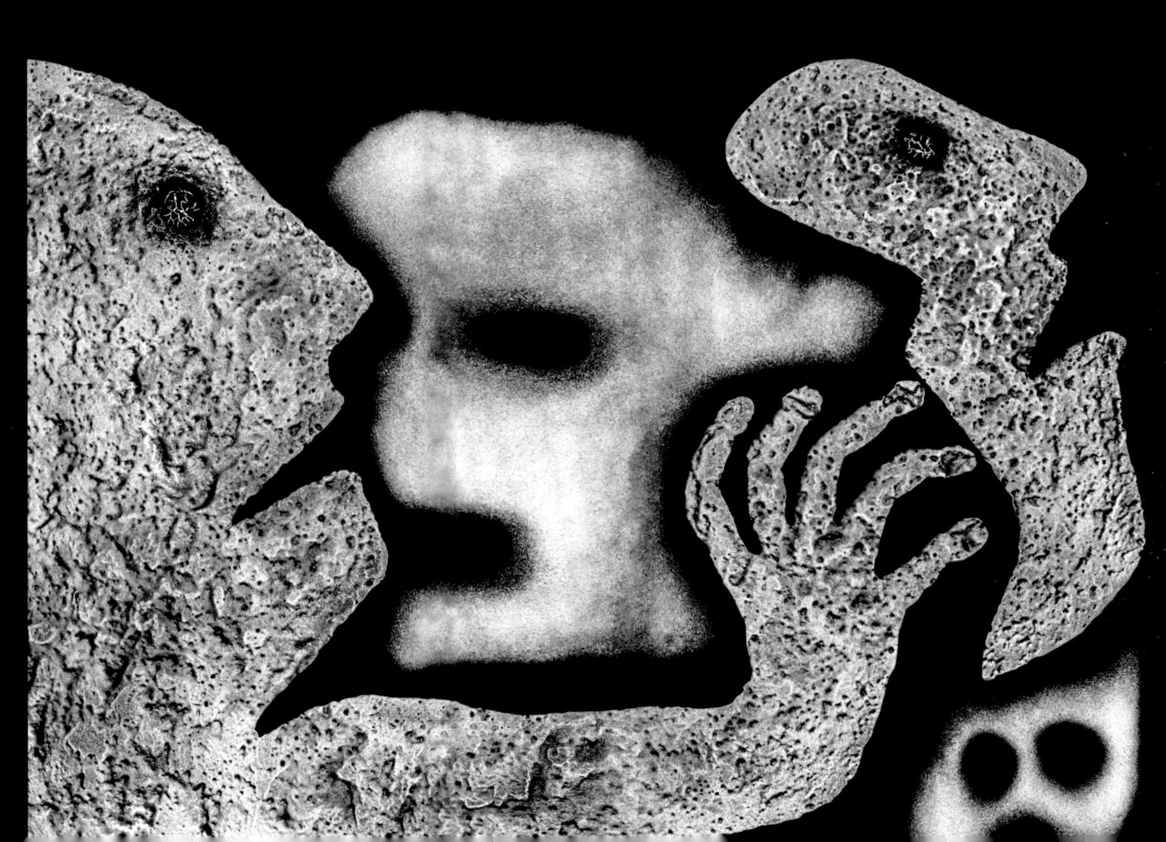

Revelation, 2012

Spikey, 2007

Spikey, 2007

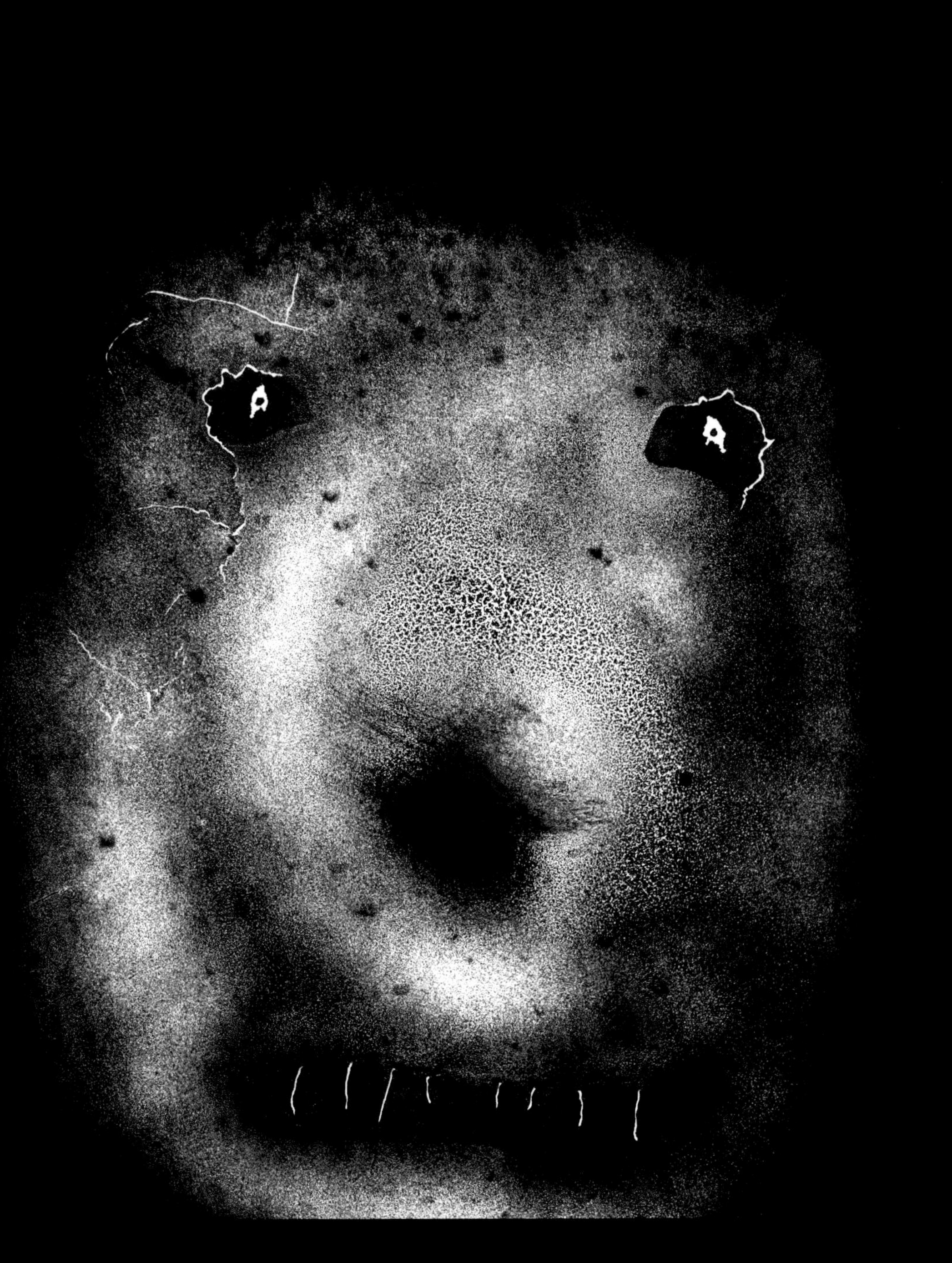

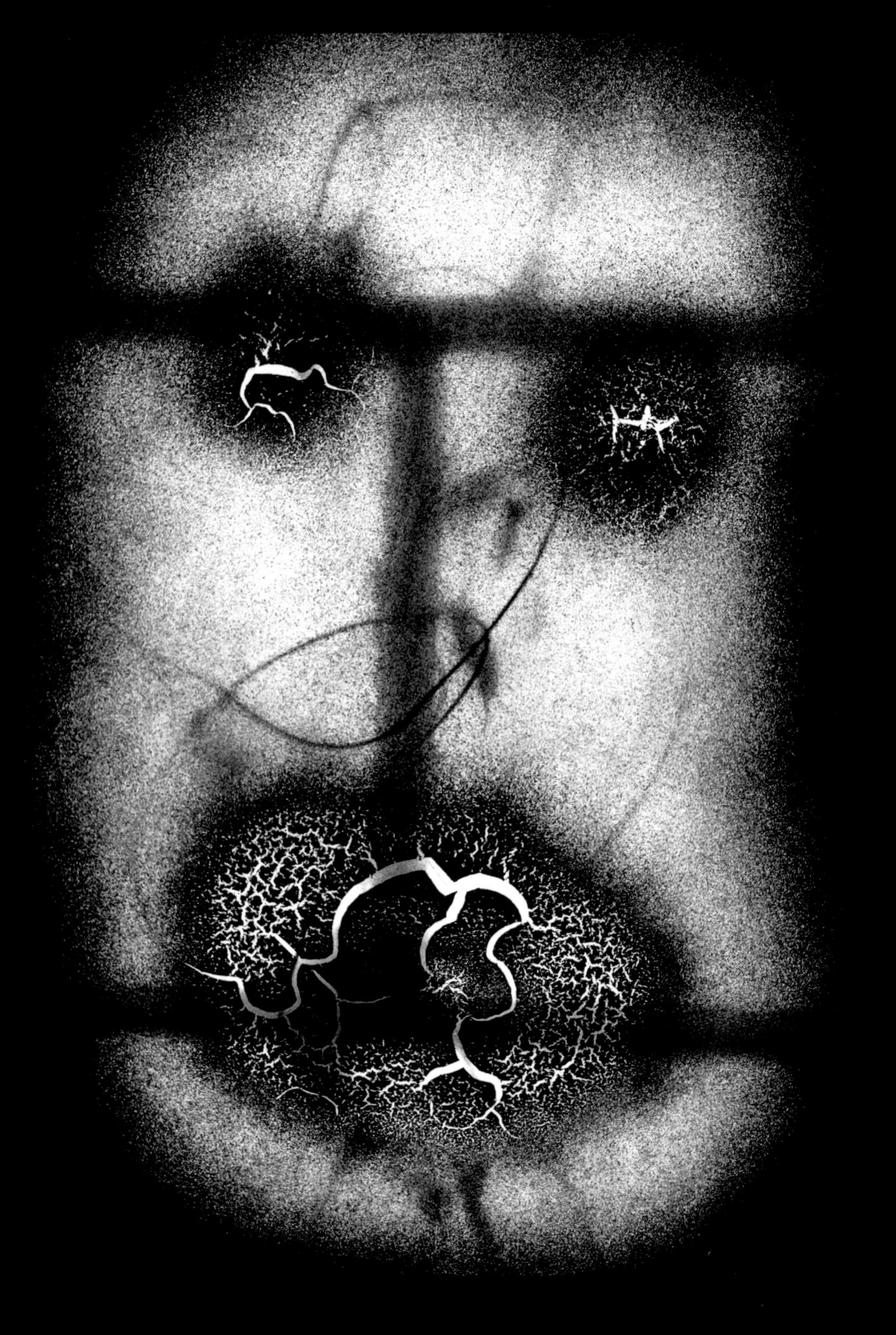

Stare, 2008

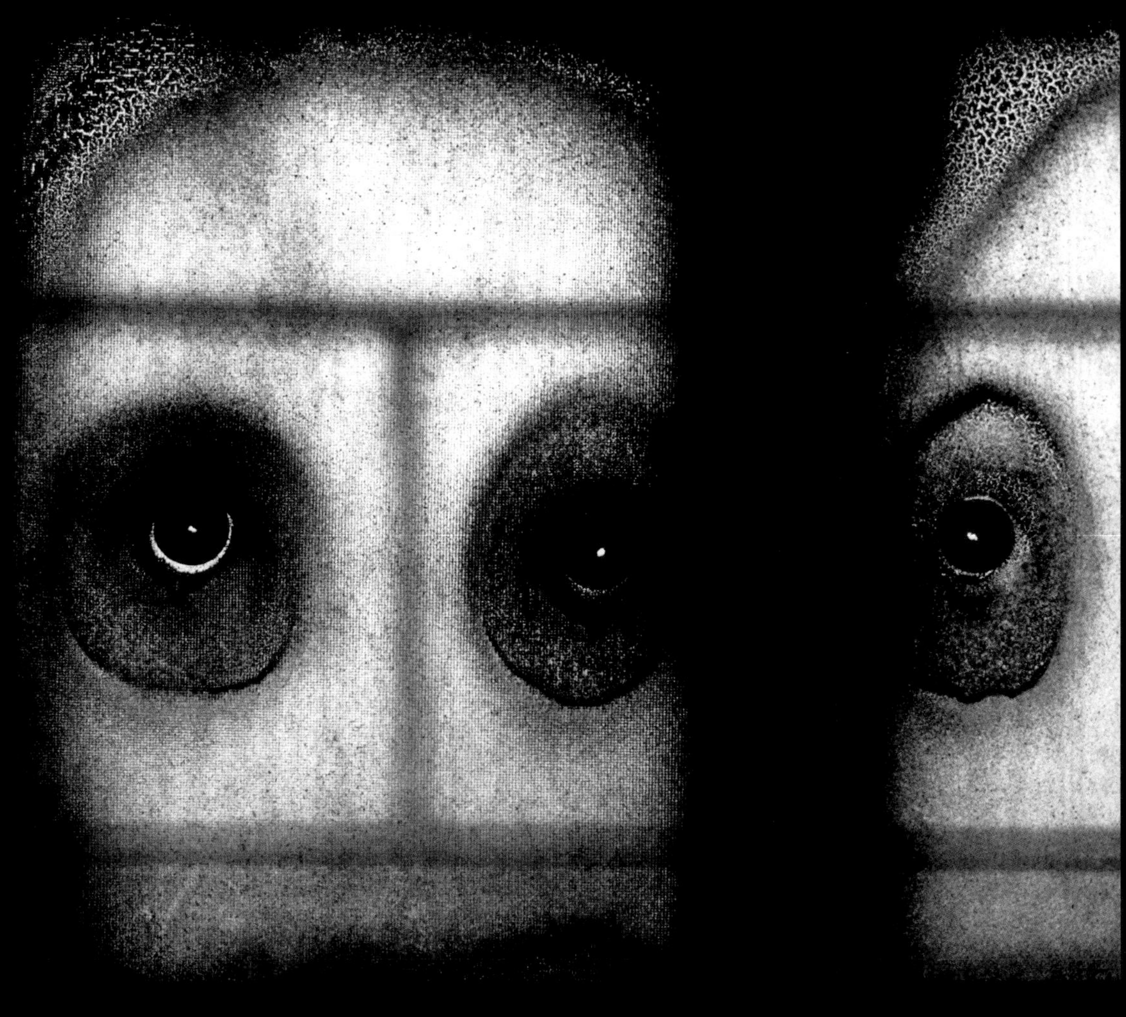

Voices, 2012
overleaf: Forewarned, 2012

Voices, 2012
overleaf: Forewarned, 2012

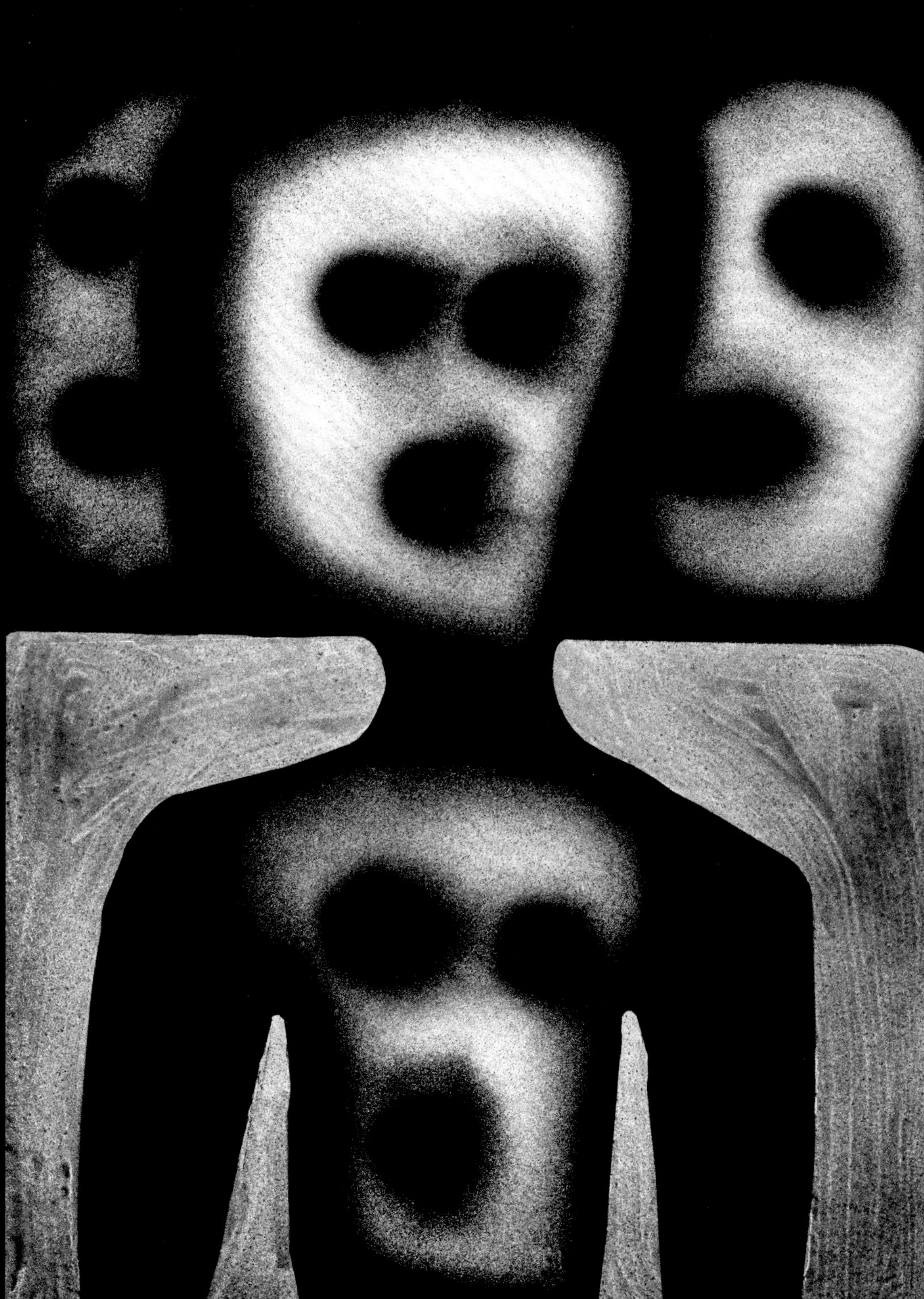

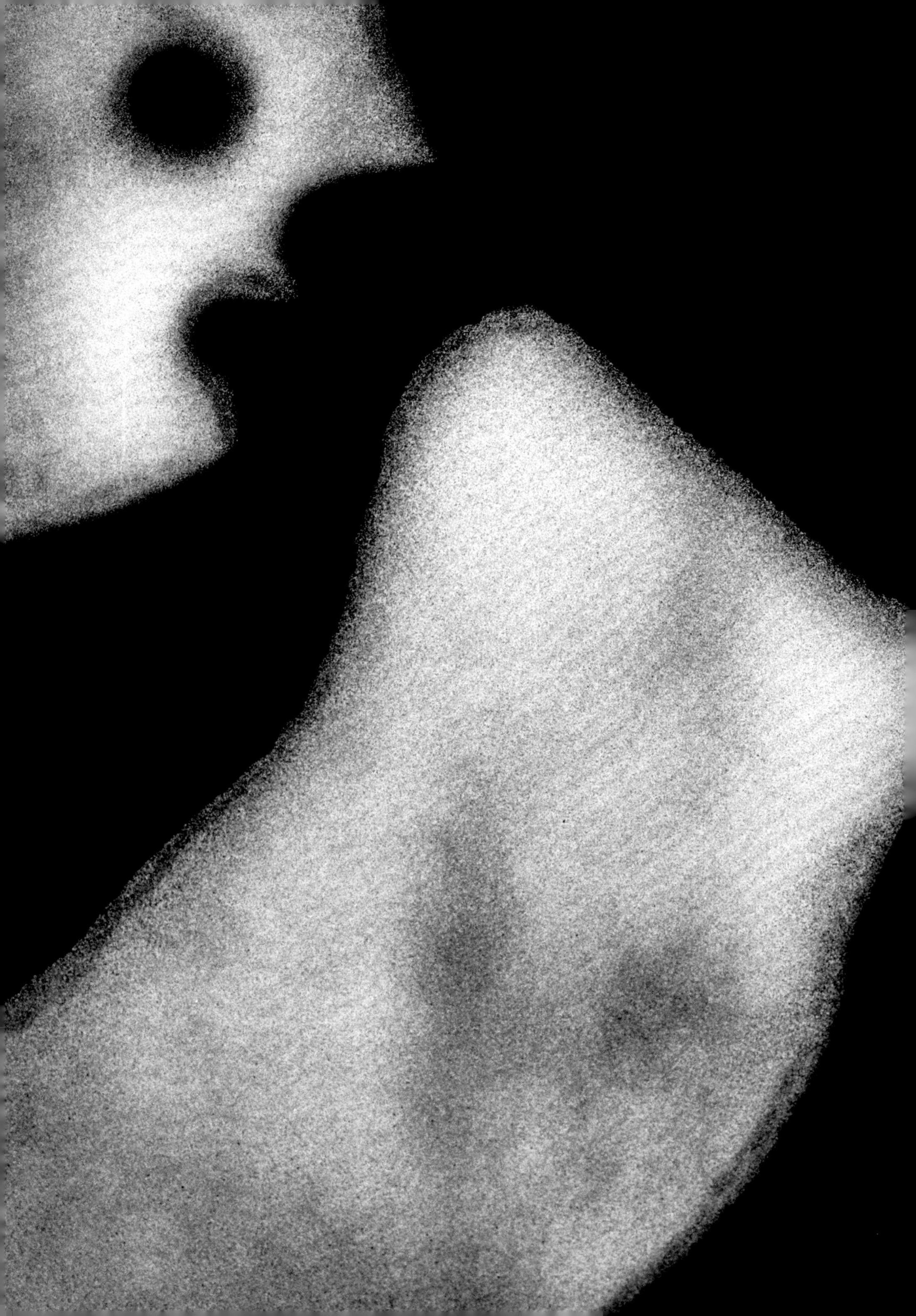

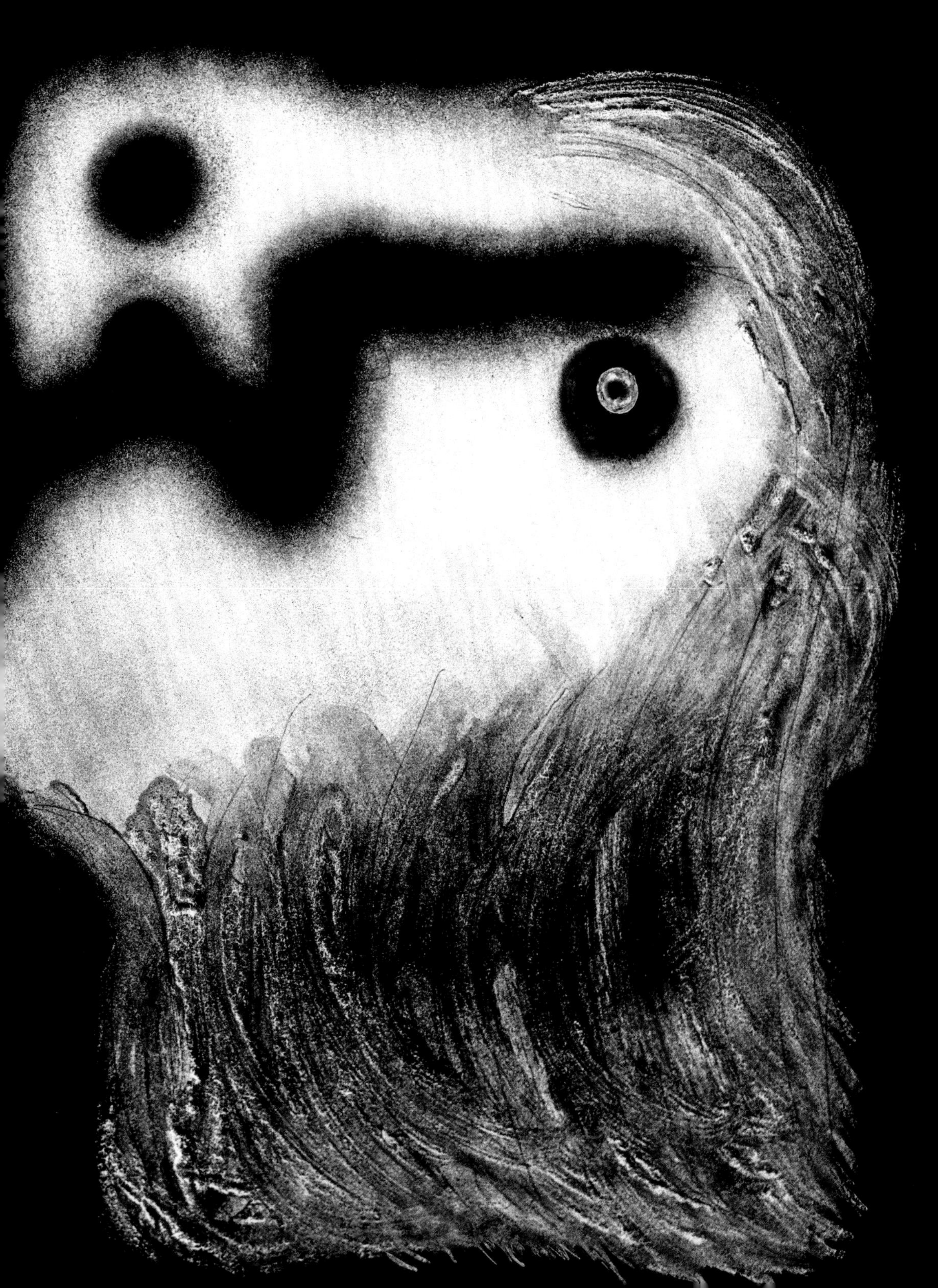

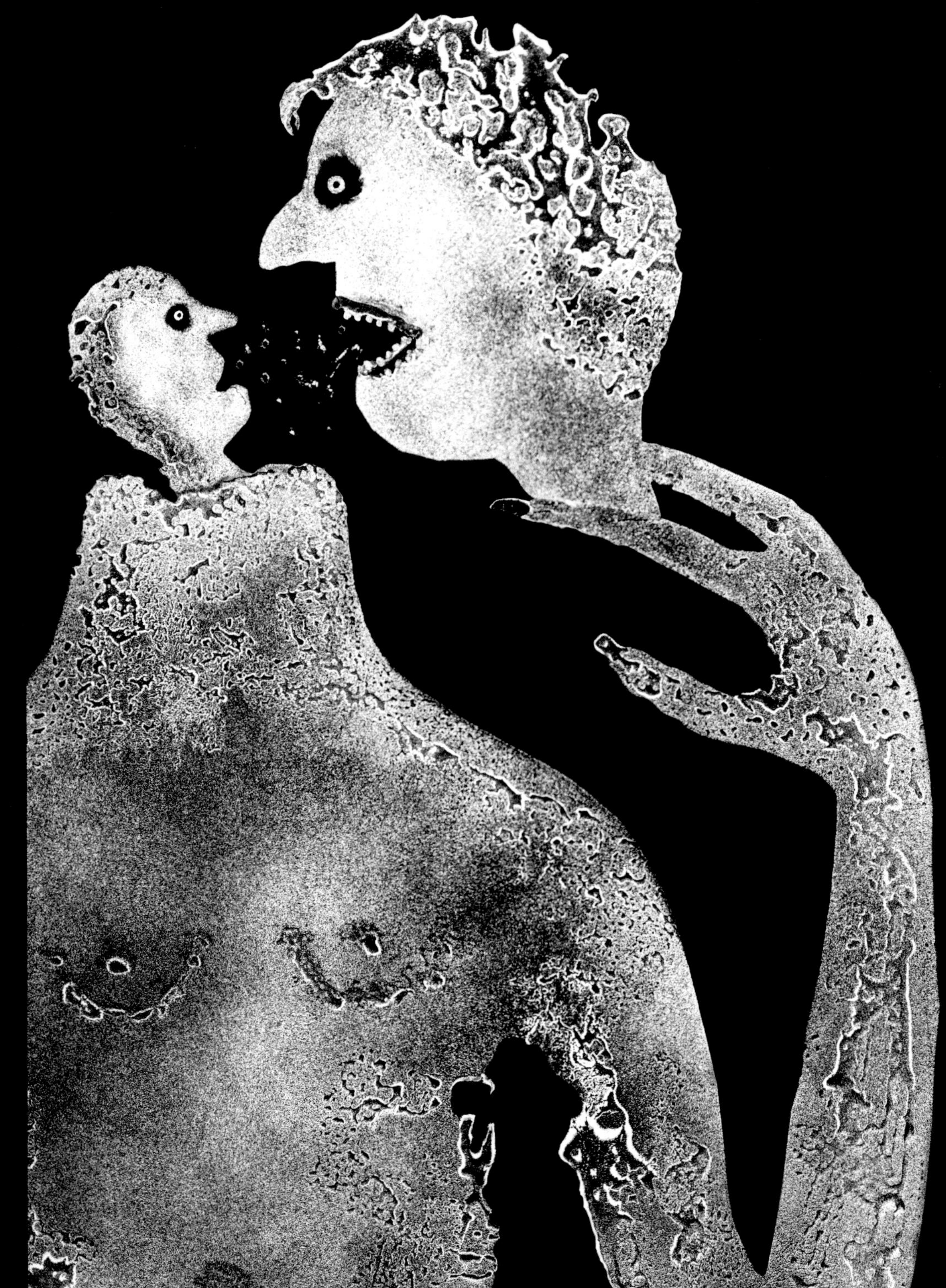

Assembly, 2011

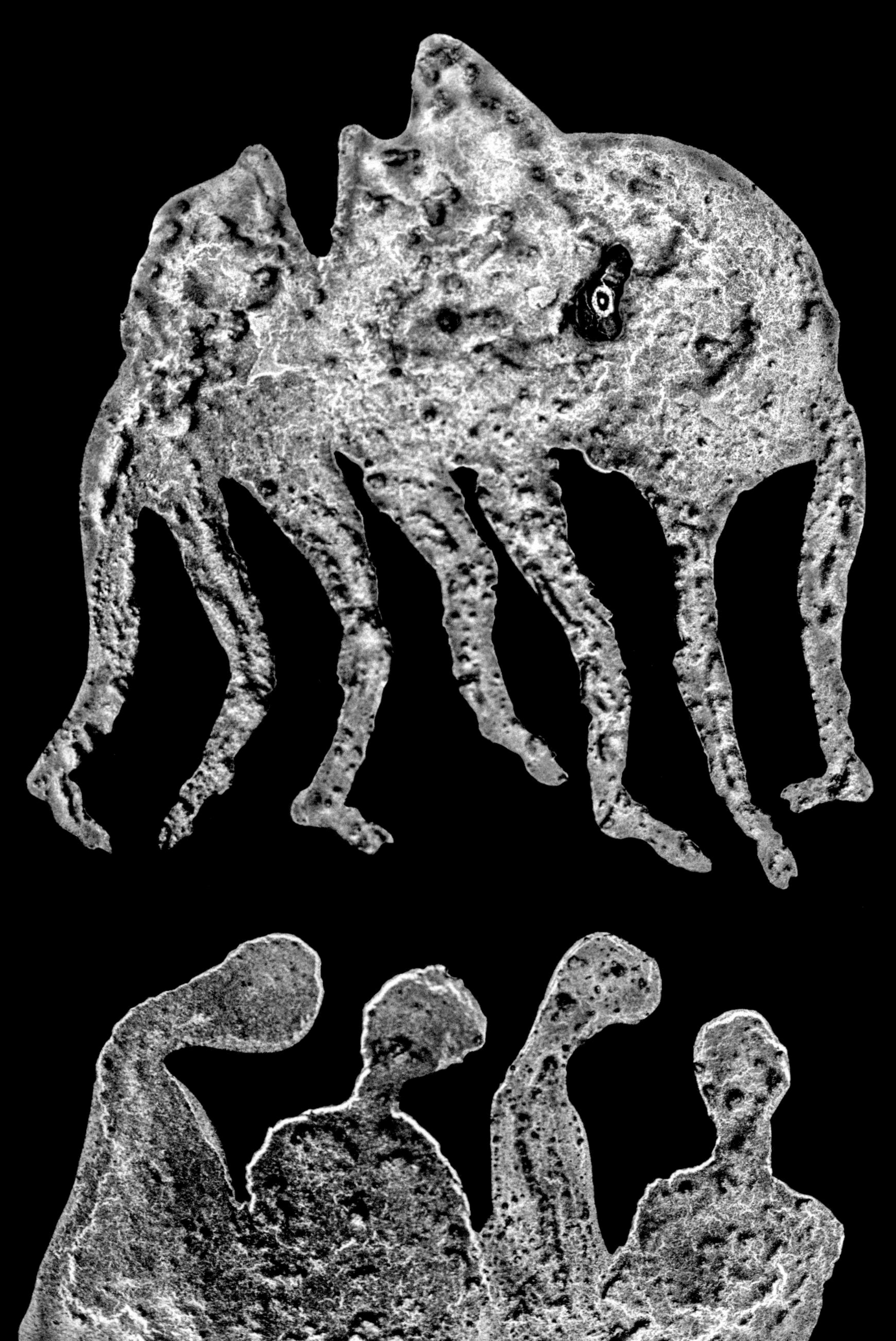

ACT TWO

burlesque

Burlesque, 2011

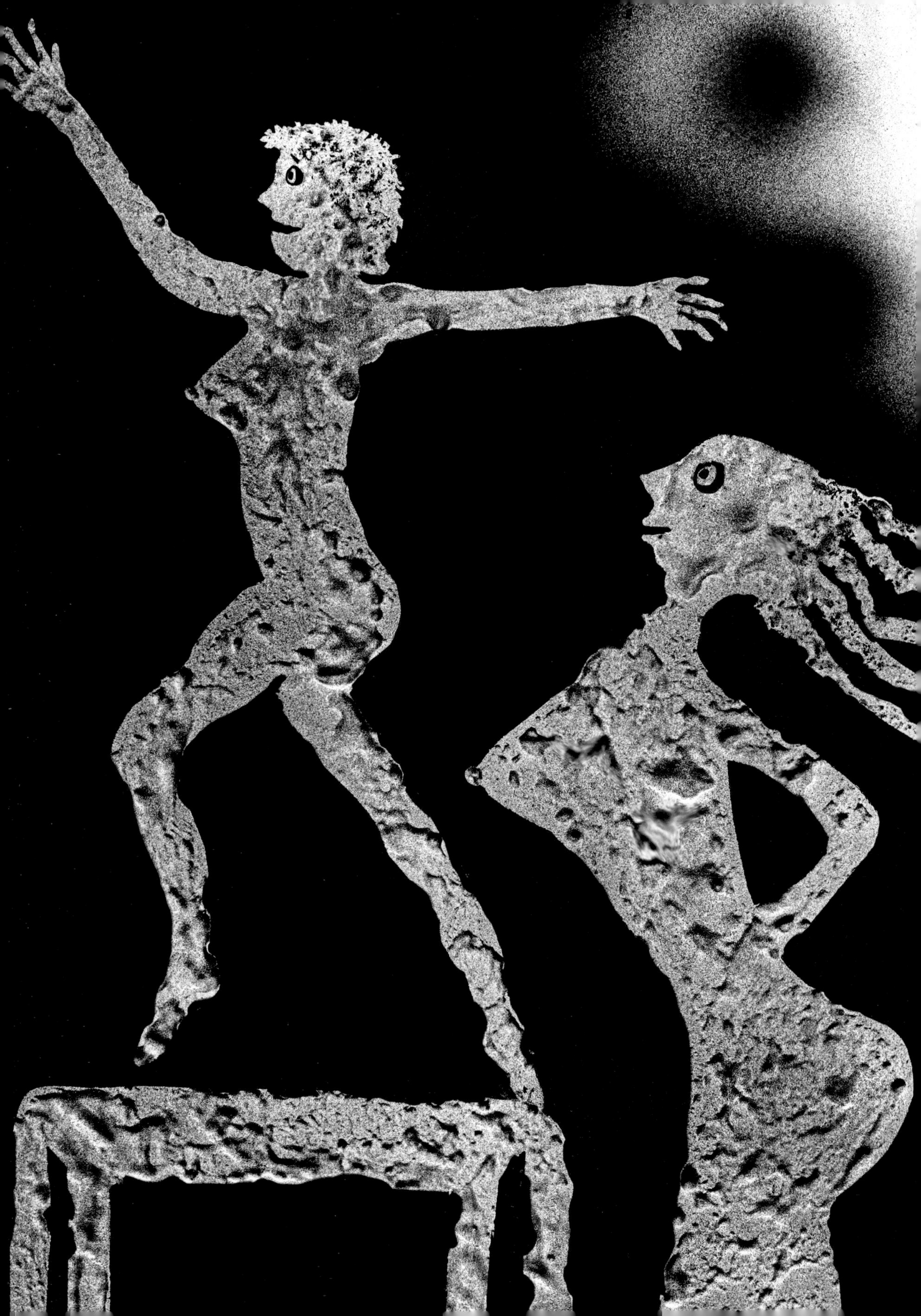

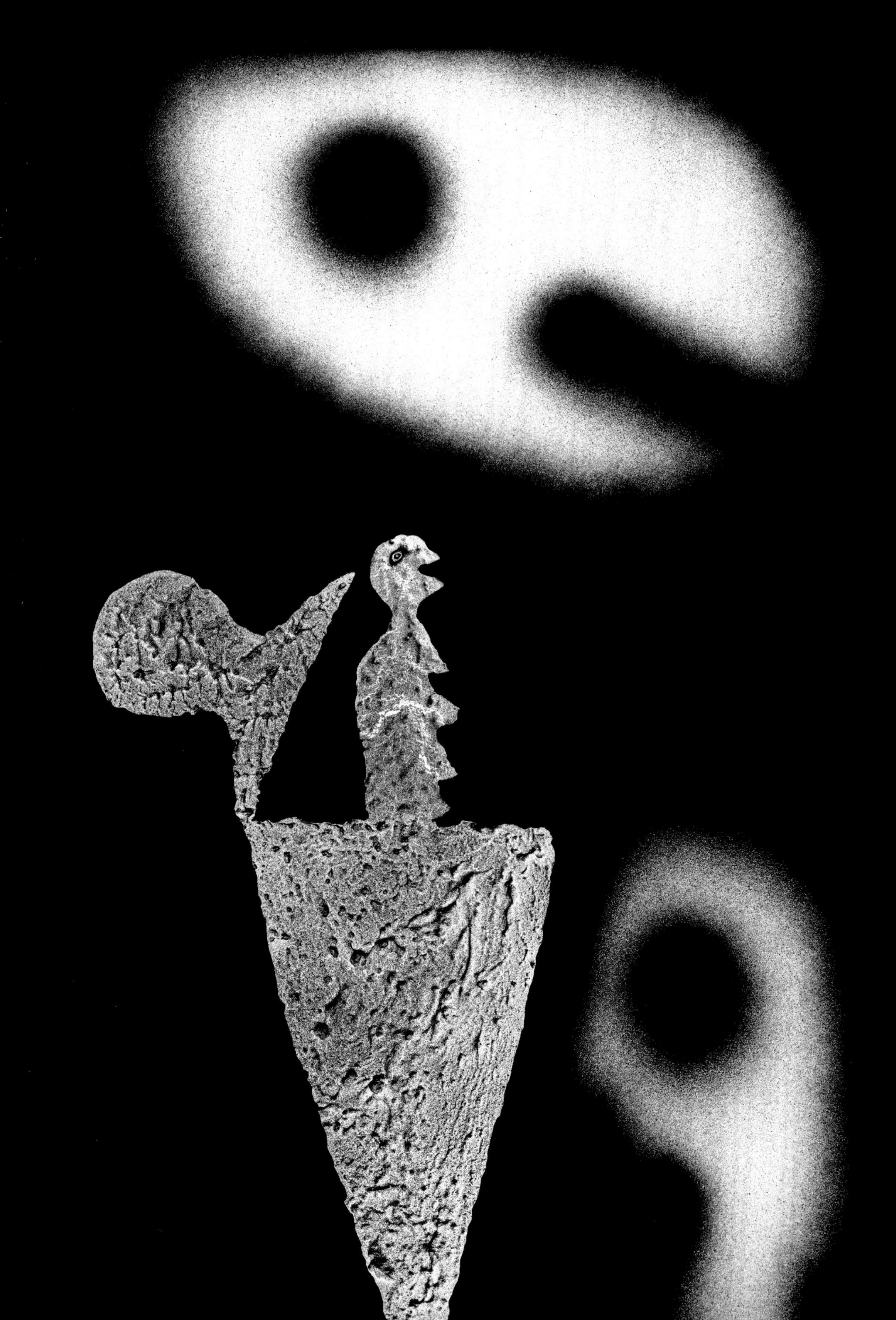

Blurp, 2011

Incident, 2011

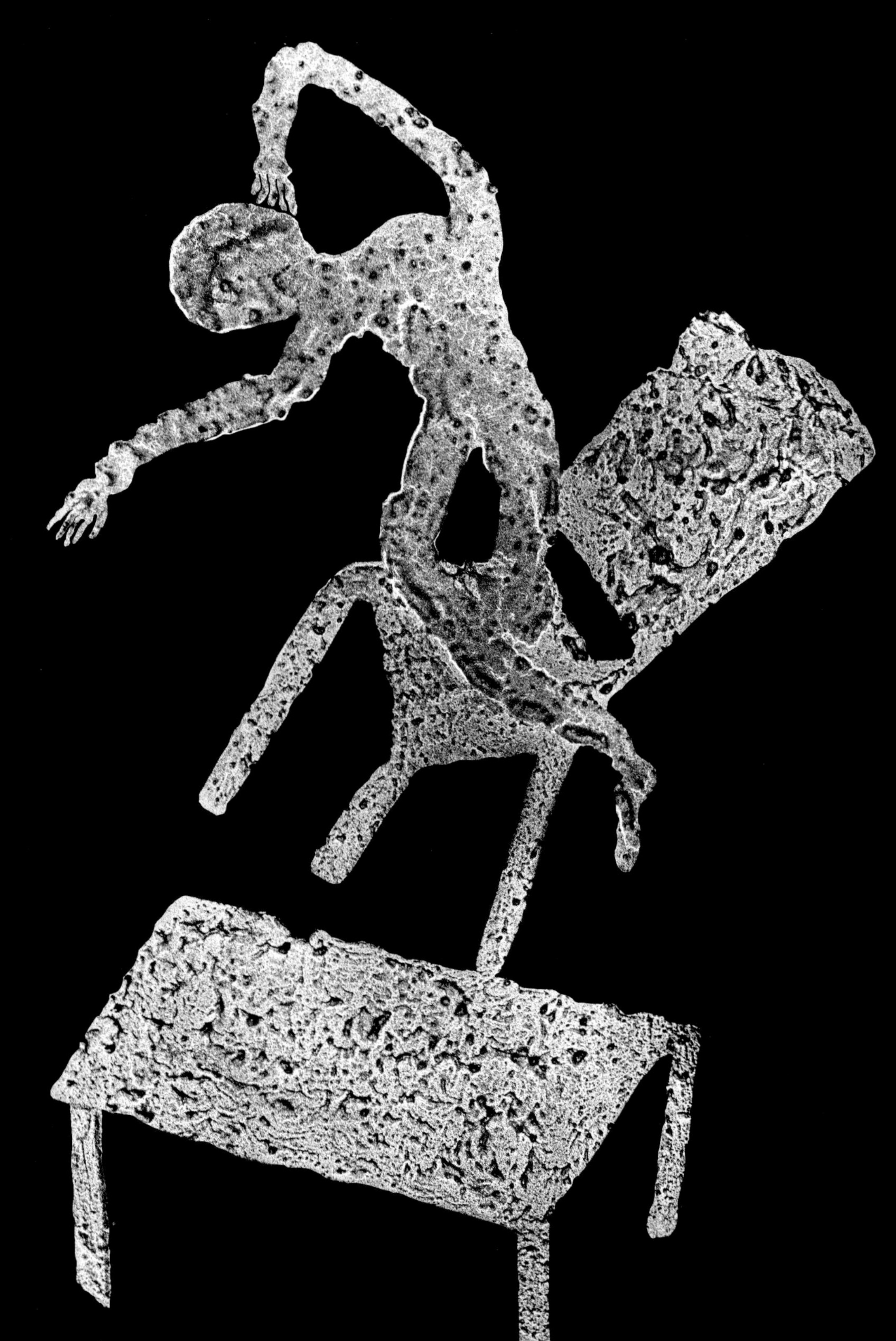

Outreach, 2012

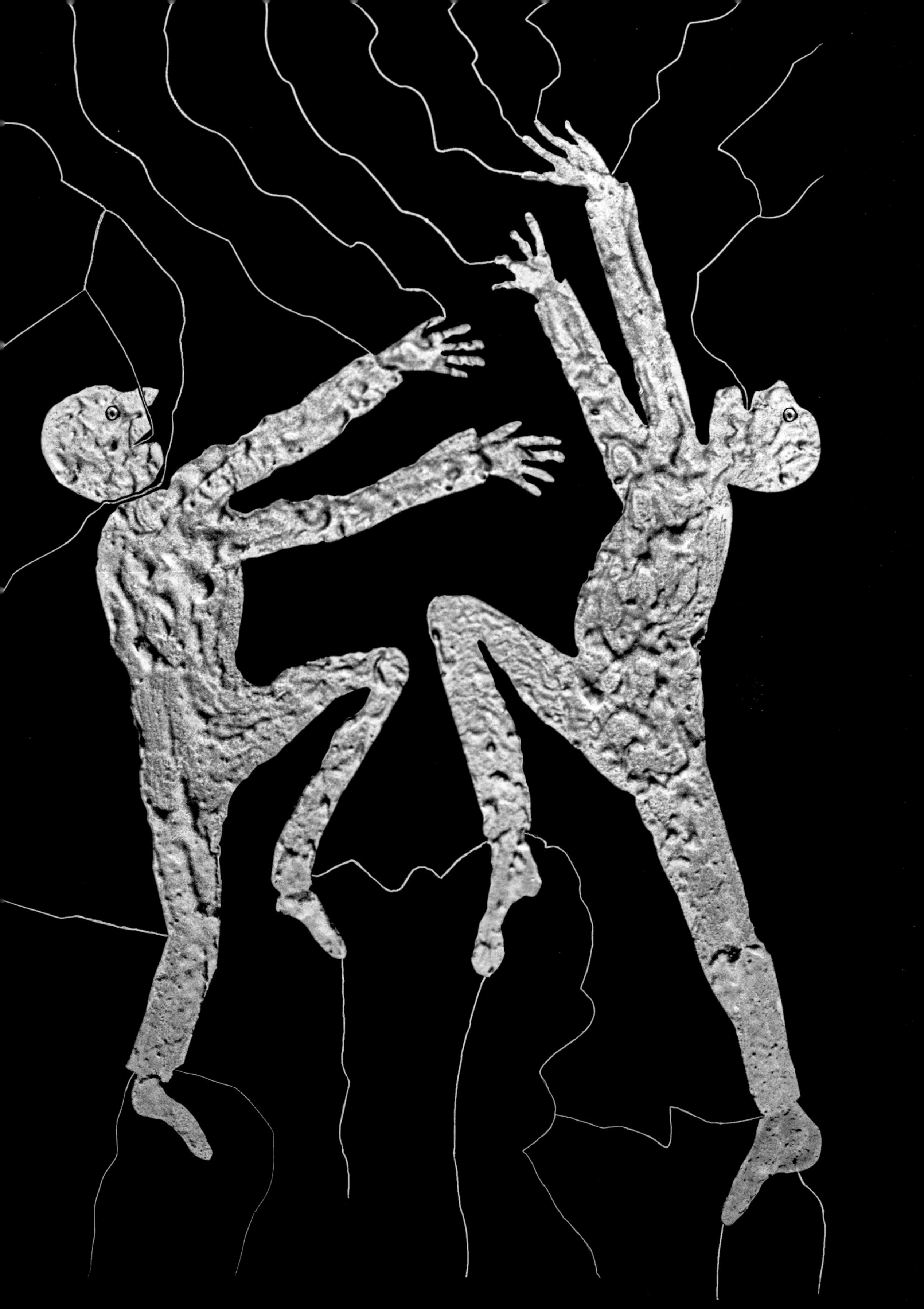

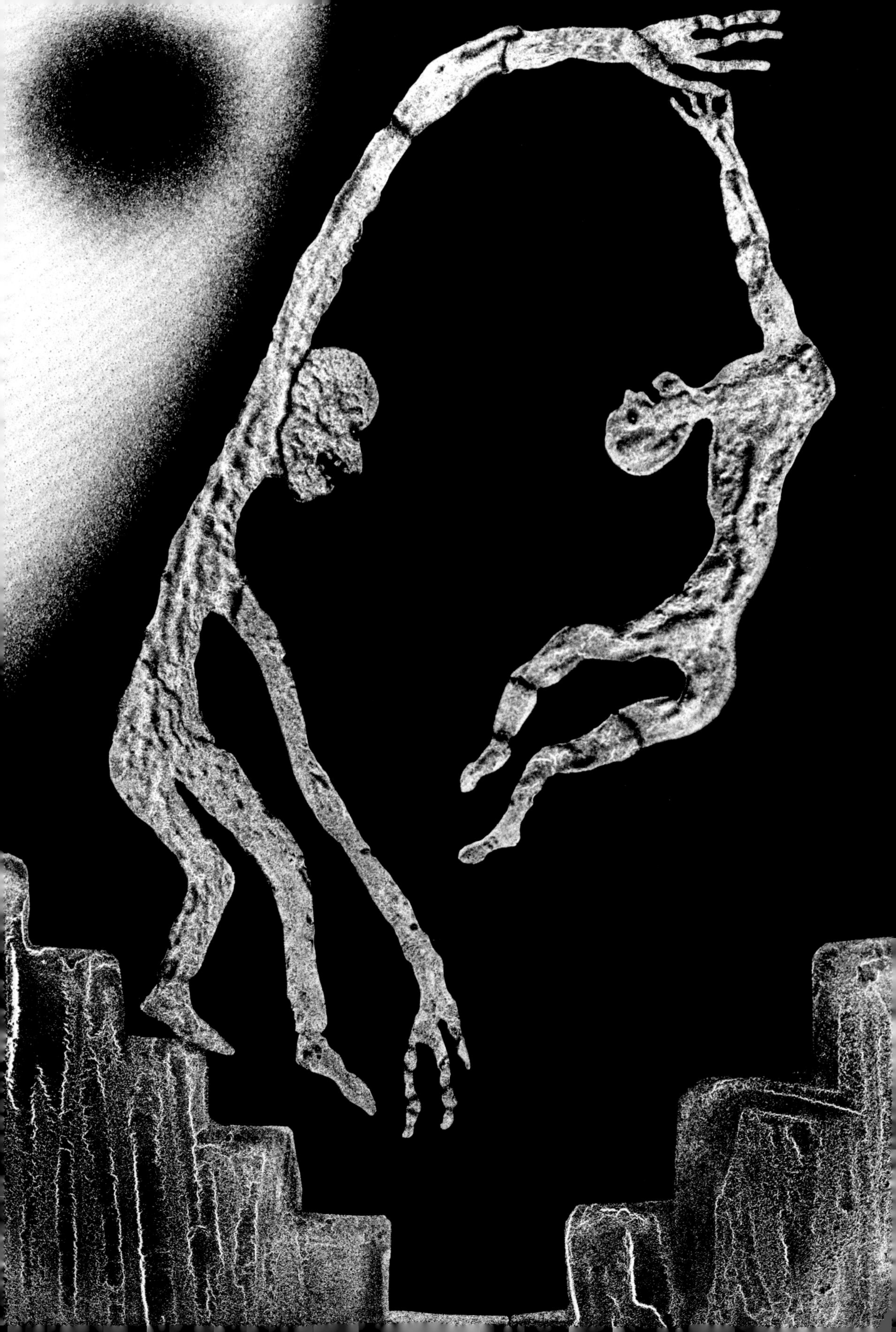

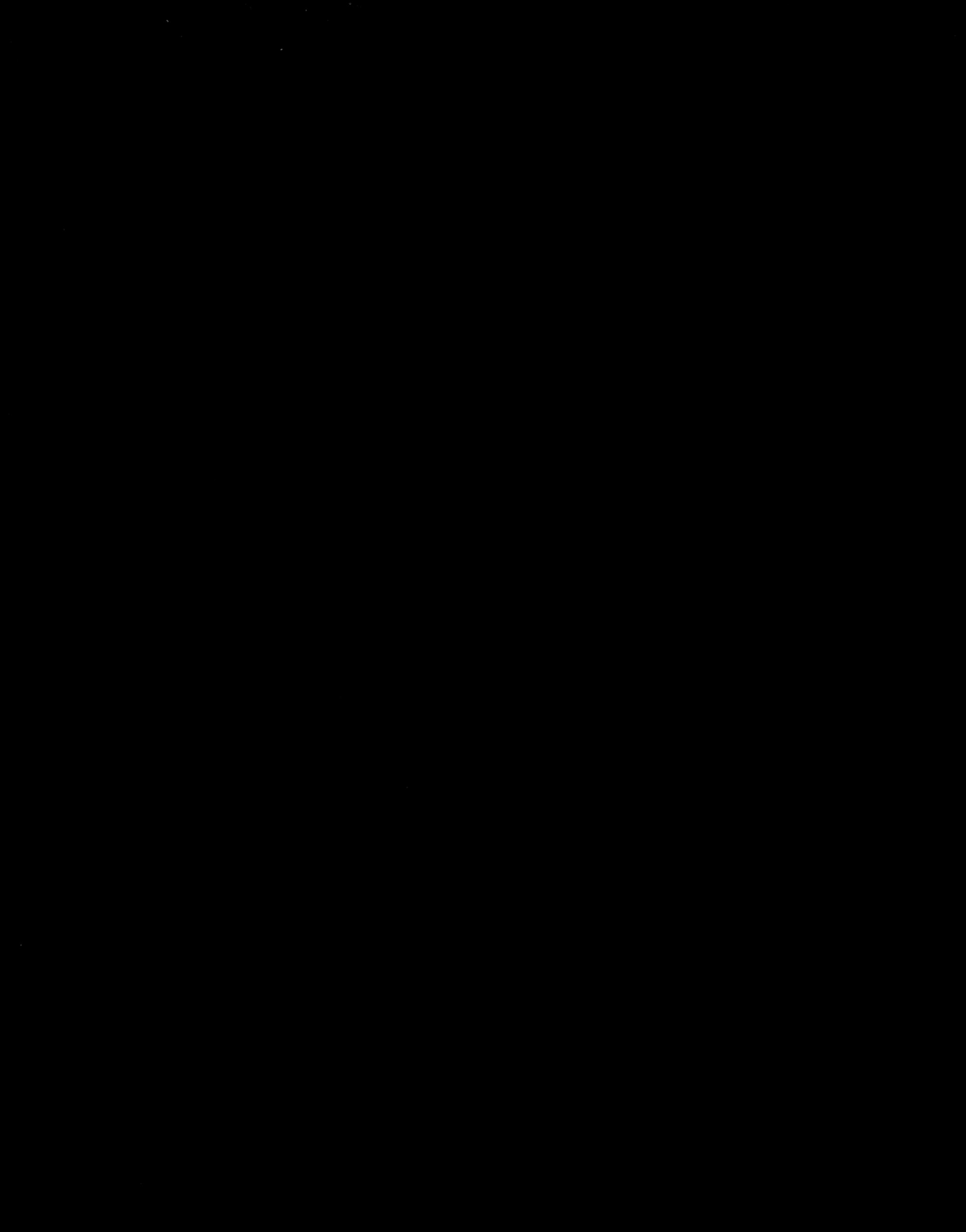

Hallucination, 2010

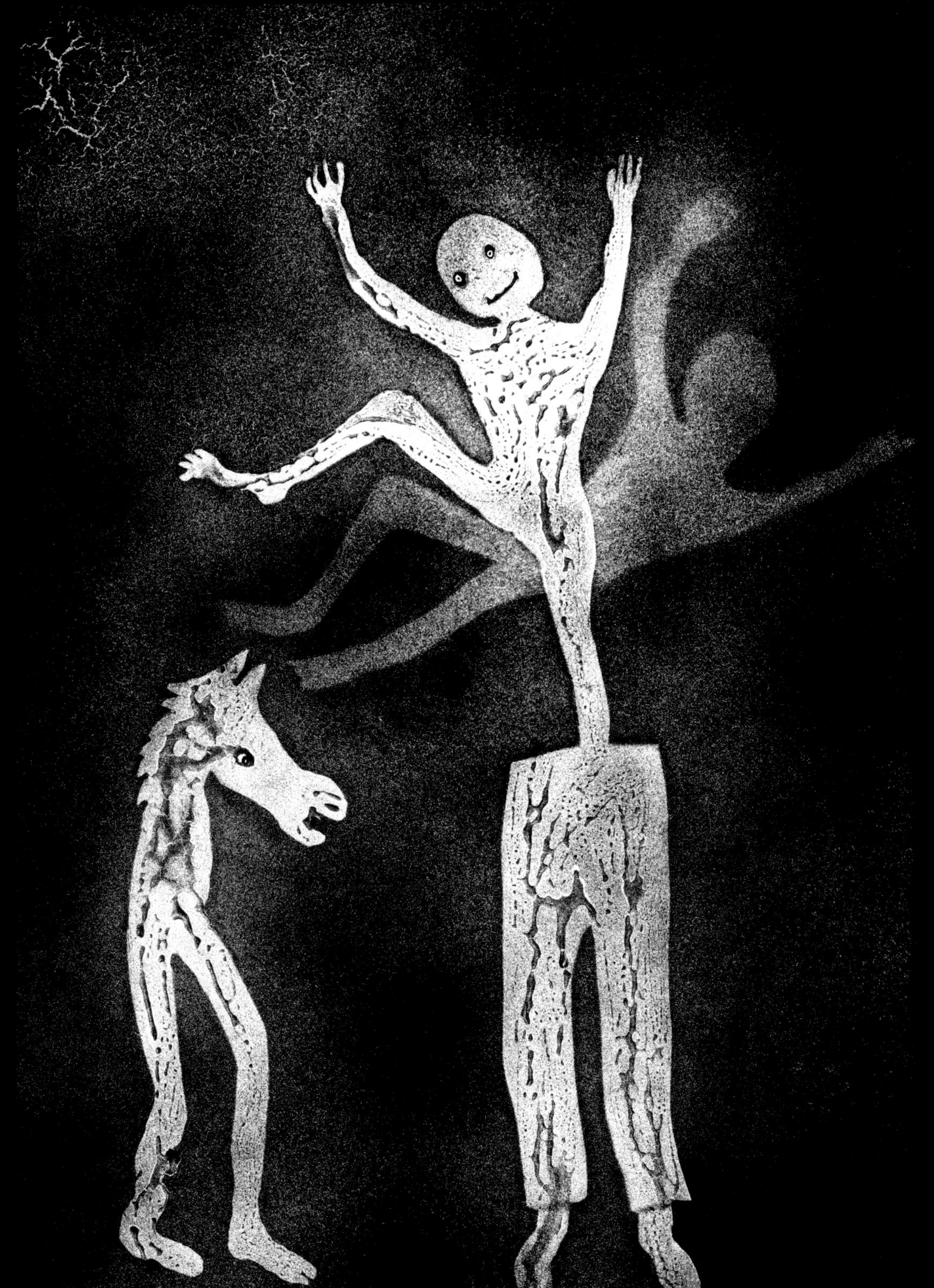

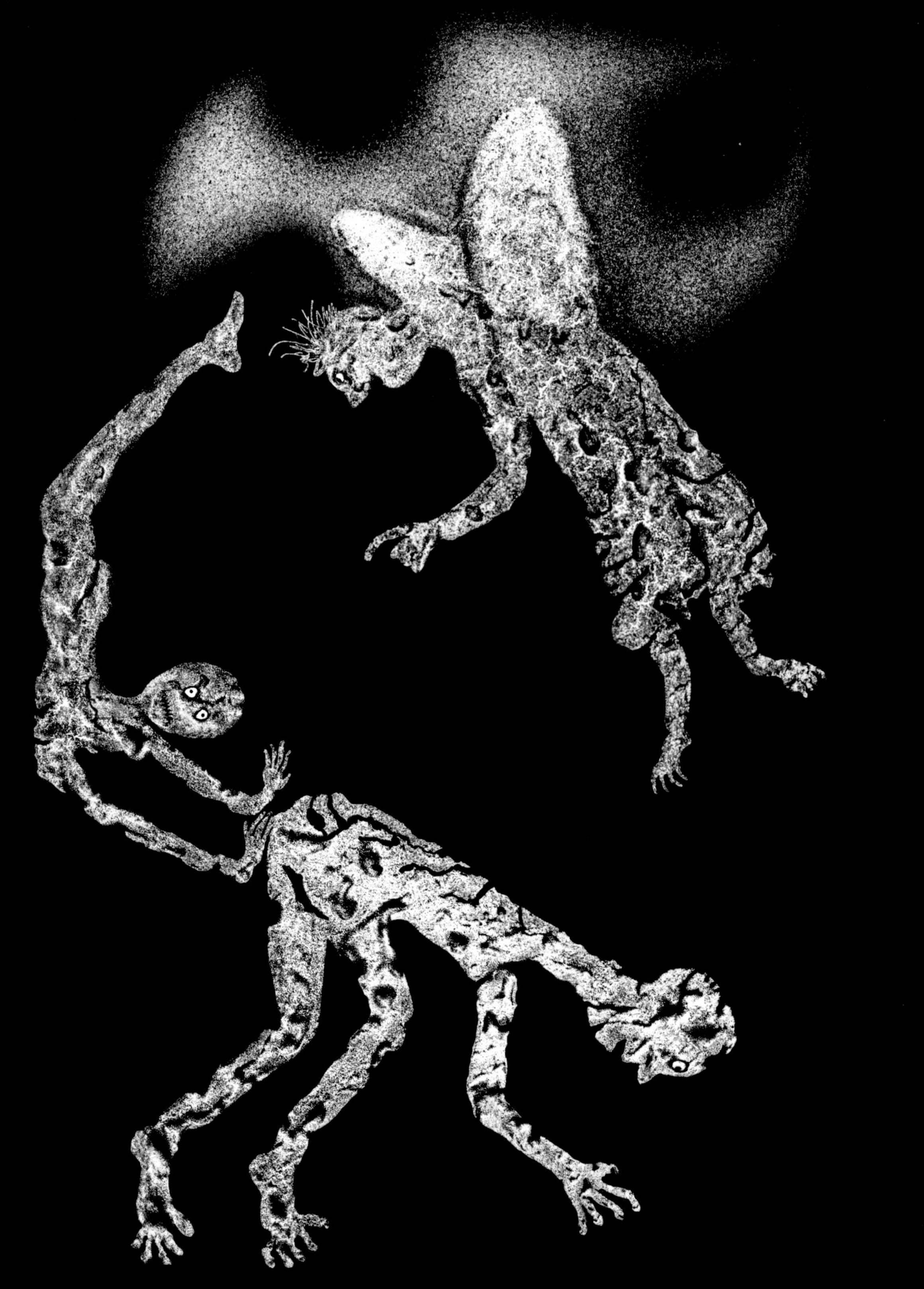

Admonishment, 2011

Bombastic, 2012

Bombastic, 2012

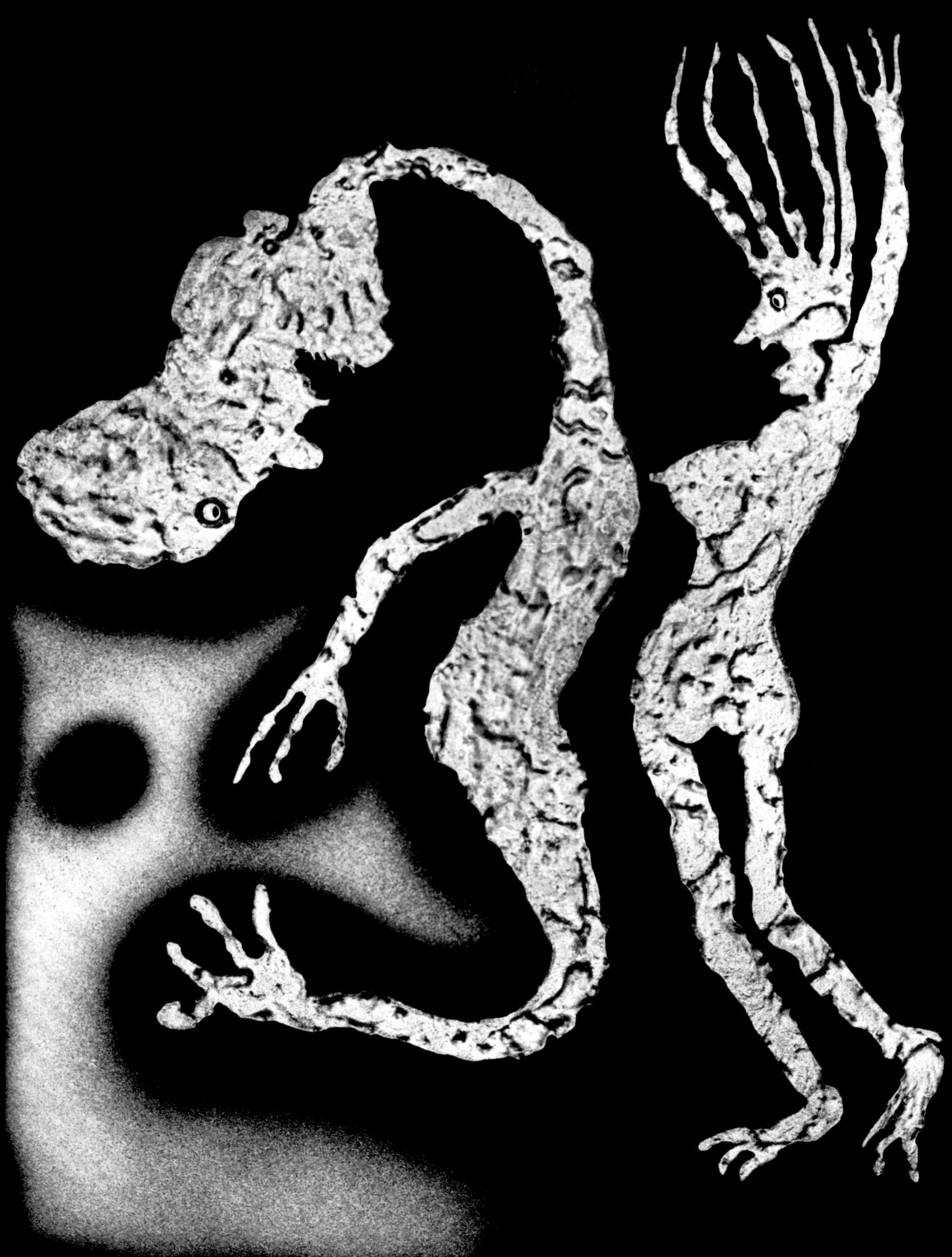

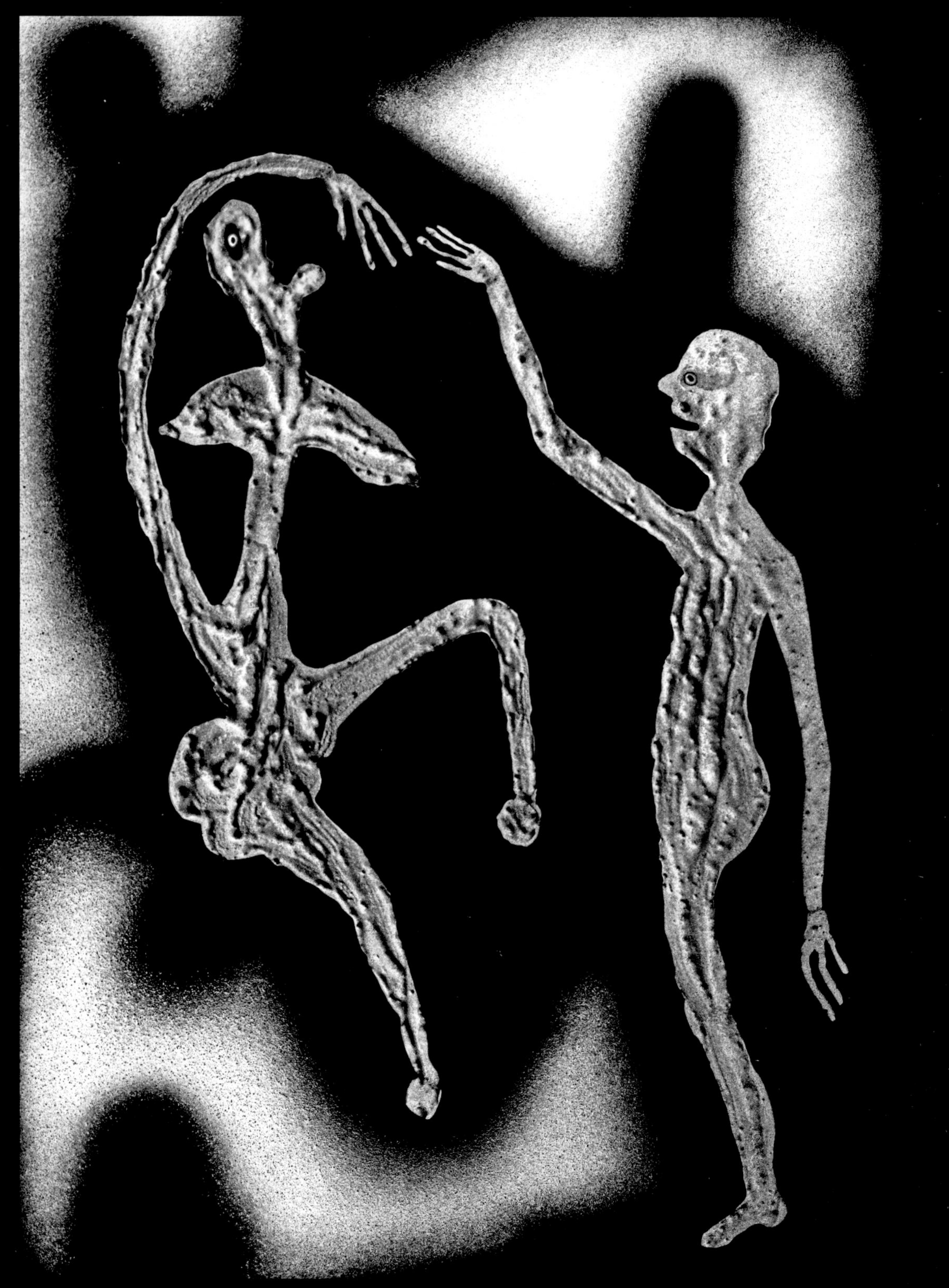

Cha Cha Cha, 2011

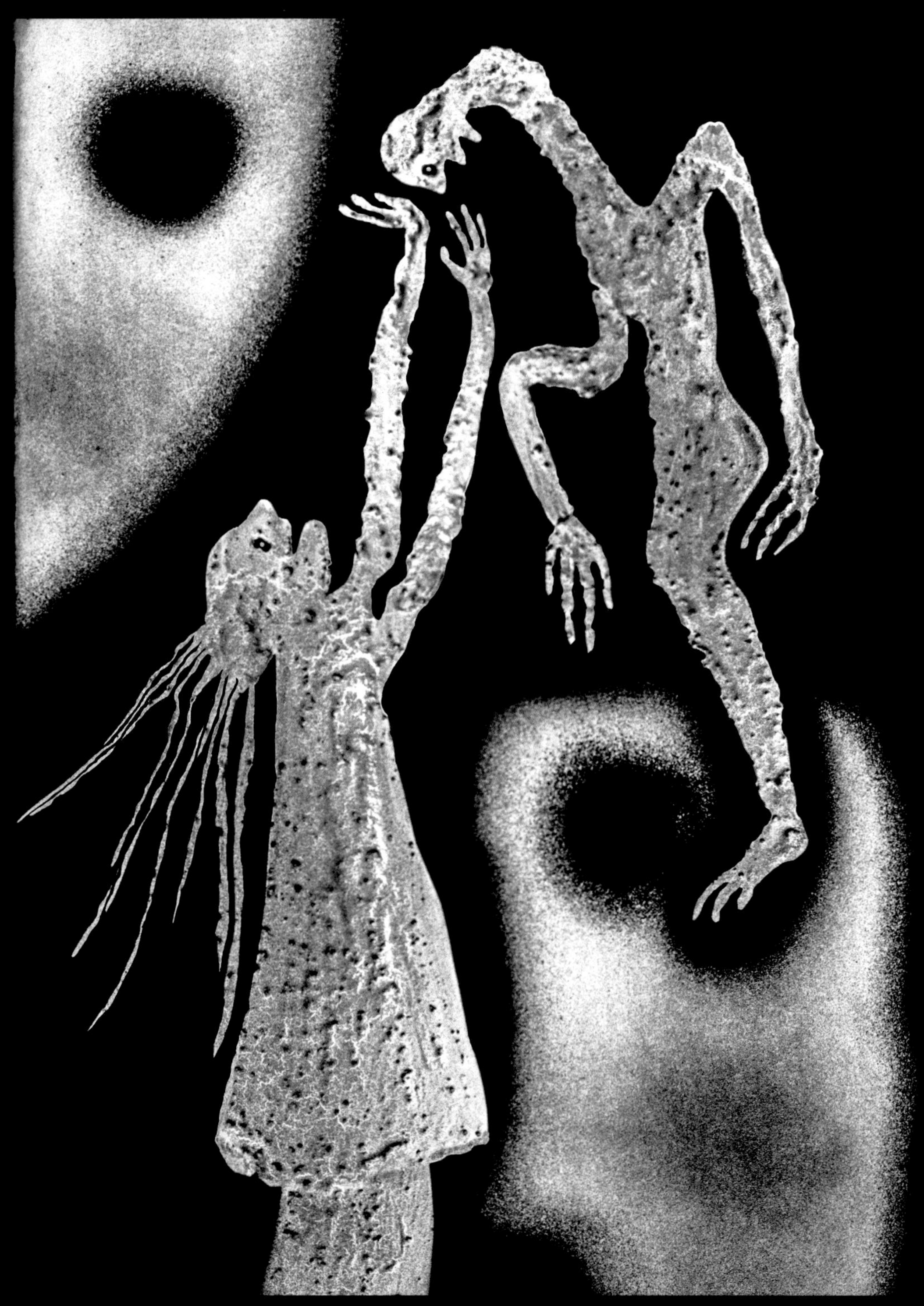

Repulsed, 2012

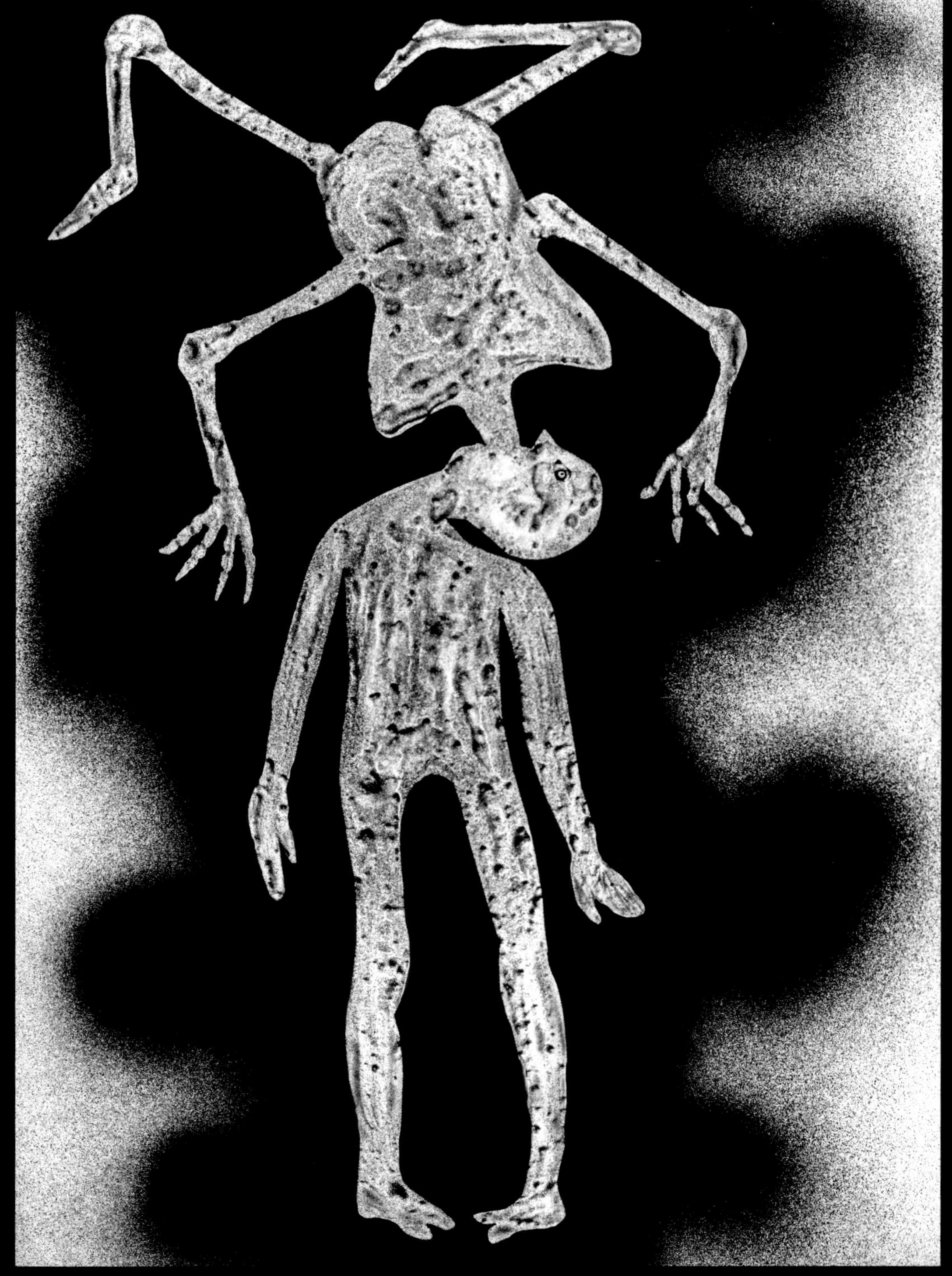

Ambrosial, 2011

Hanging, 2012

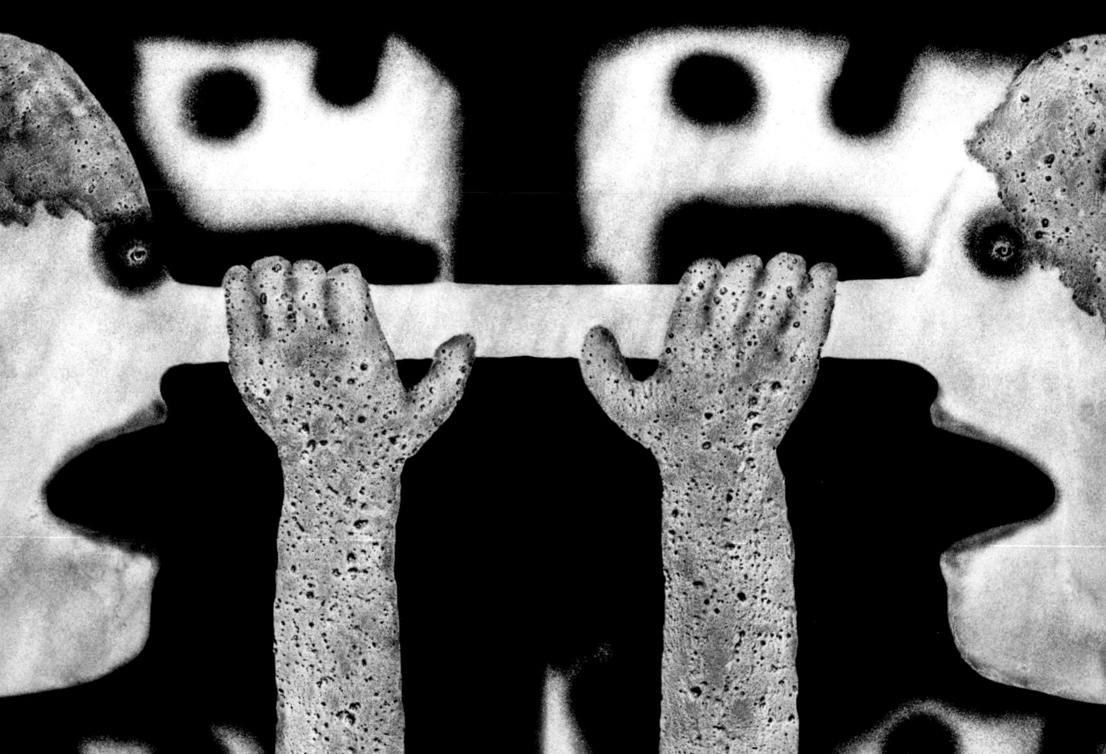

ACT THREE

eros

Foreplay, 2011

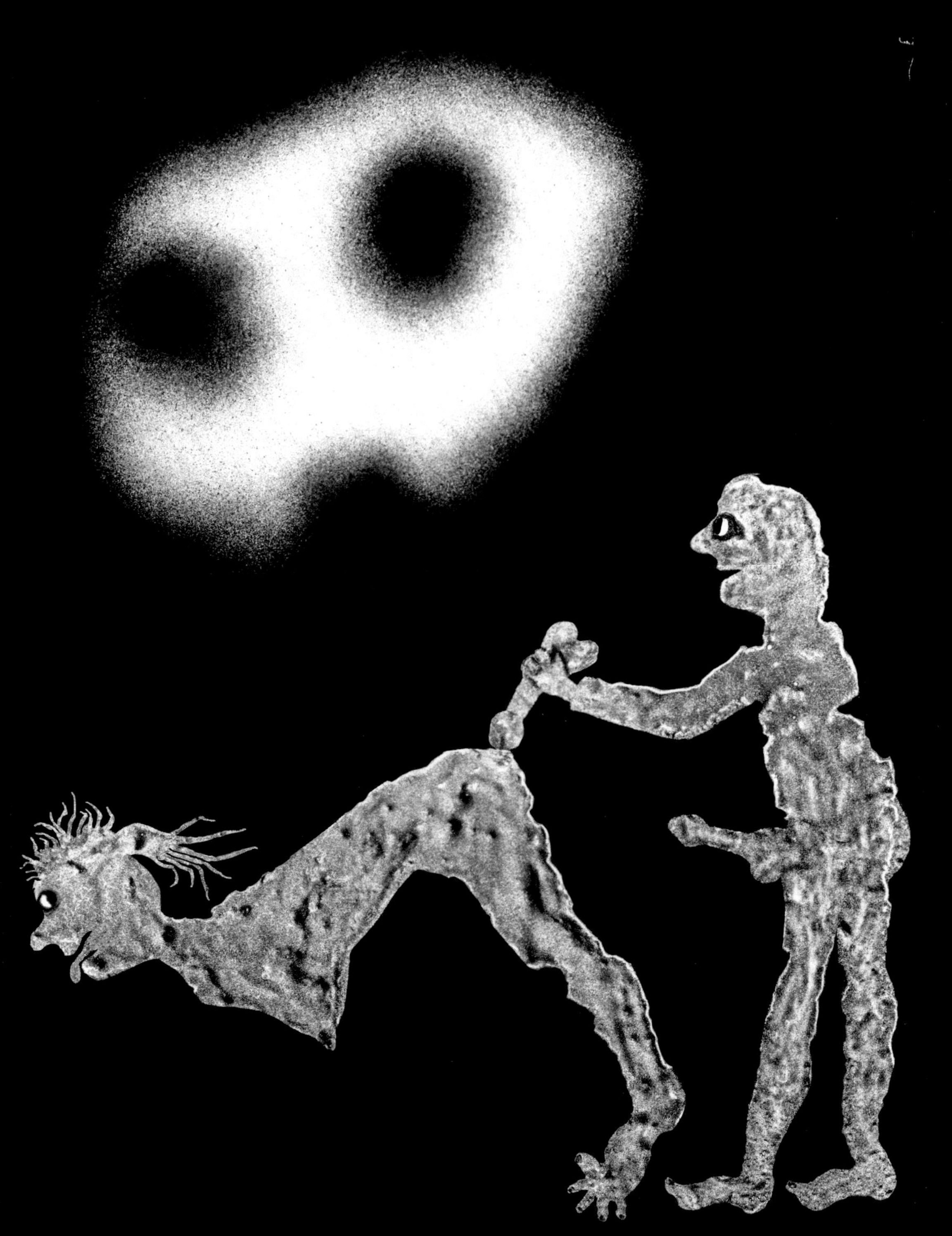

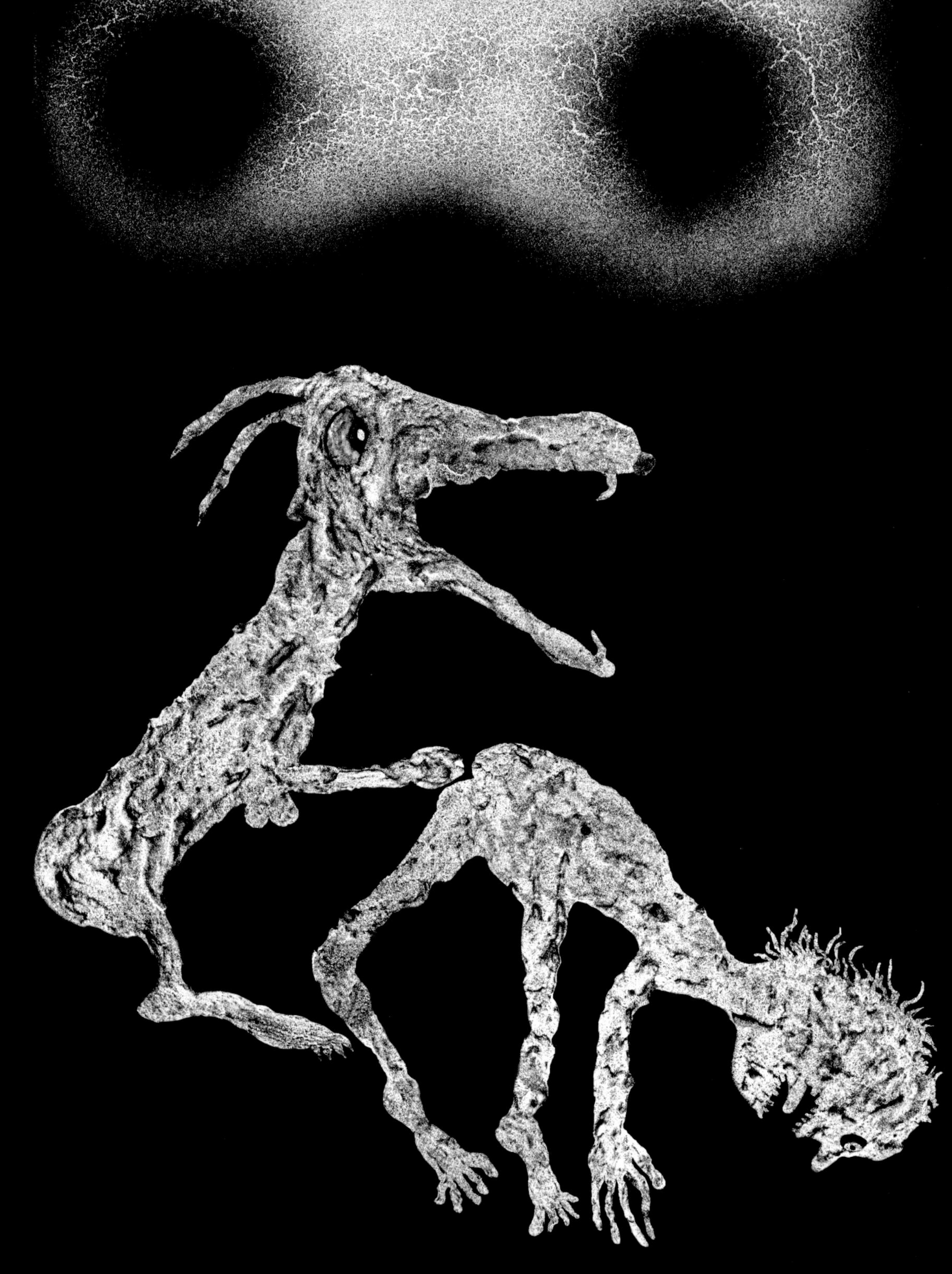

Bestiality, 2010

End to End, 2011
overleaf: Hand Over, 2012

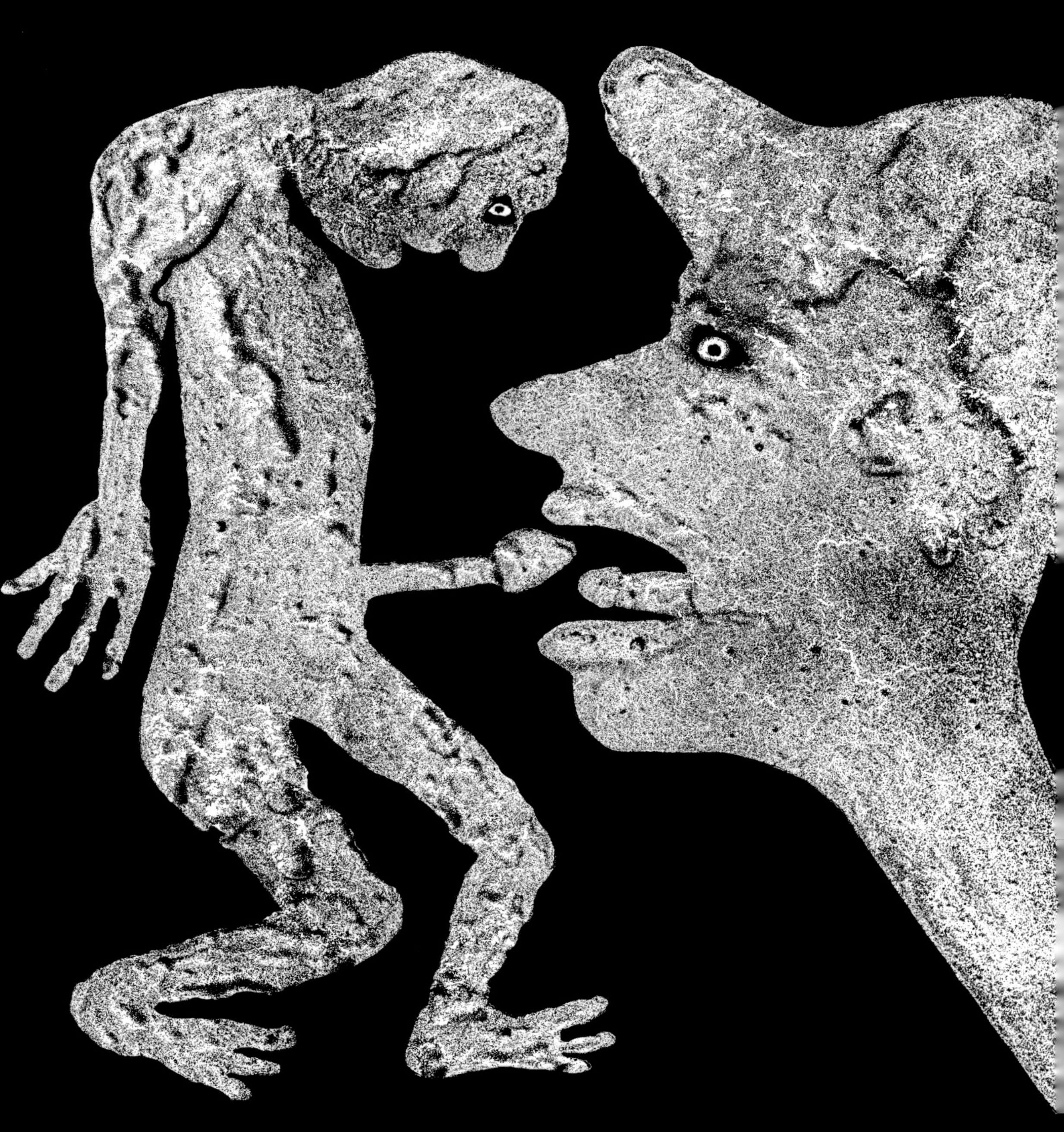

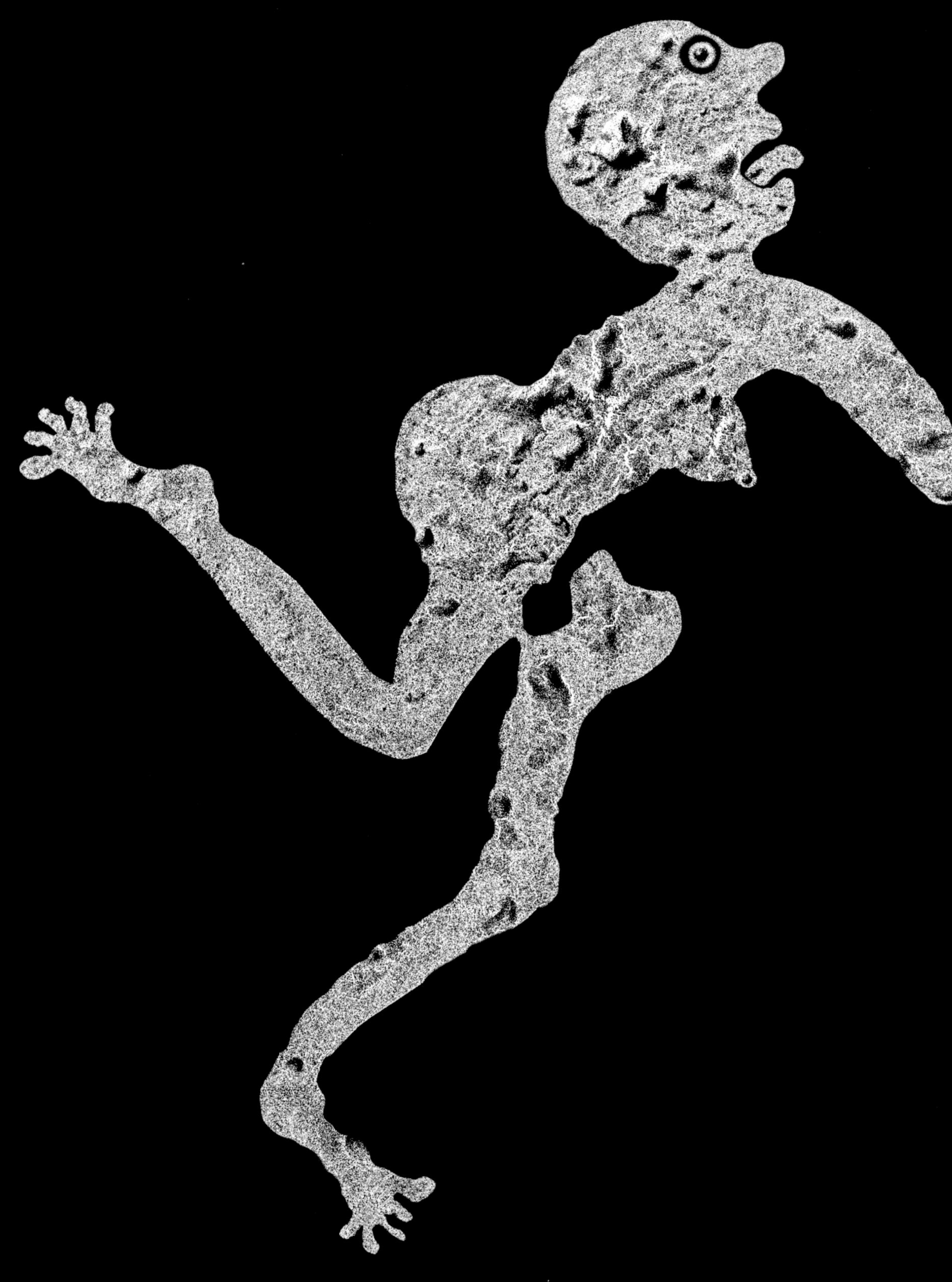

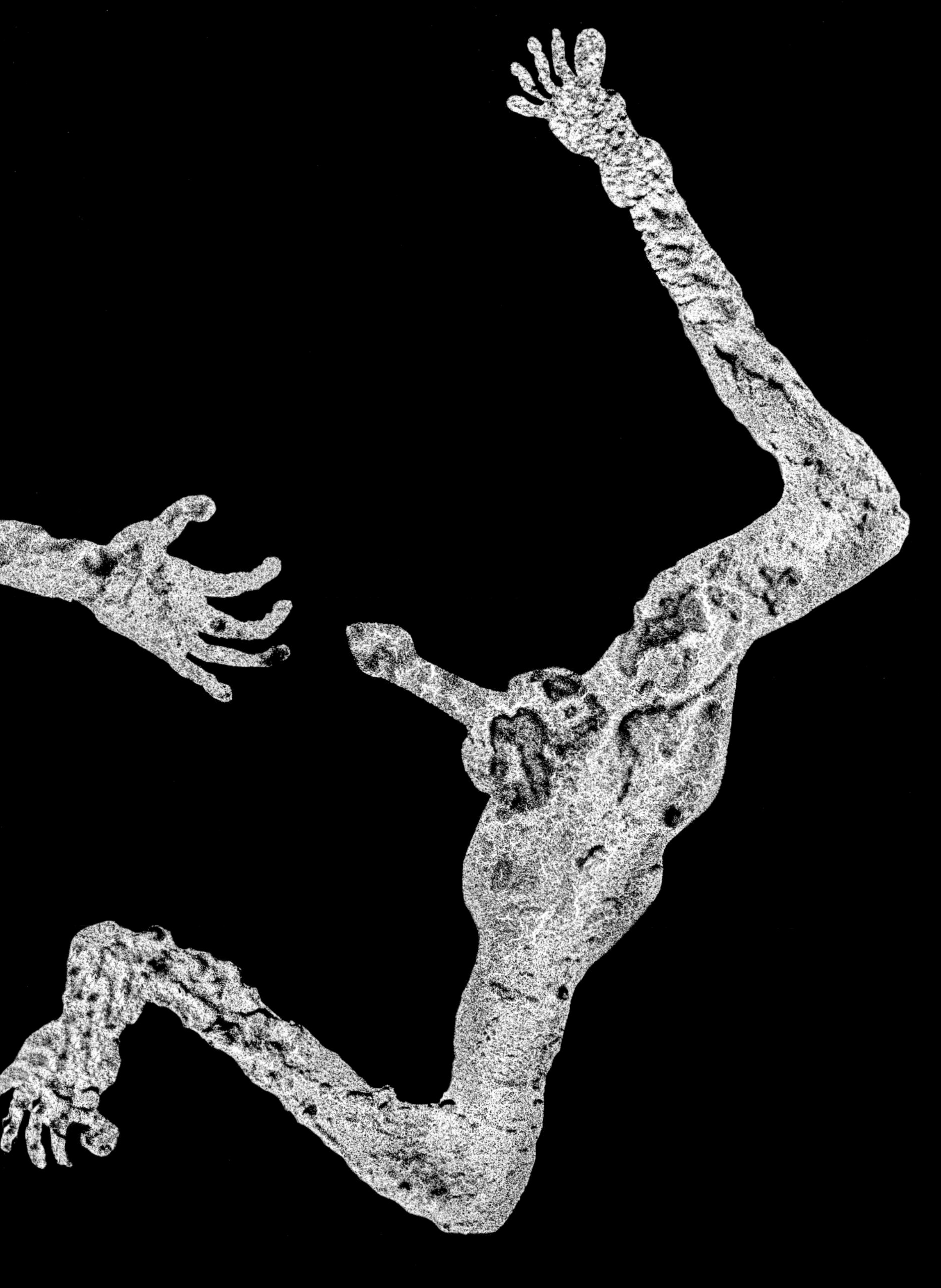

French Kiss, 2010

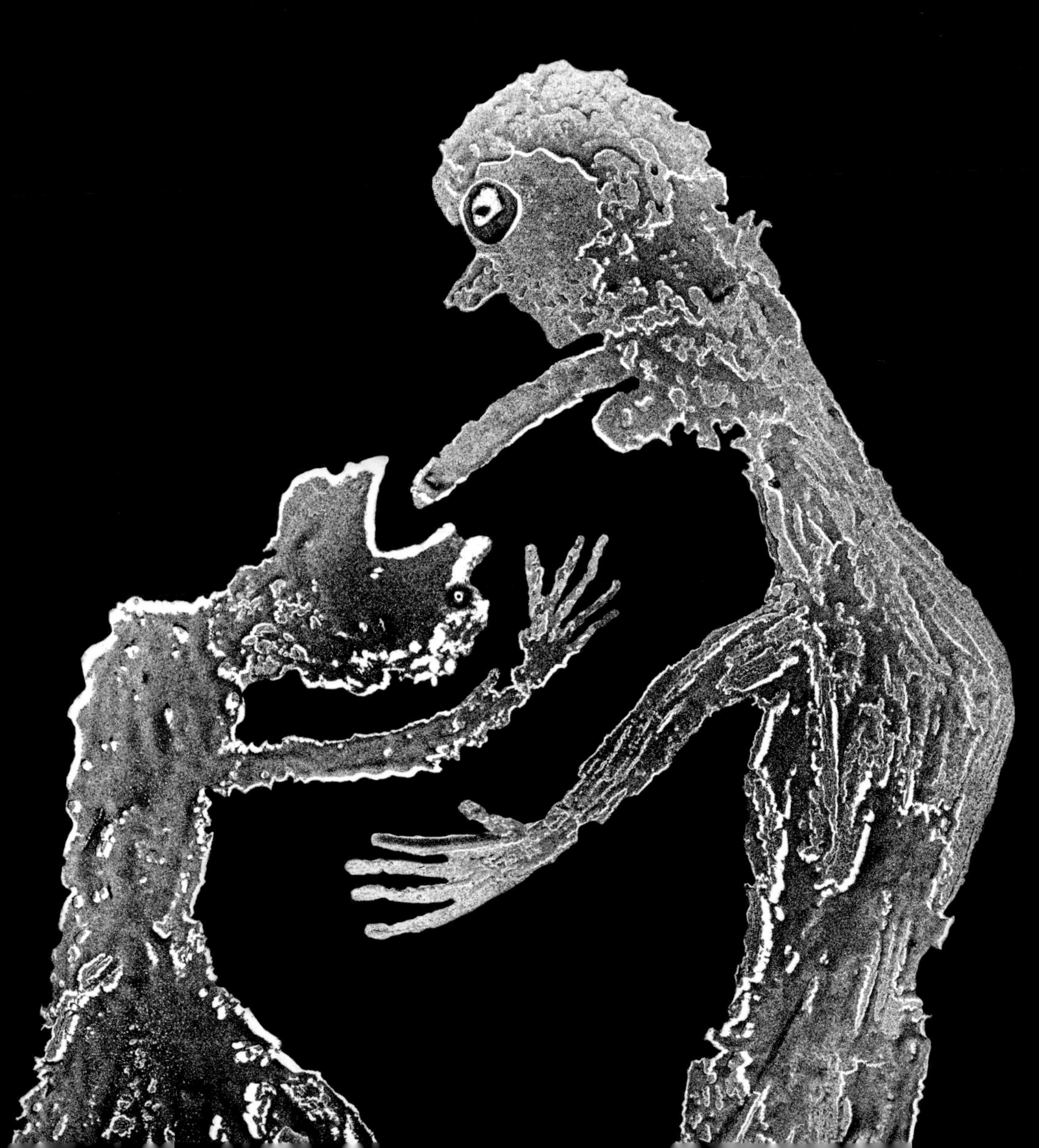

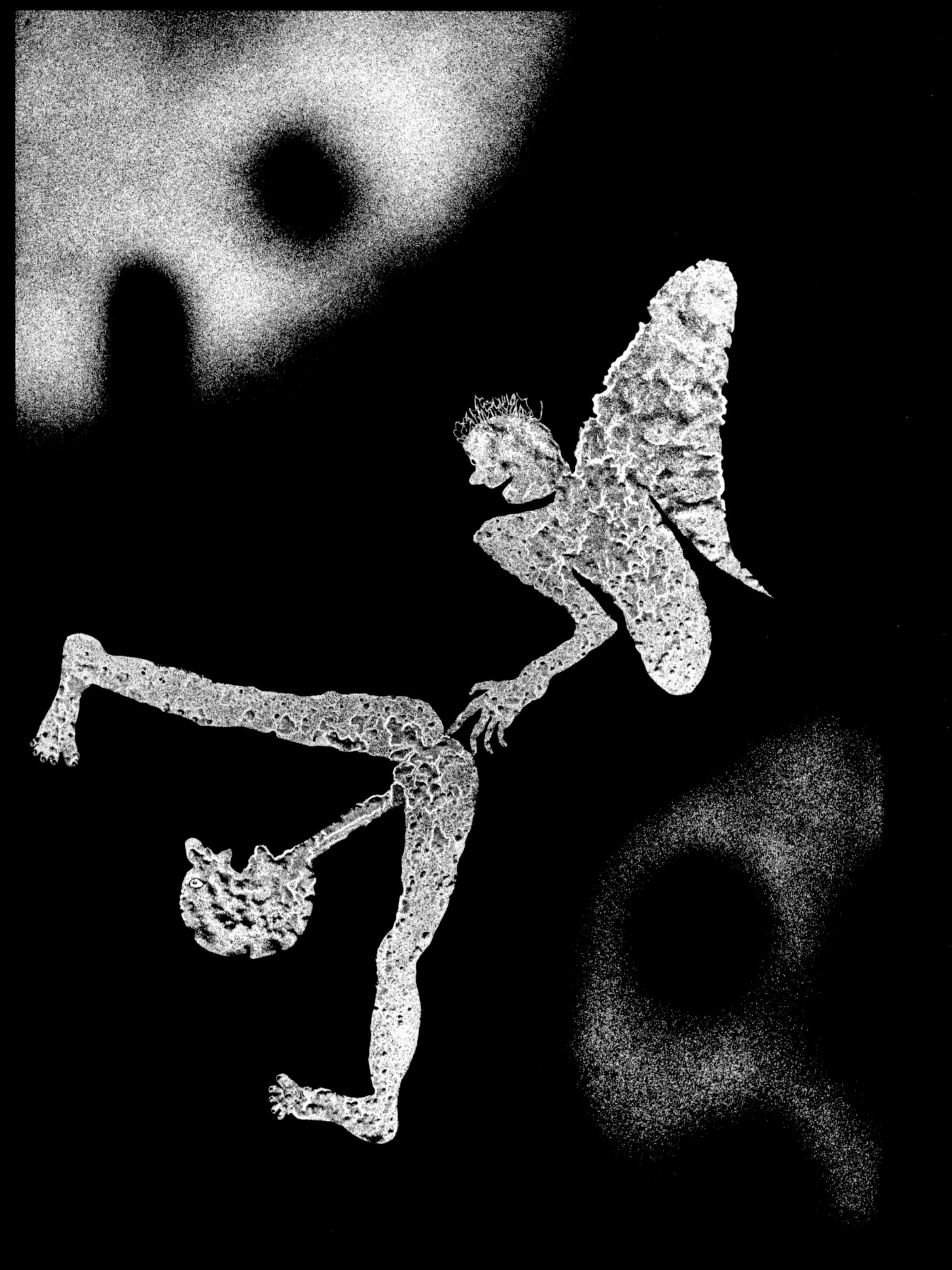

Zing, 2011
overleaf: Queue, 2011

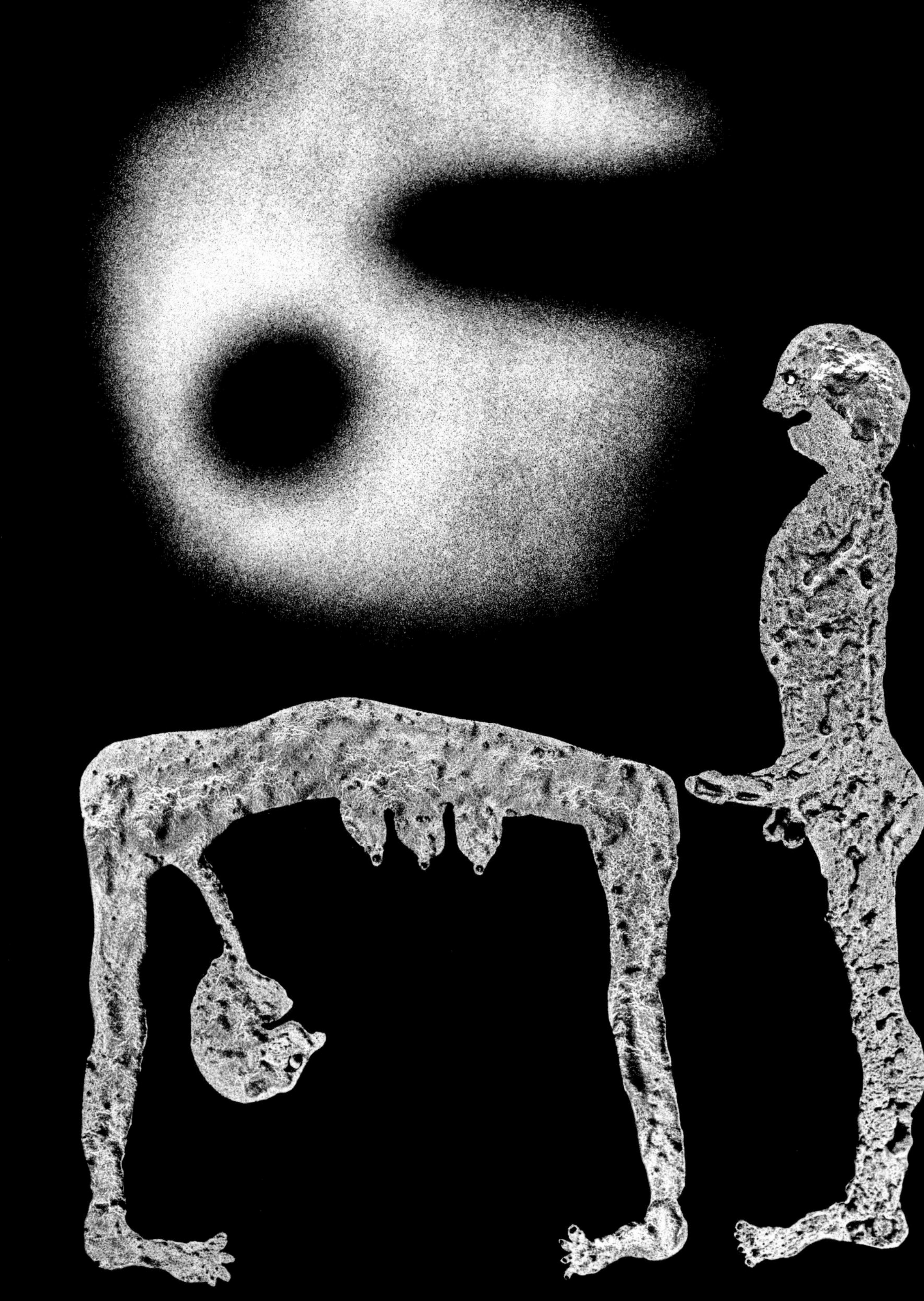

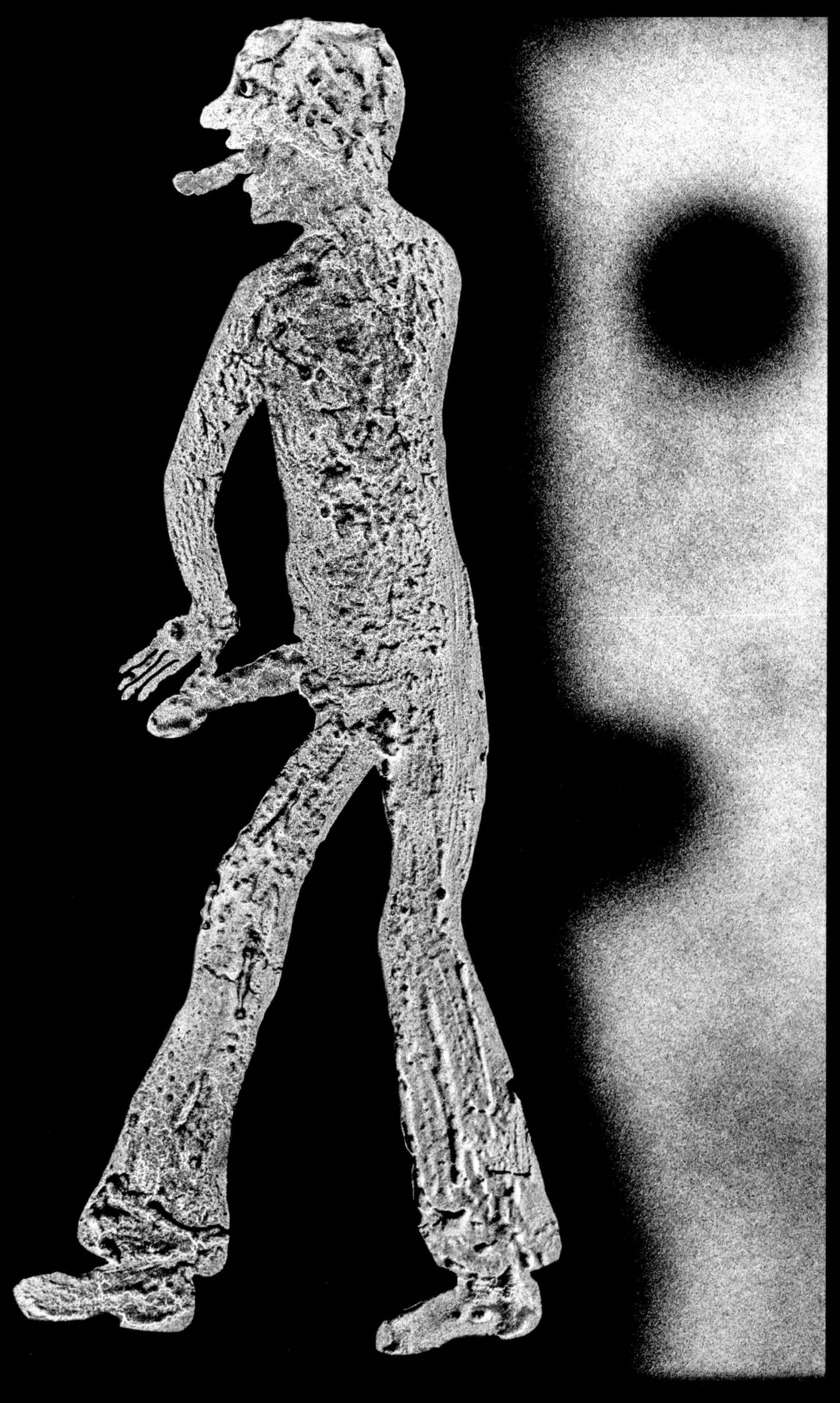

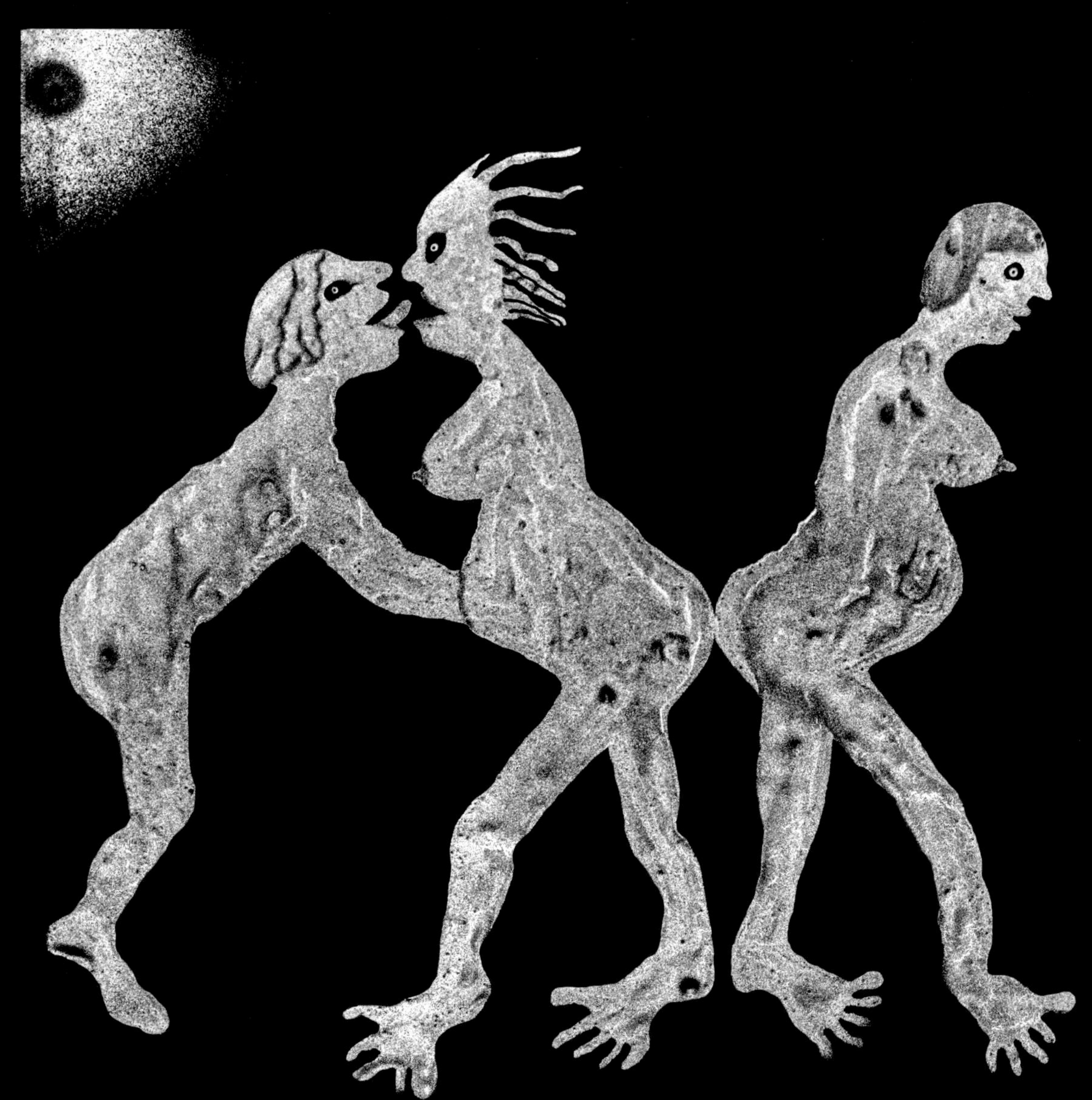

Reject, 2011

Tantalize, 2011

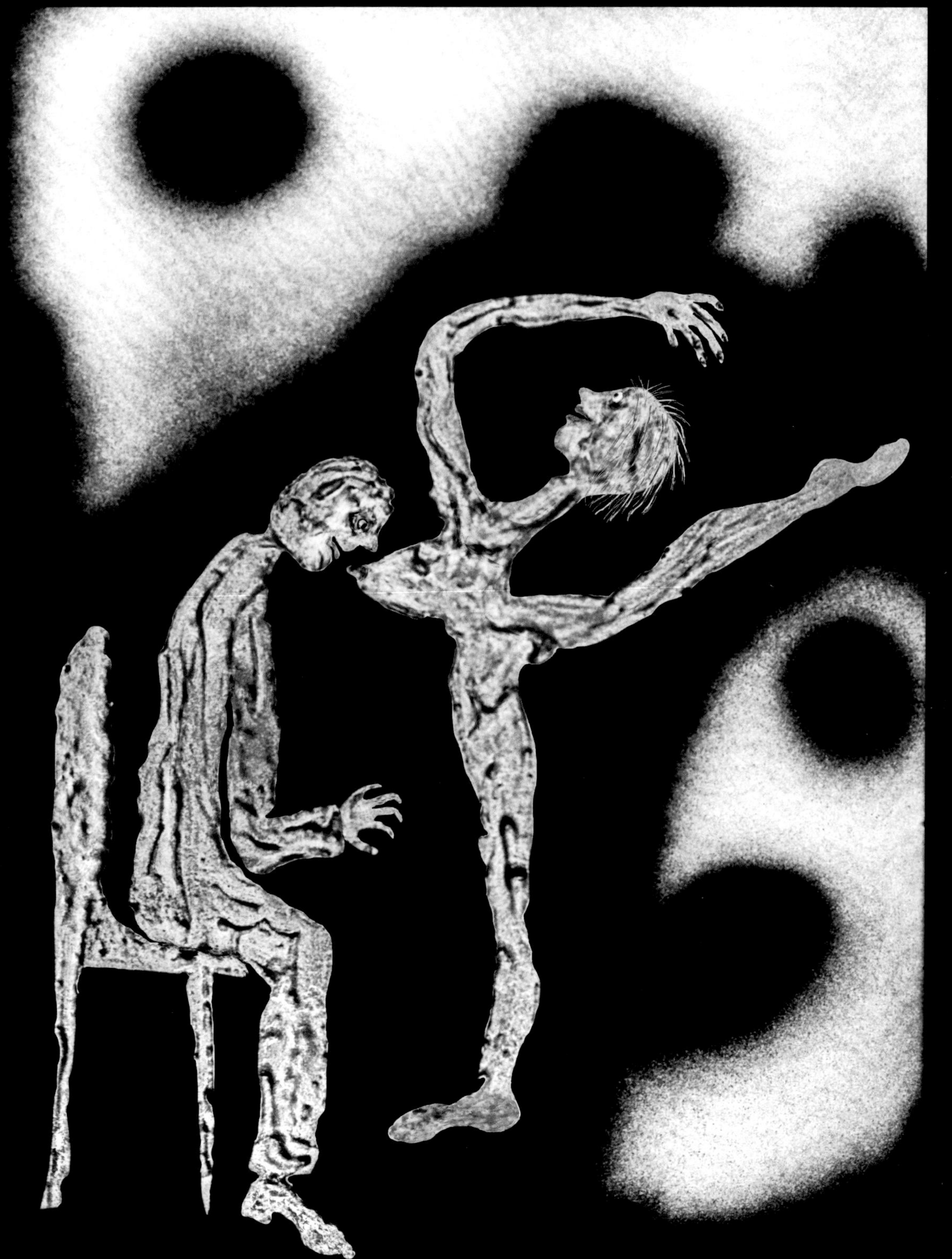

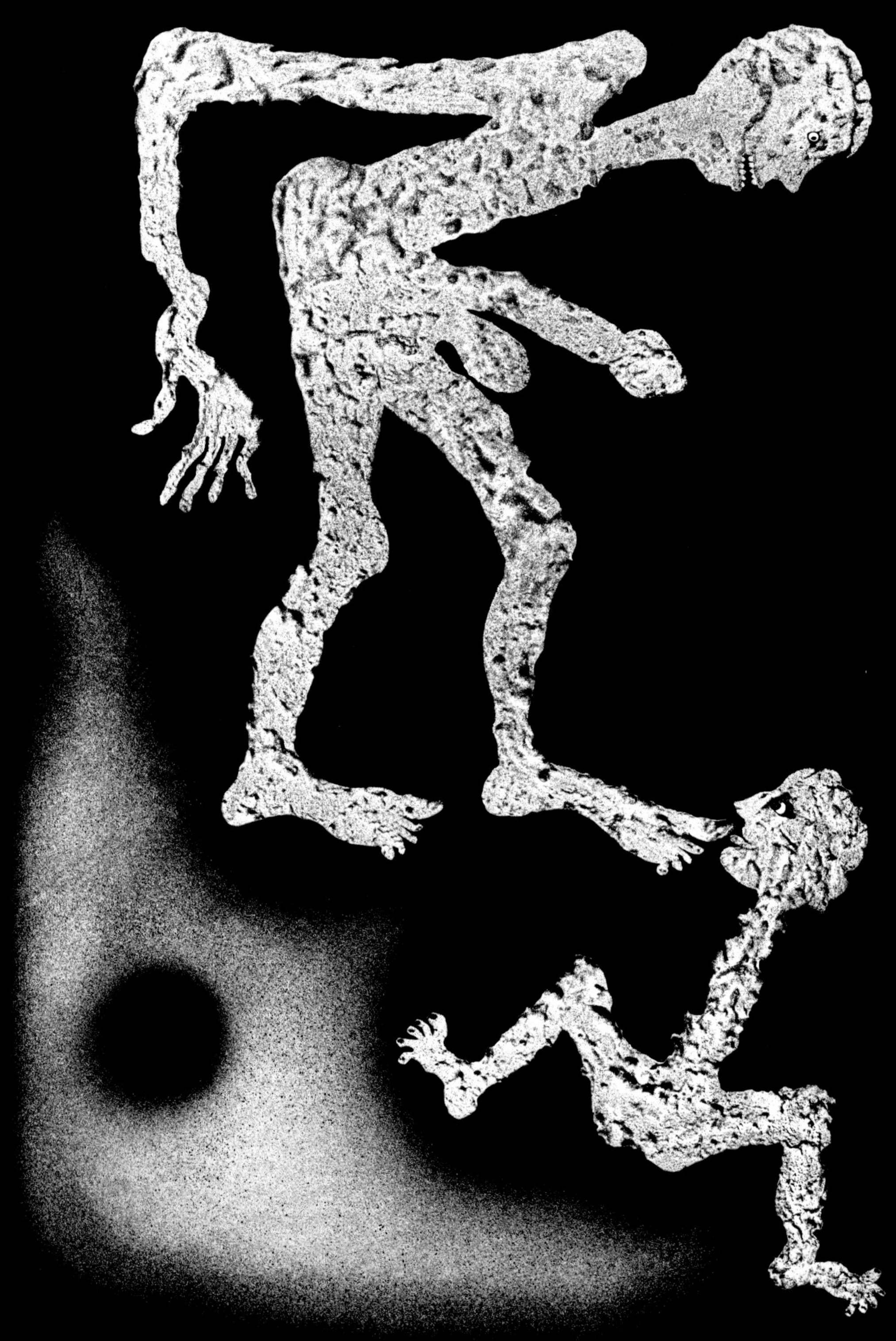

Protégé, 2012

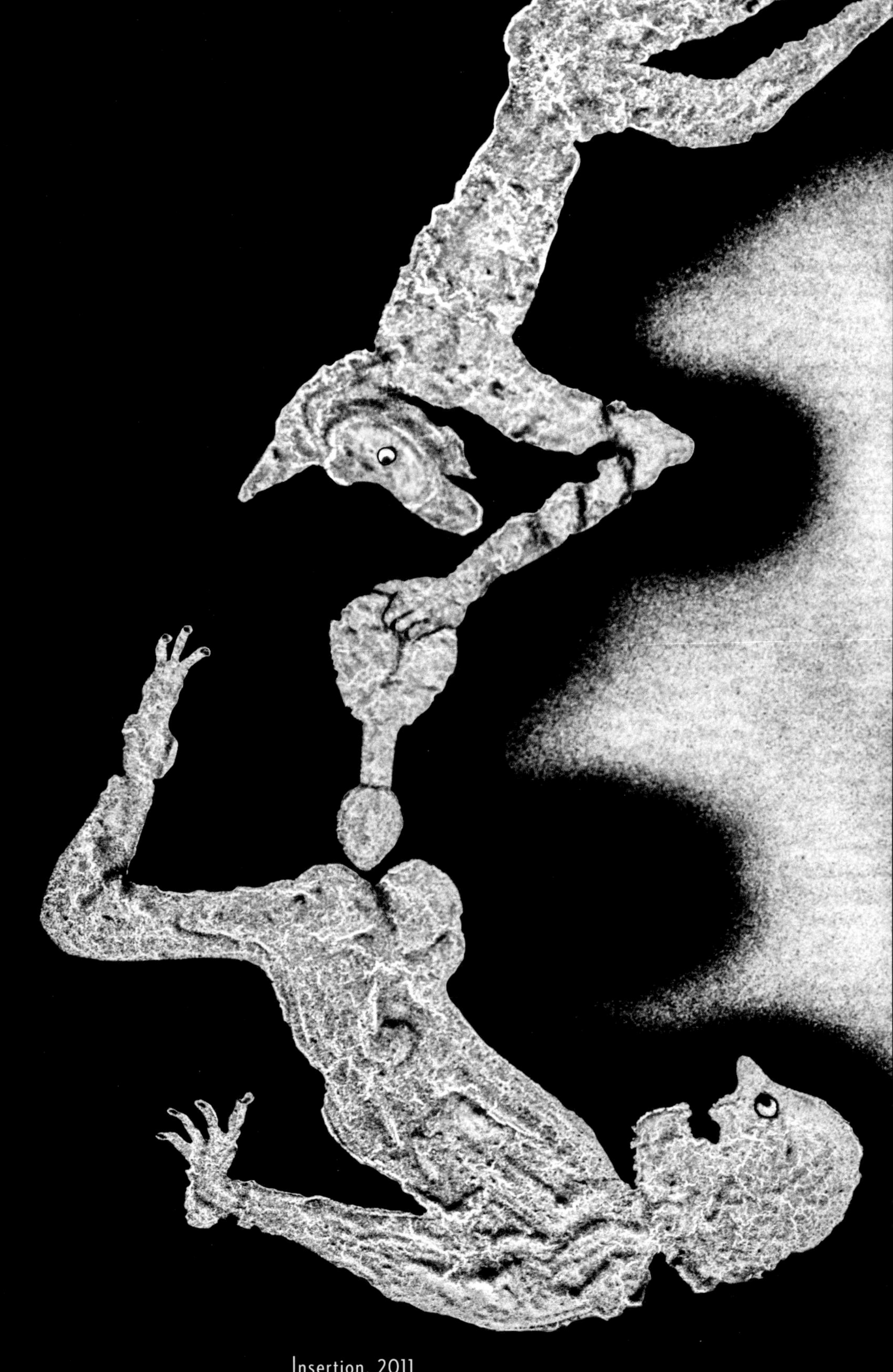

Insertion, 2011

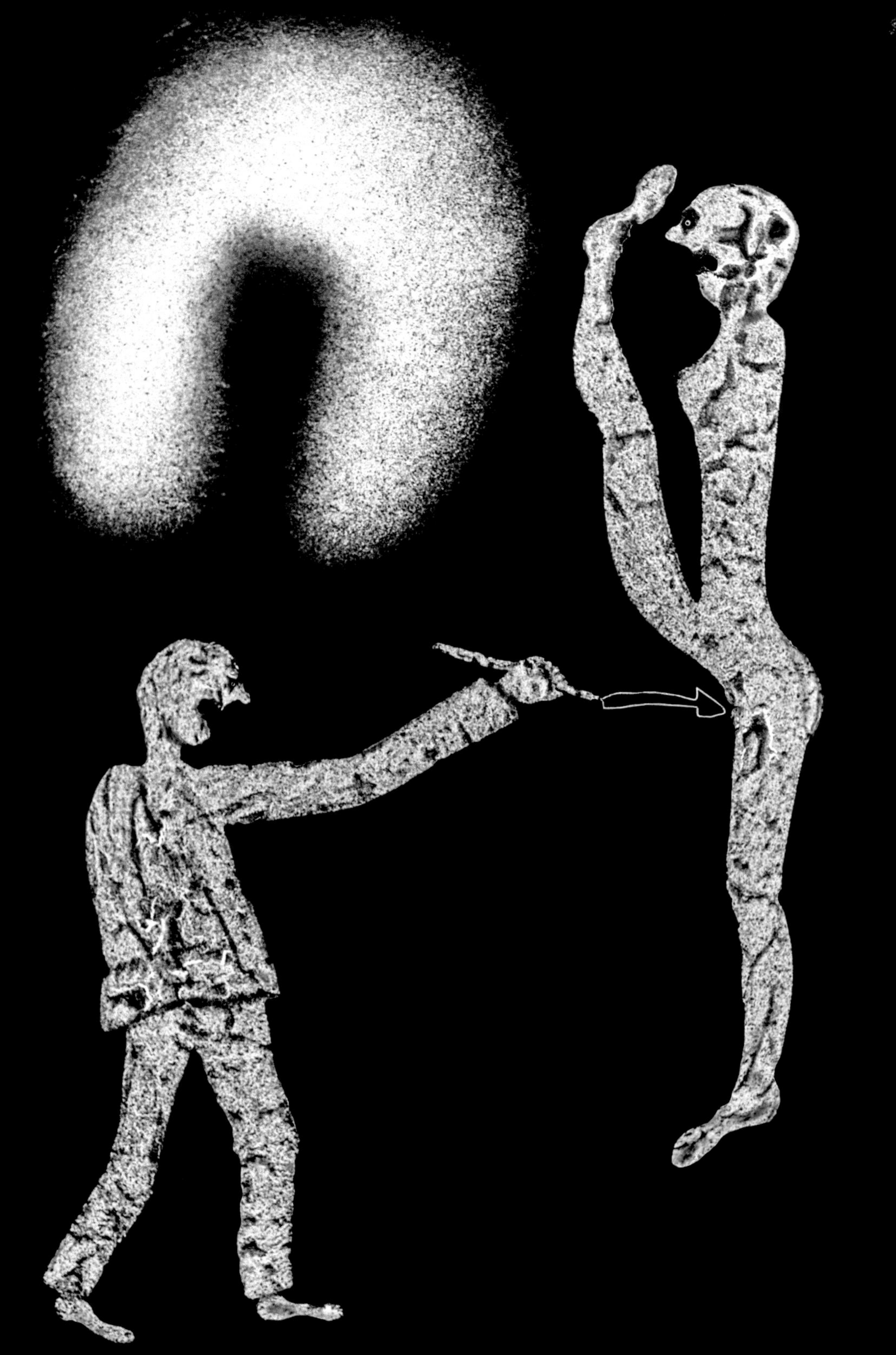

Marking, 2011

Felatio, 2011

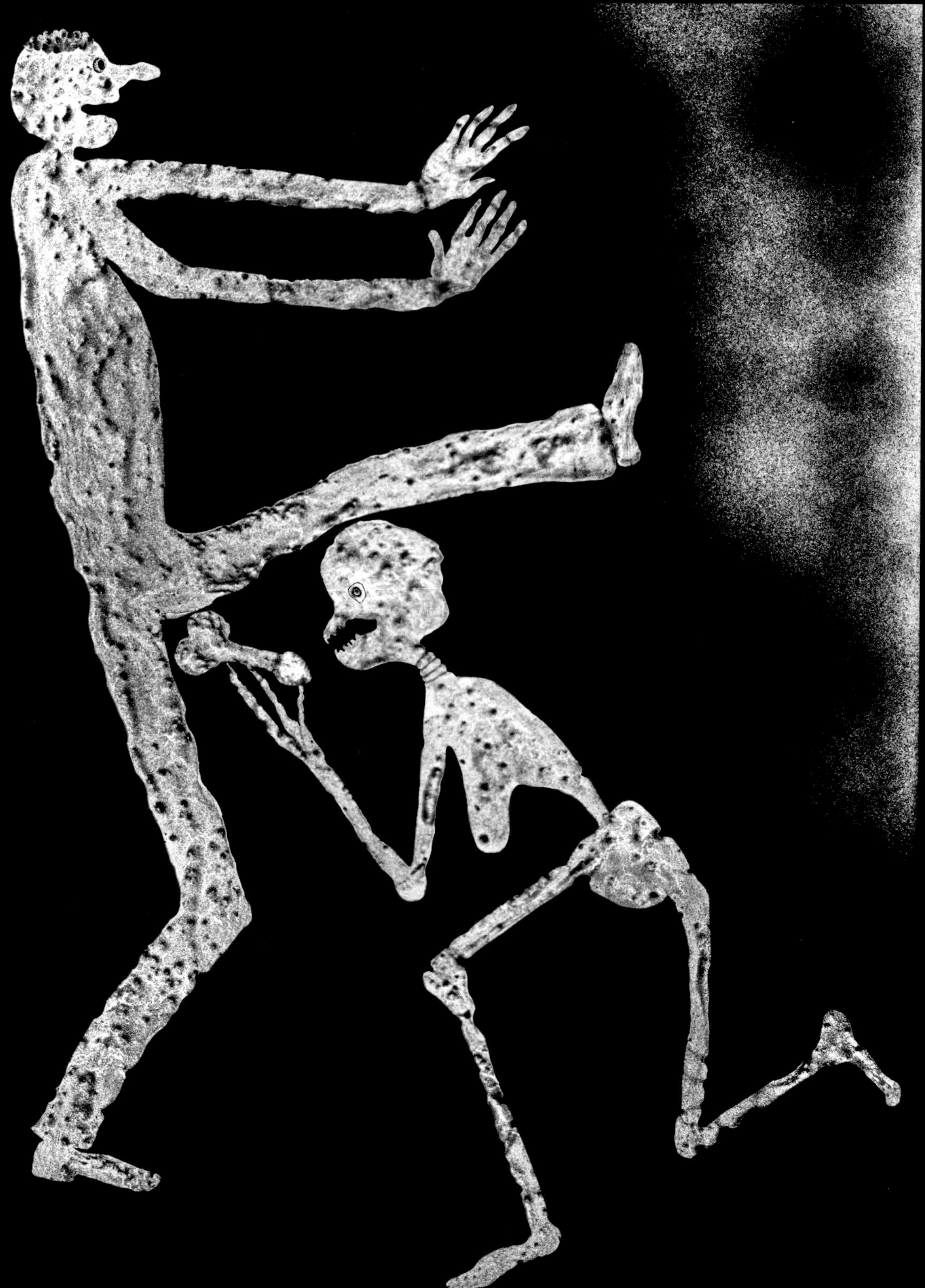

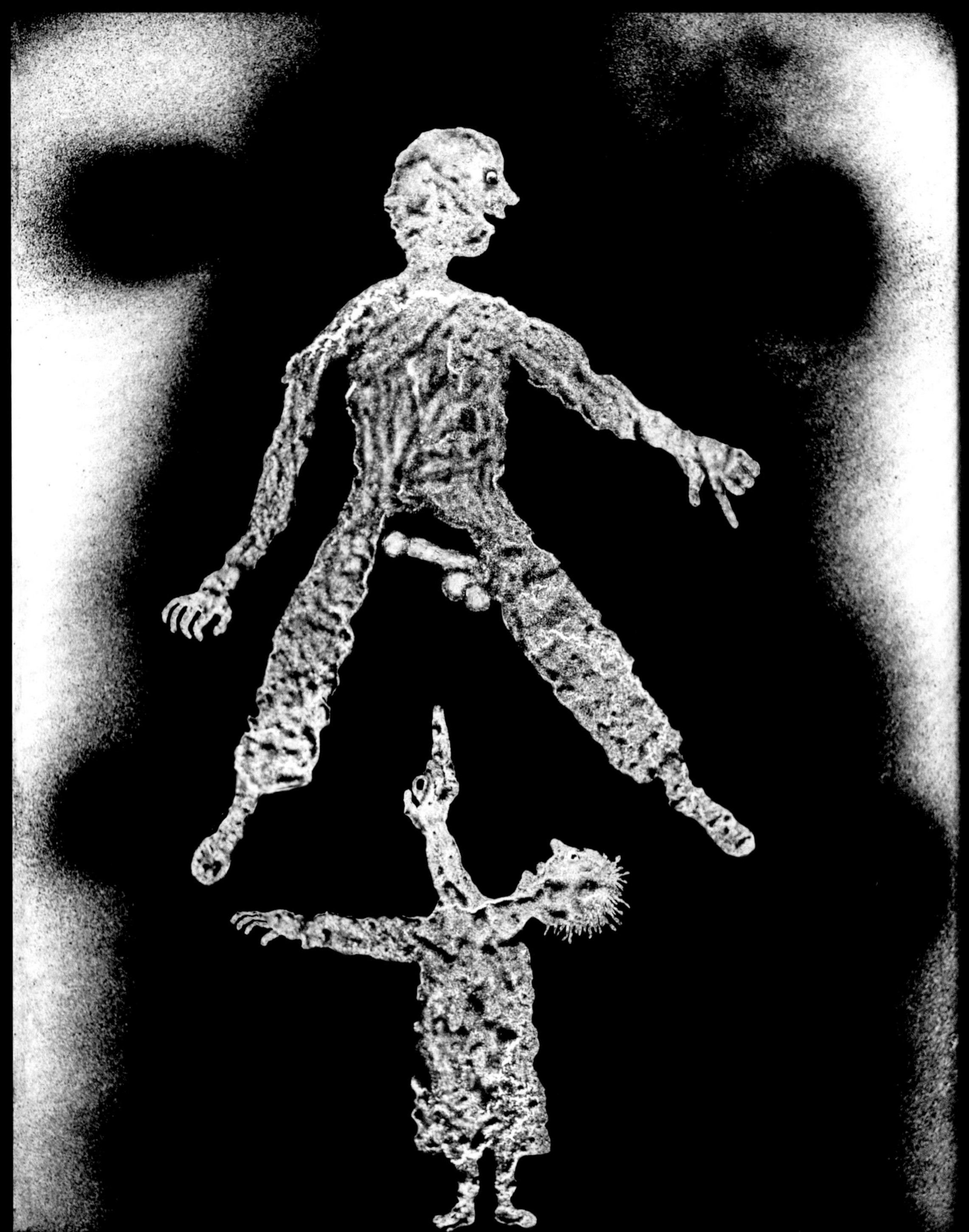

Hold Up, 2011

Sacrifice, 2011

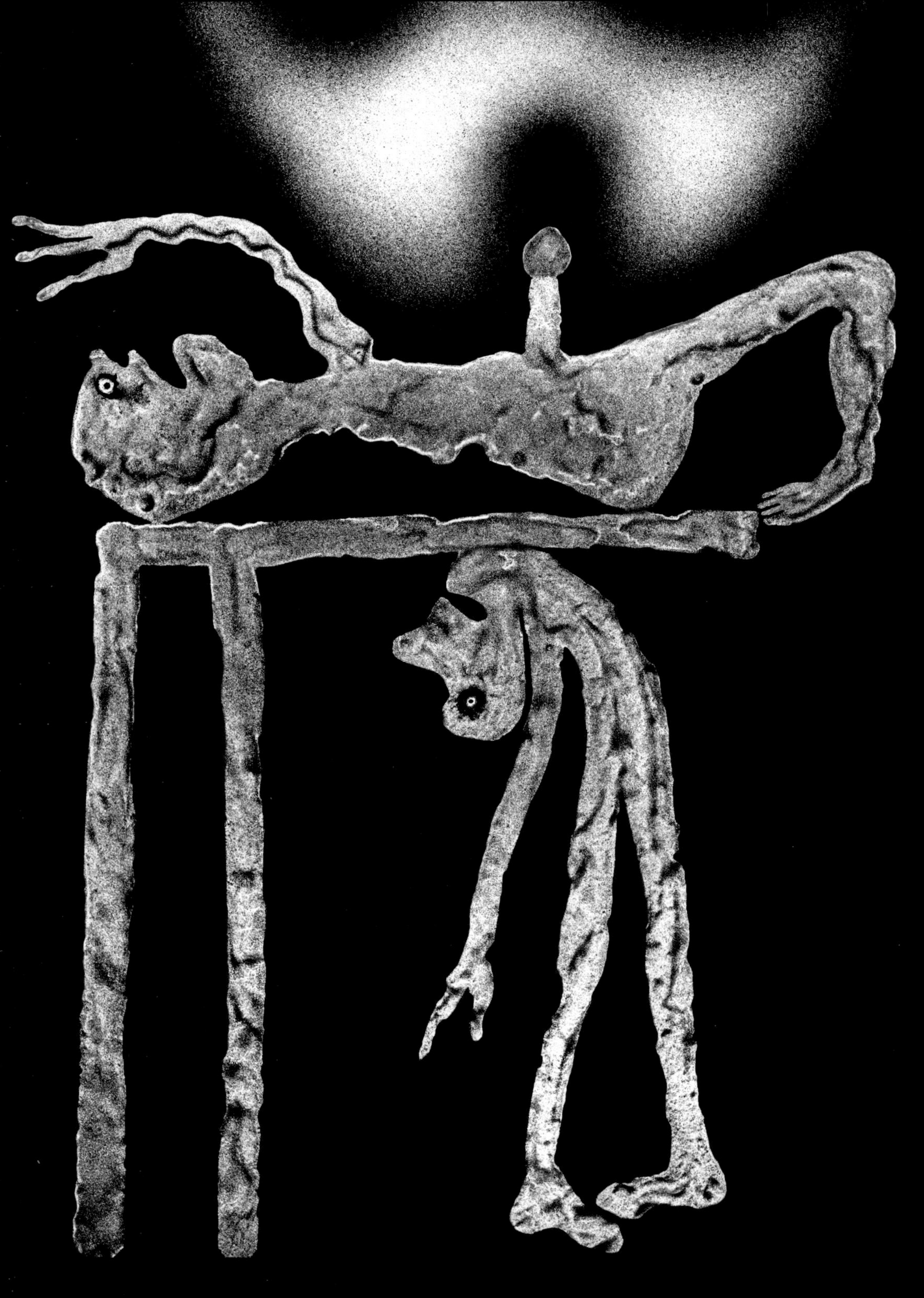

ACT FOUR

transmuted

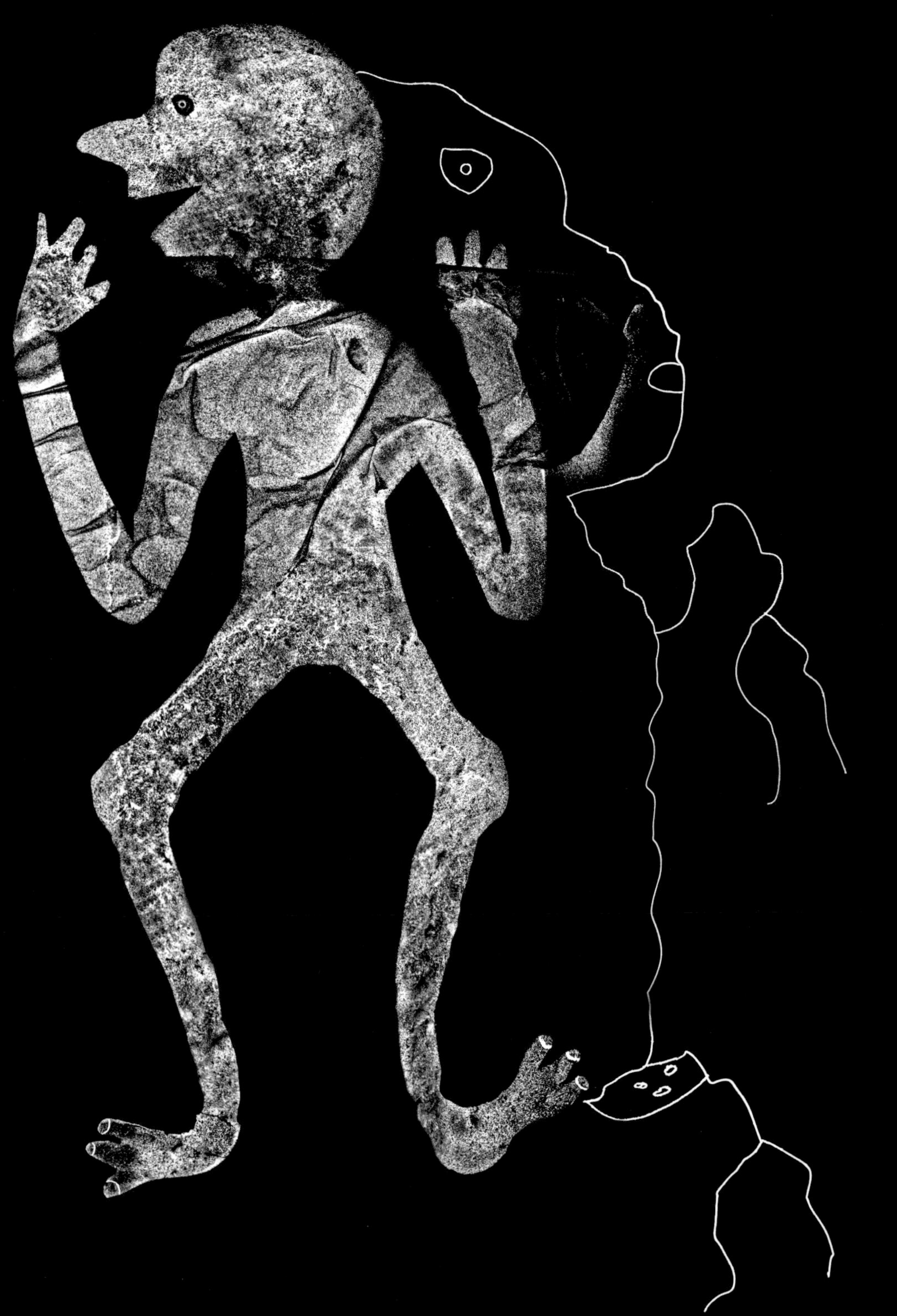

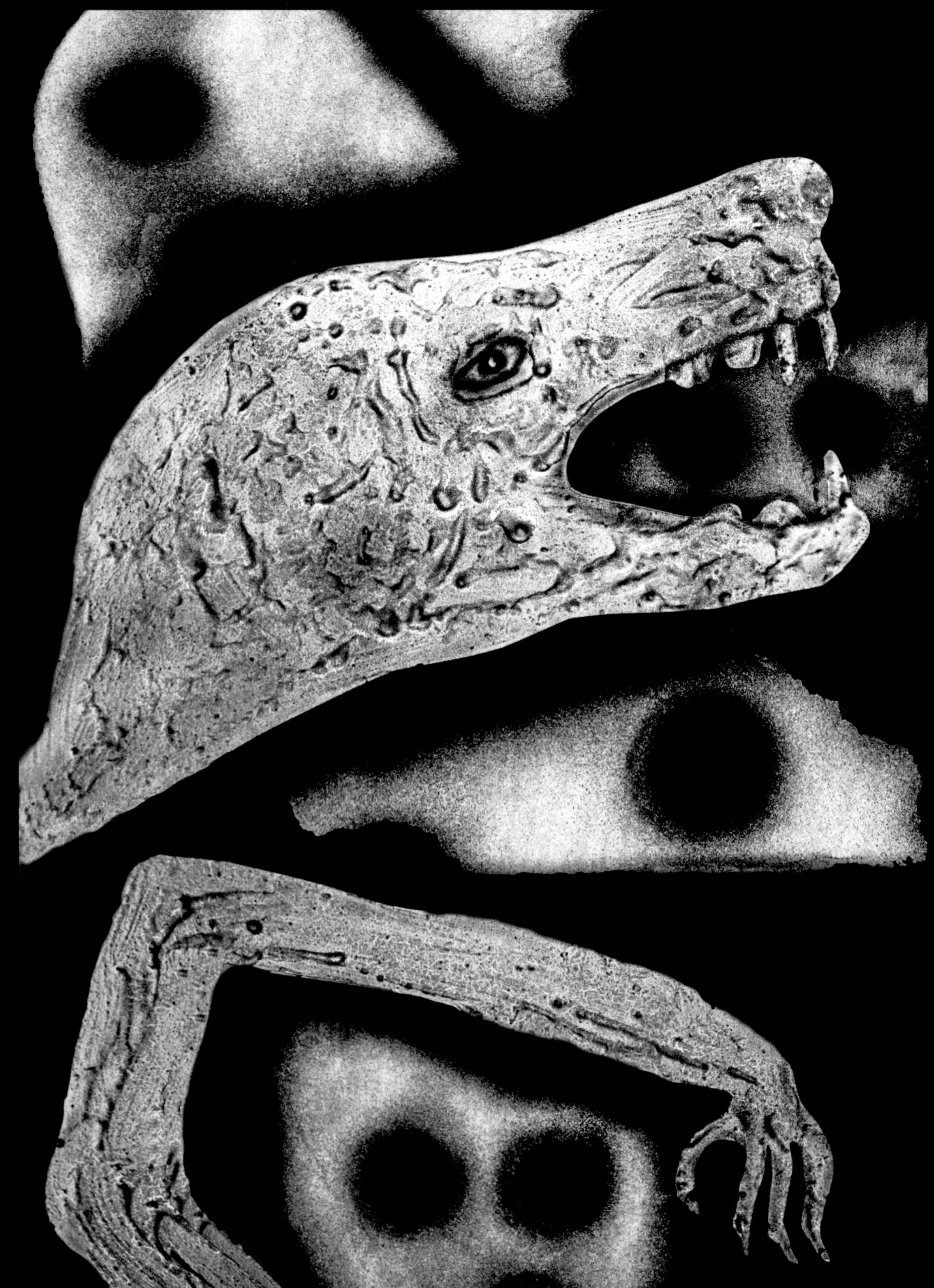

Lion's Den, 2012

Feeding, 2012

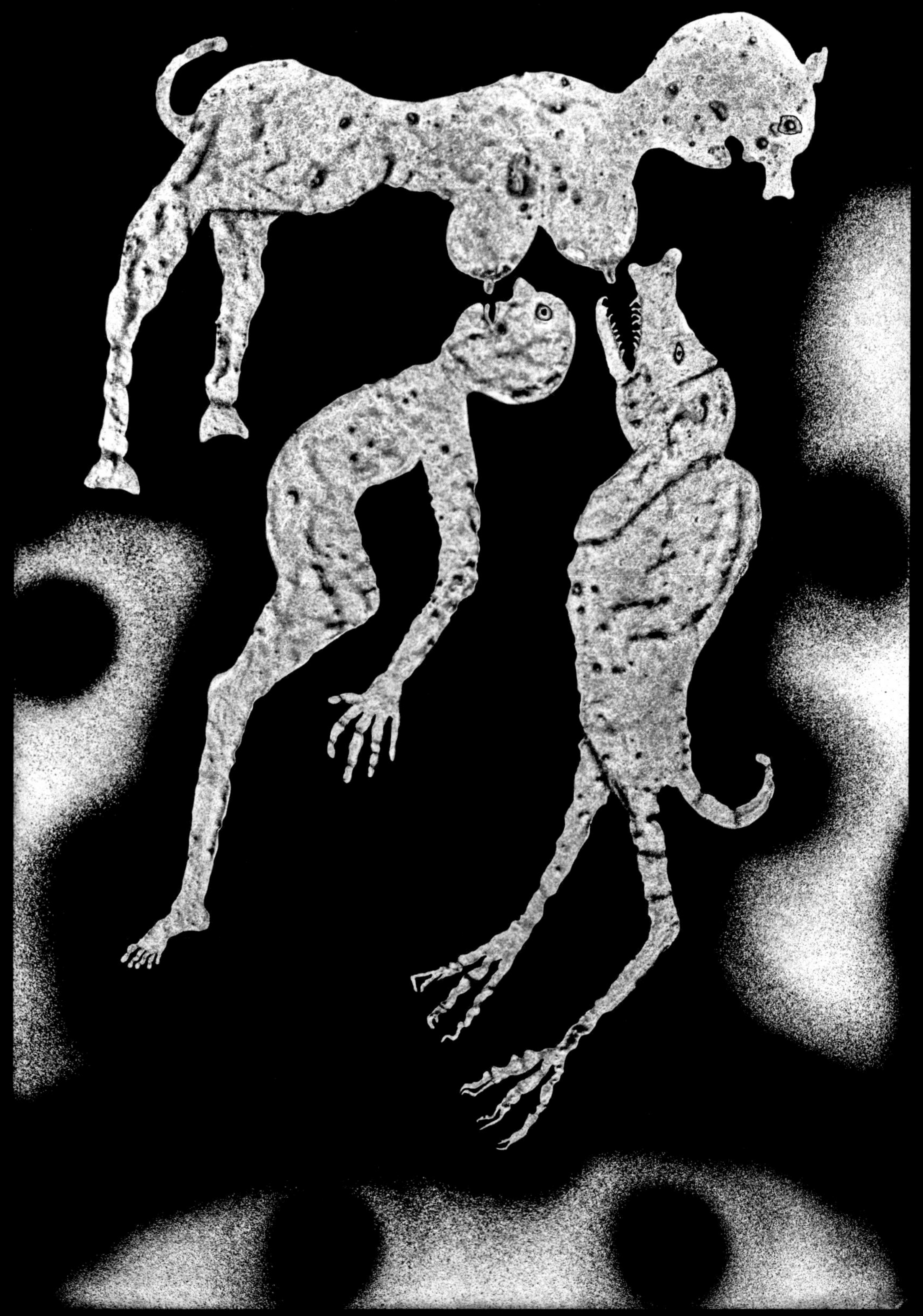

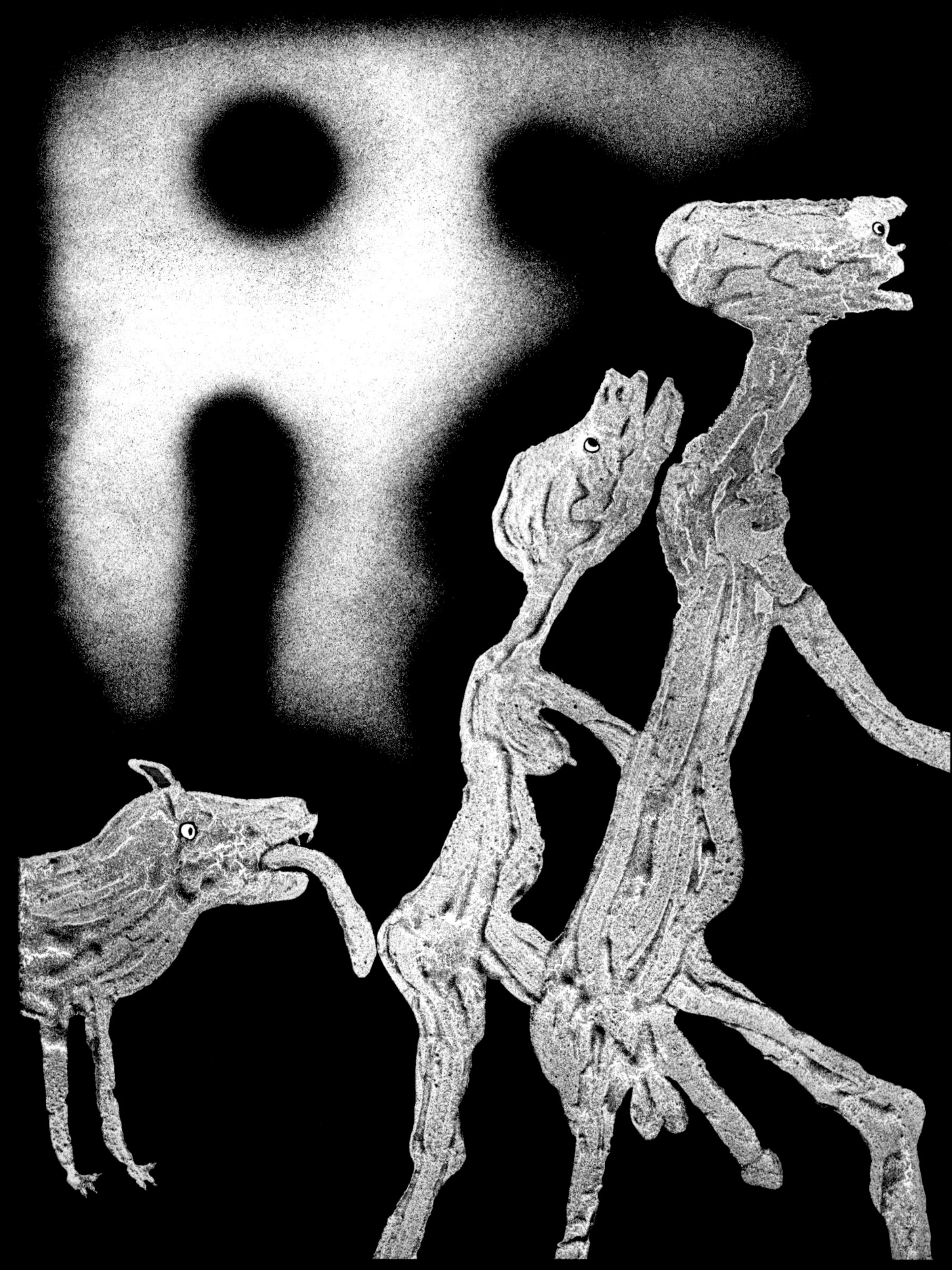

Lick, 2012

Lick, 2012

Ghostriding, 2011

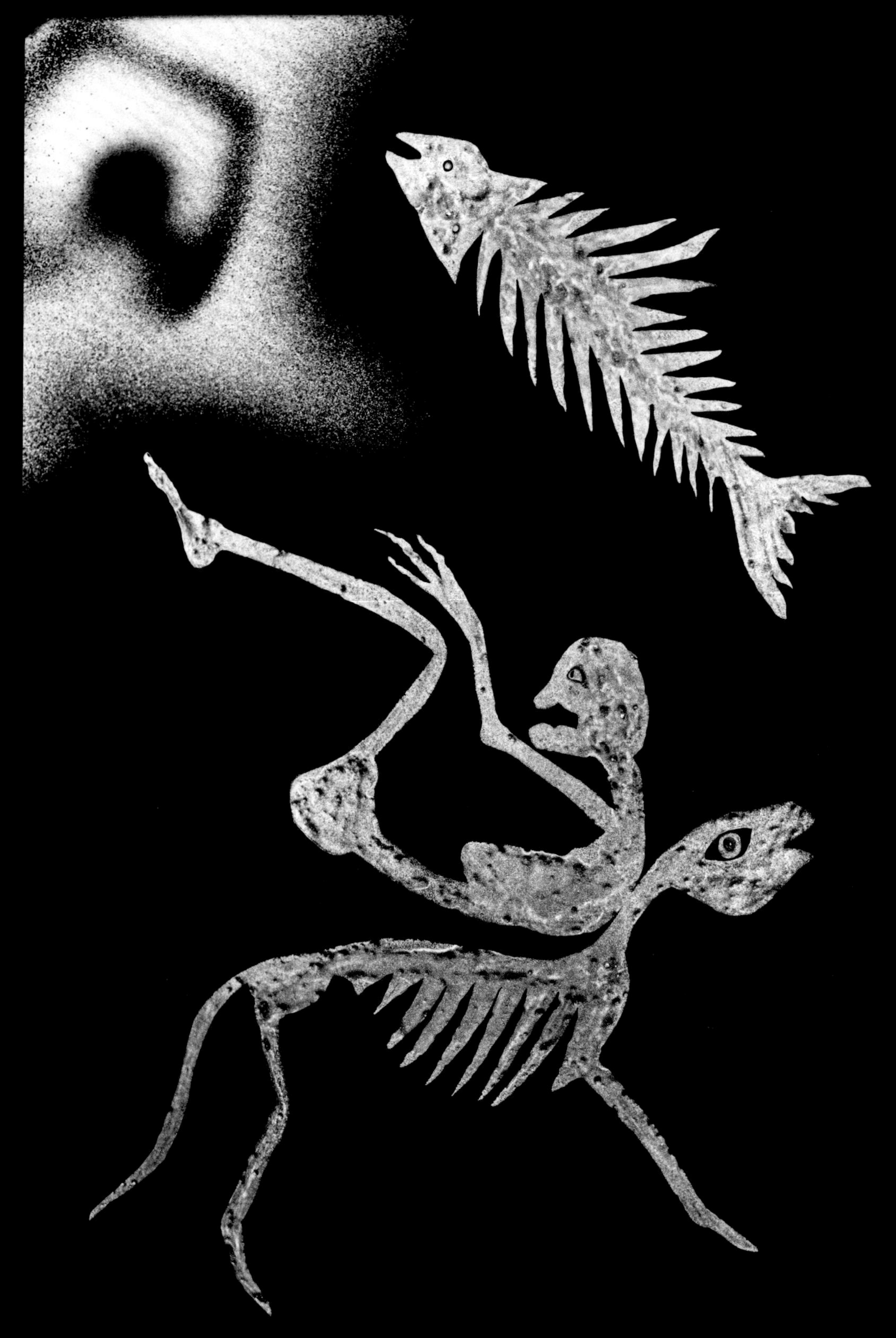

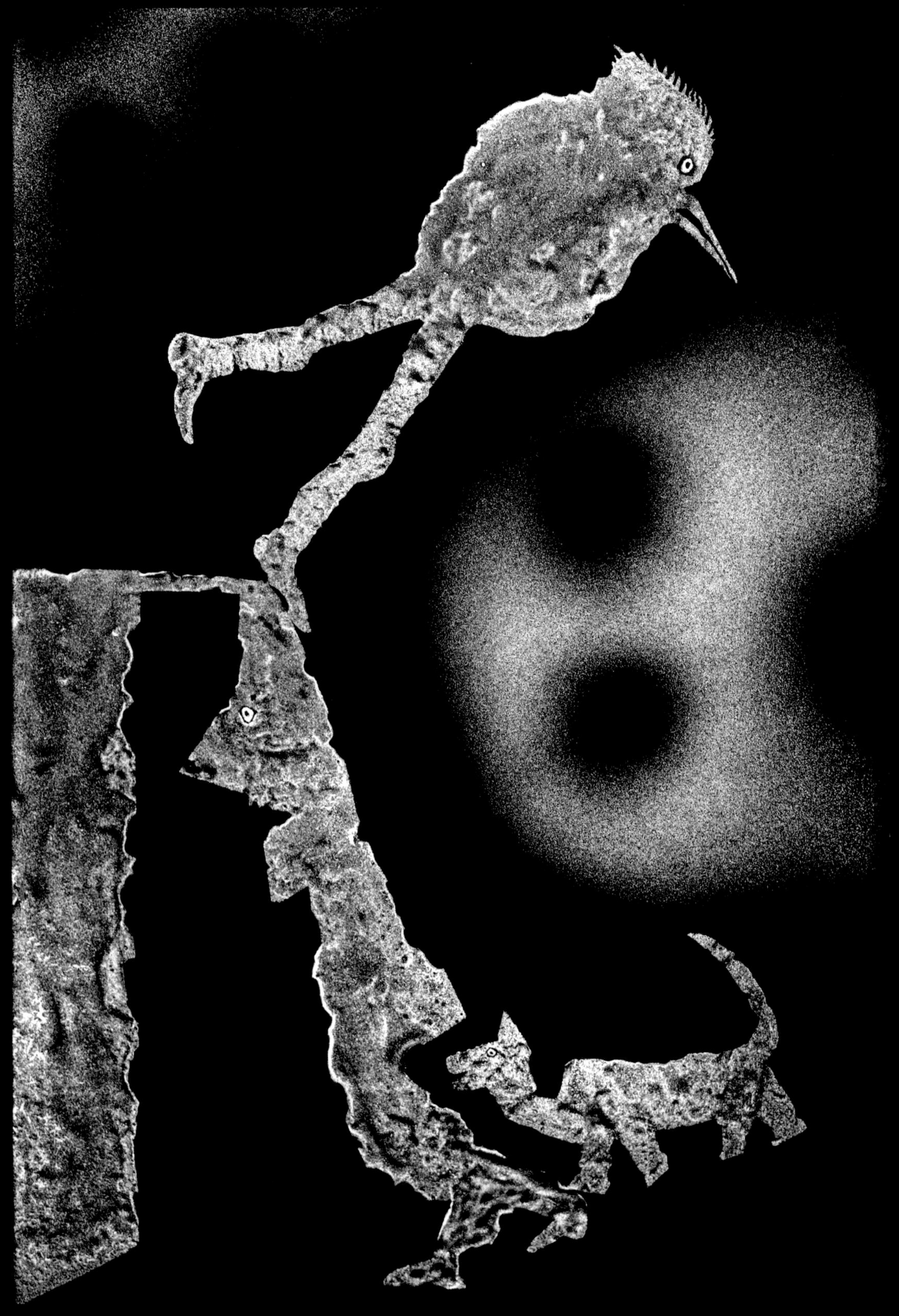

Frolicking, 2011

Ouch, 2010

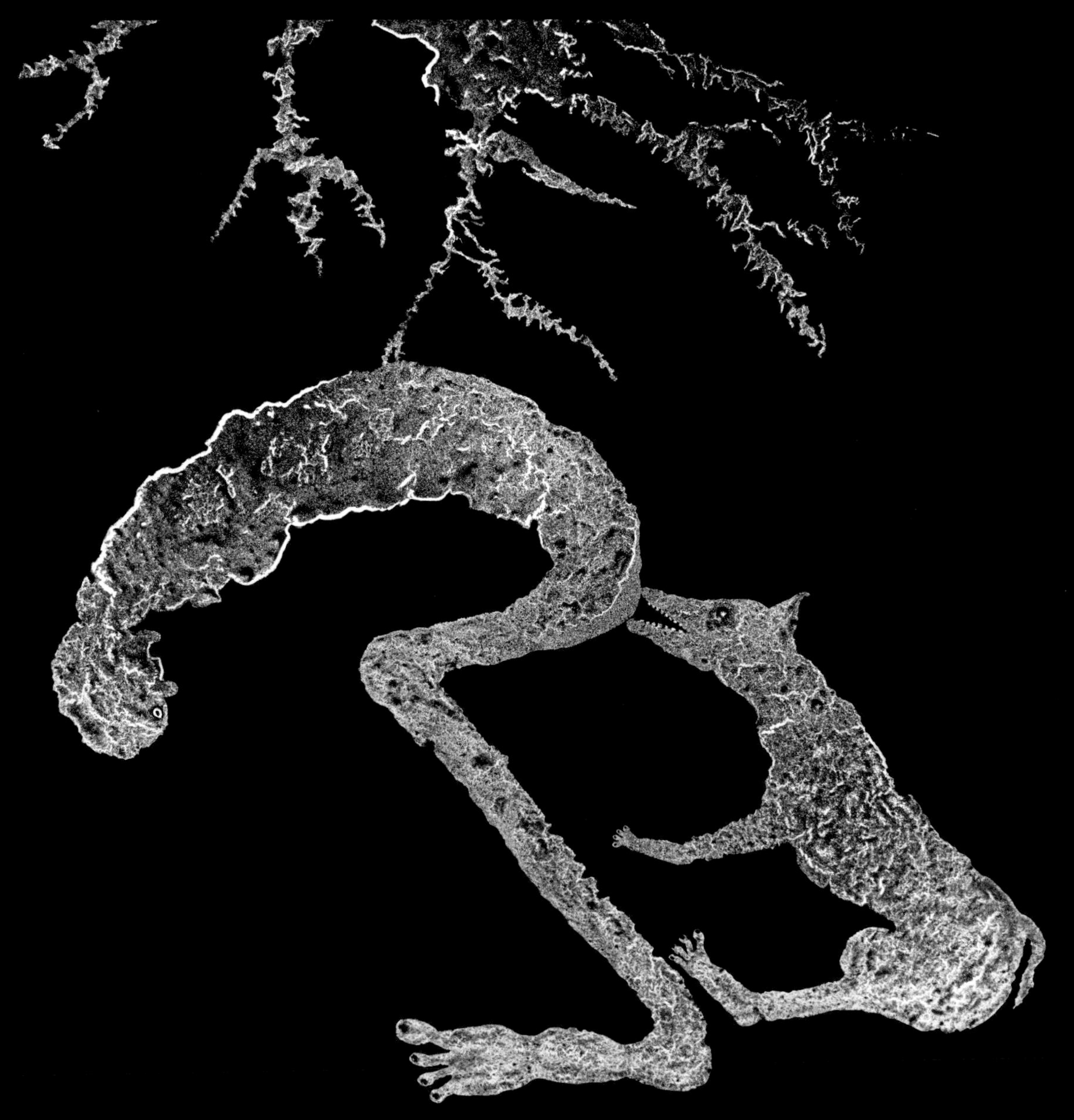

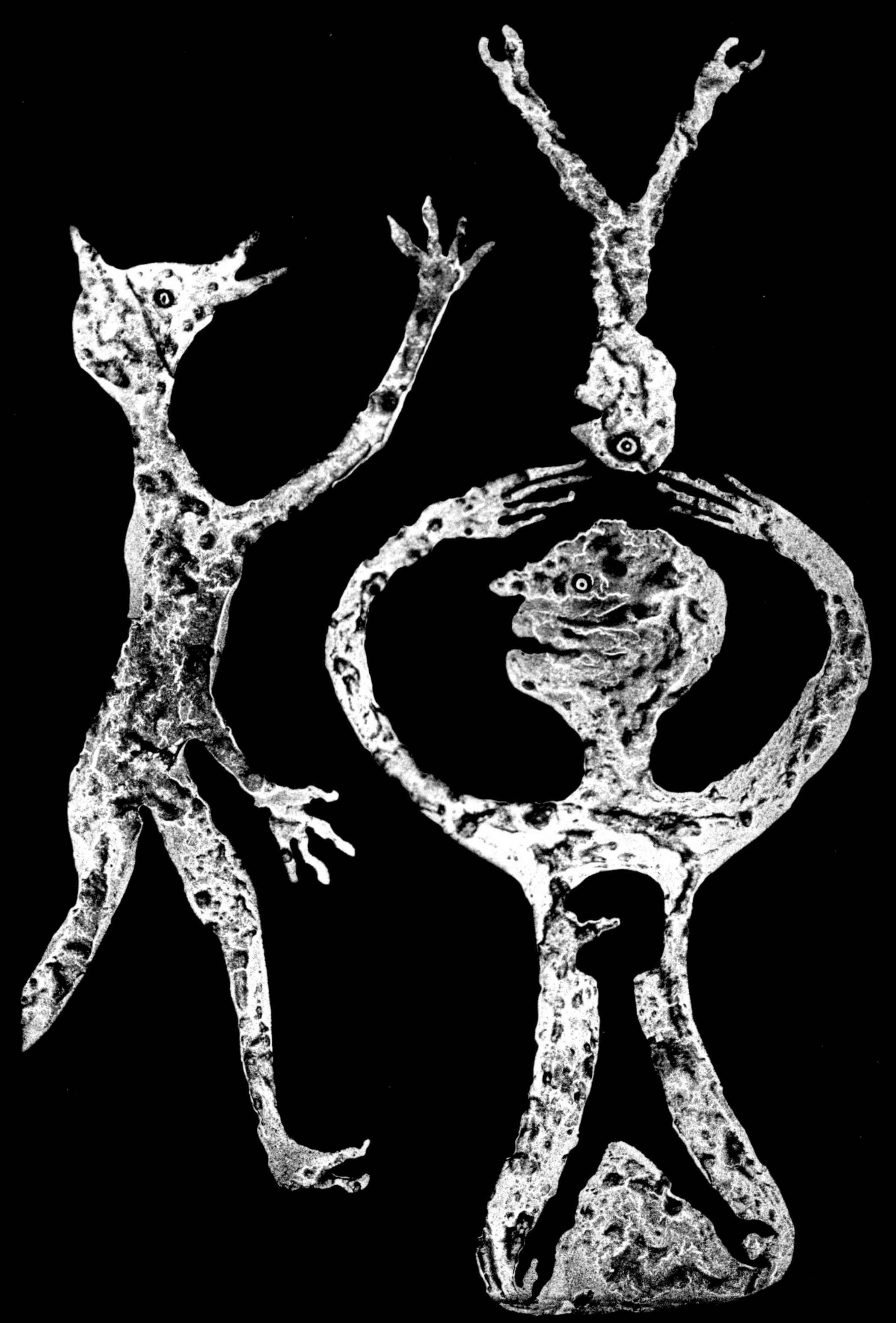

Counterpart, 2009

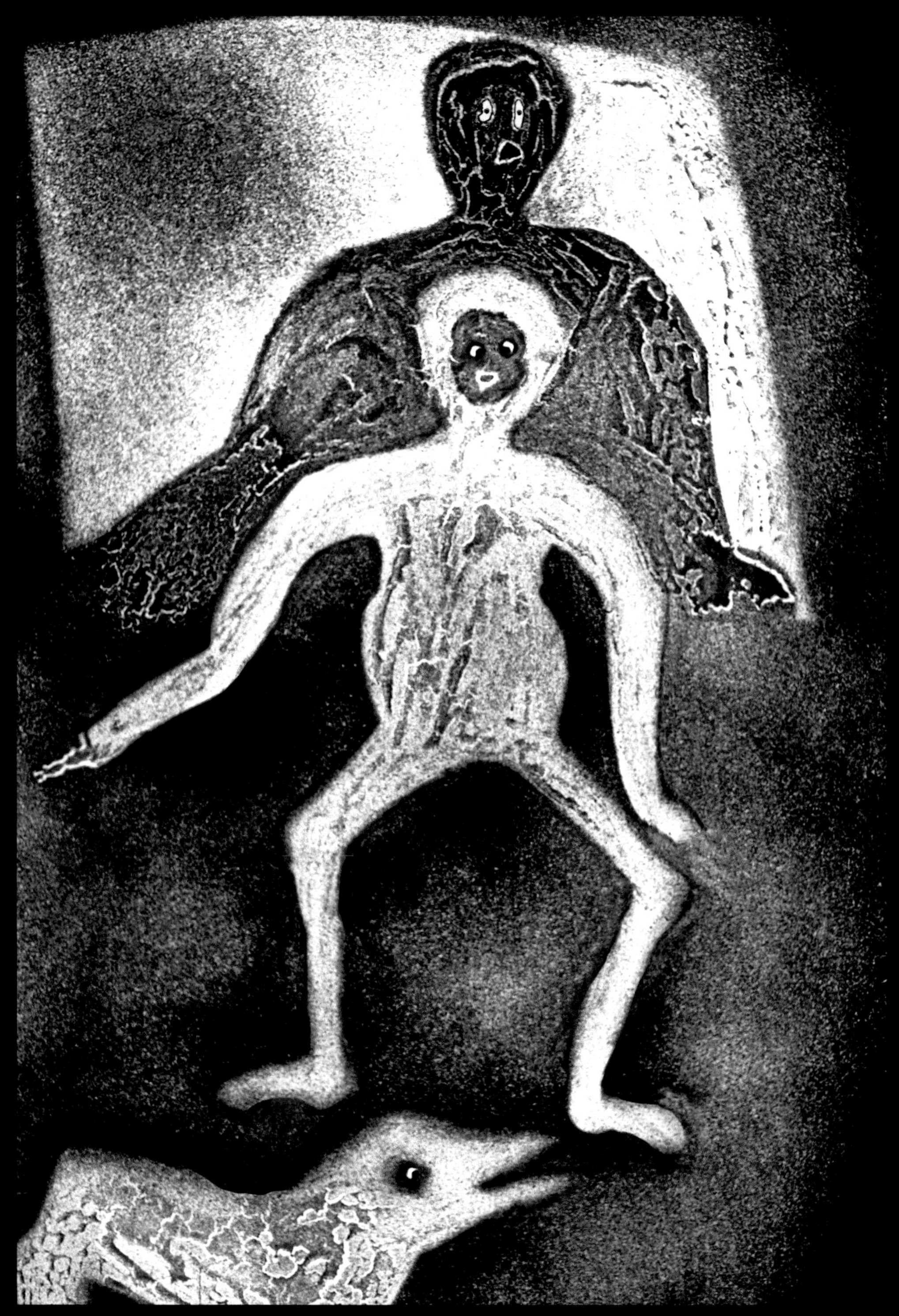

Looking Out, 2010

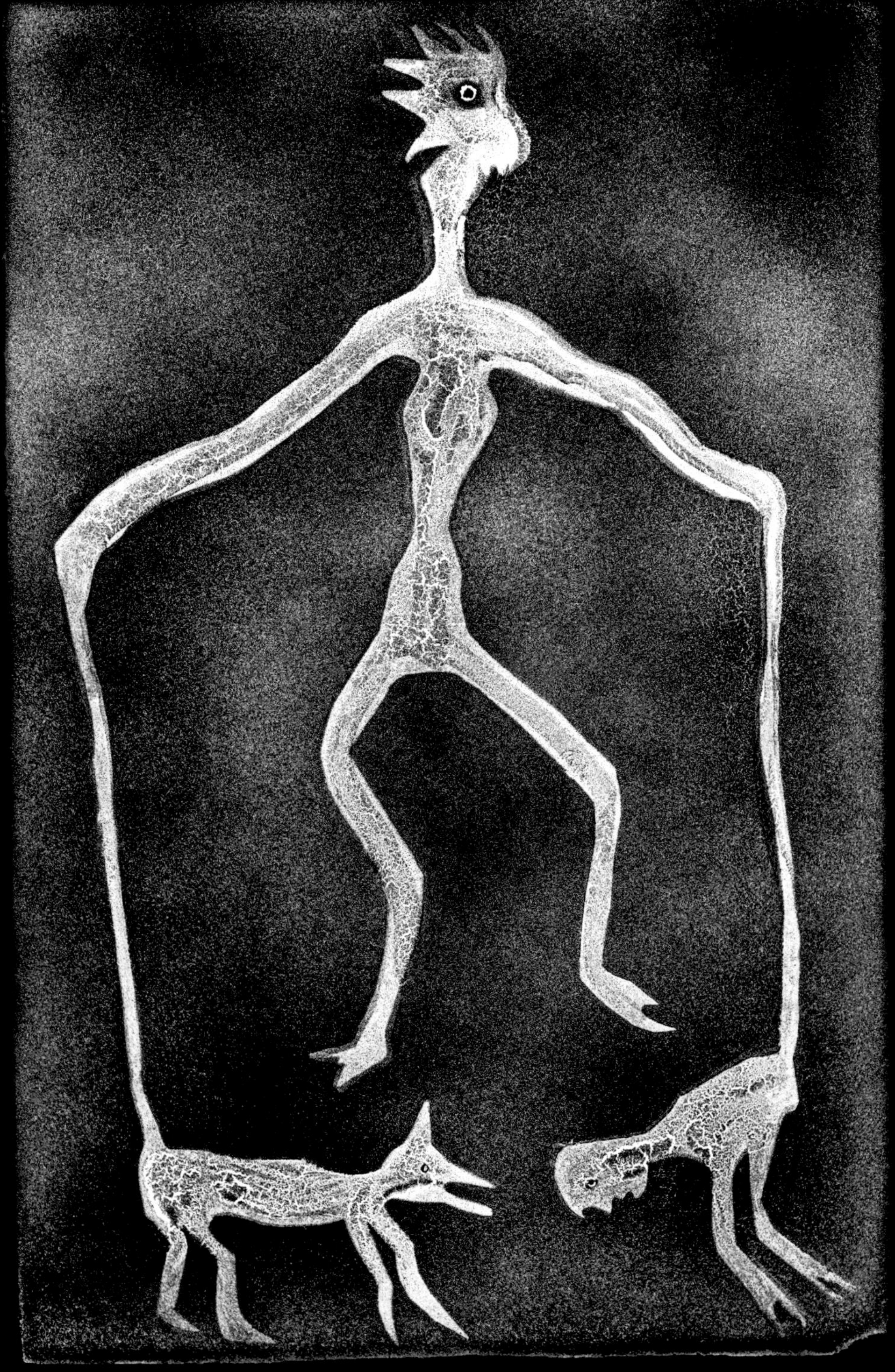

Strolling, 2010

In the Mind's Eye, 2007

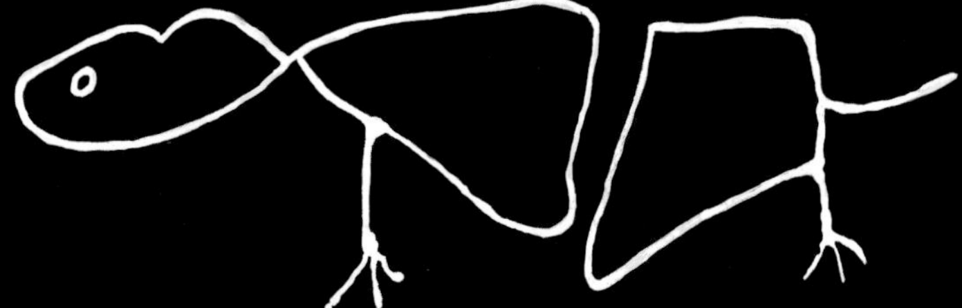

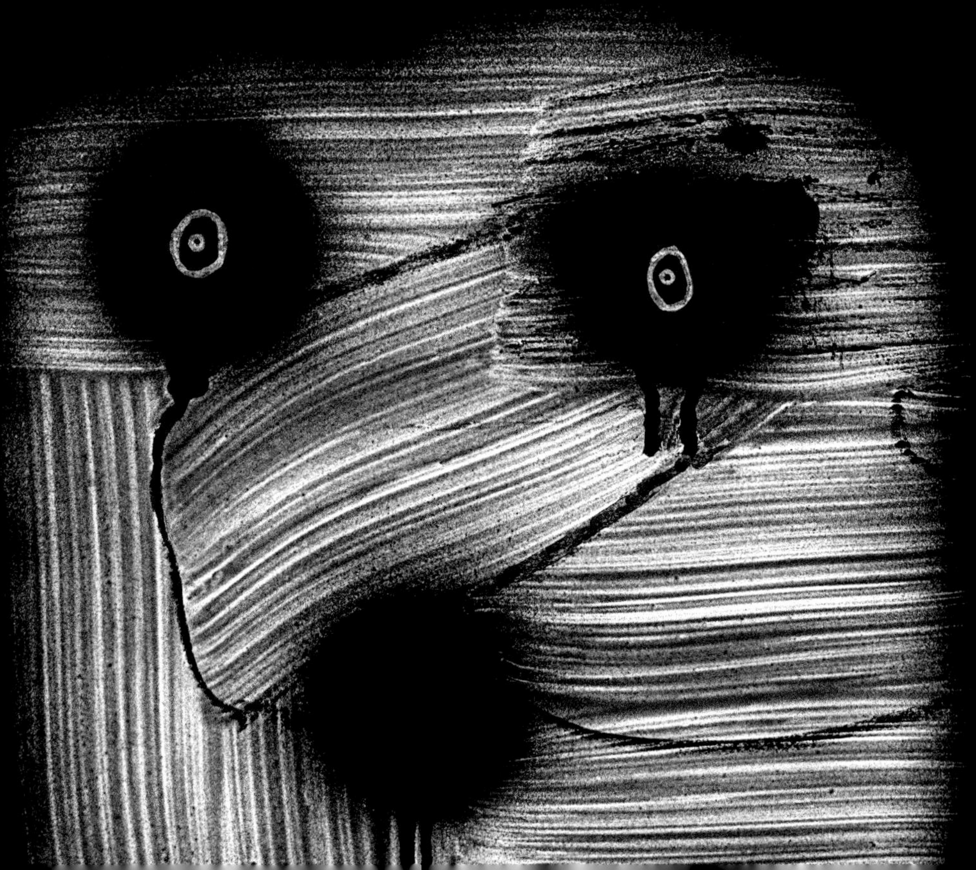

ACT FIVE

melancholy

Despair, 2010

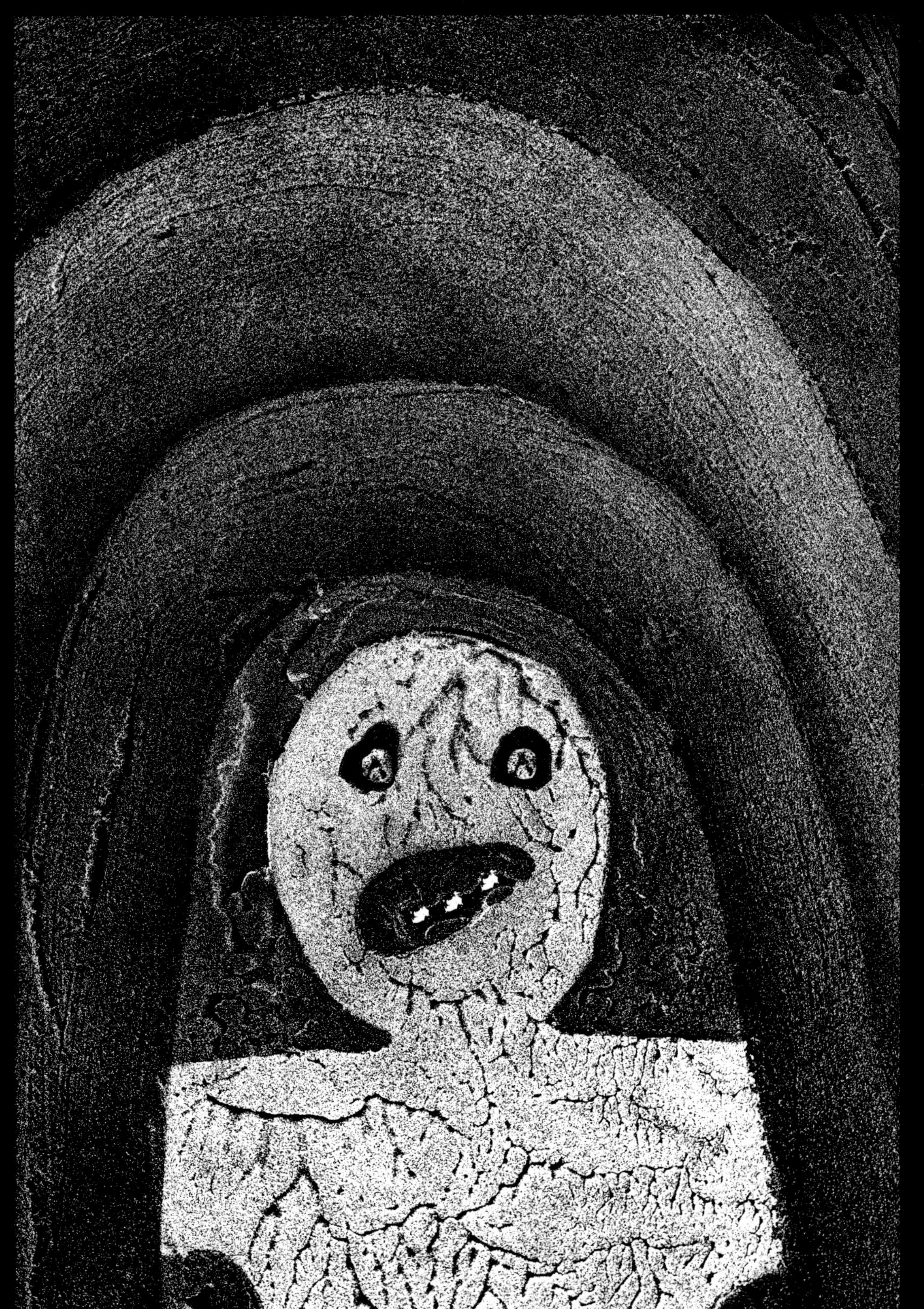

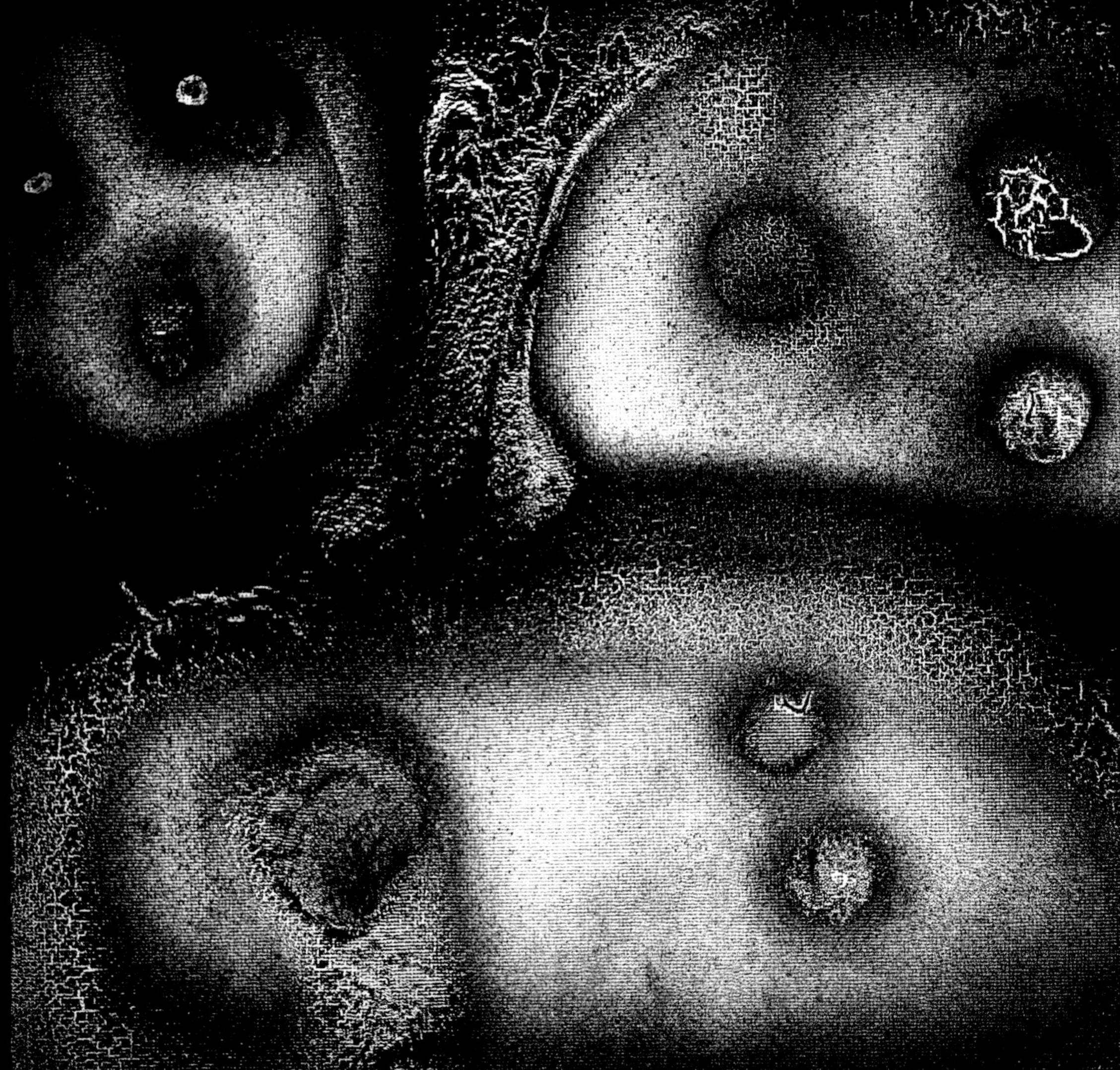

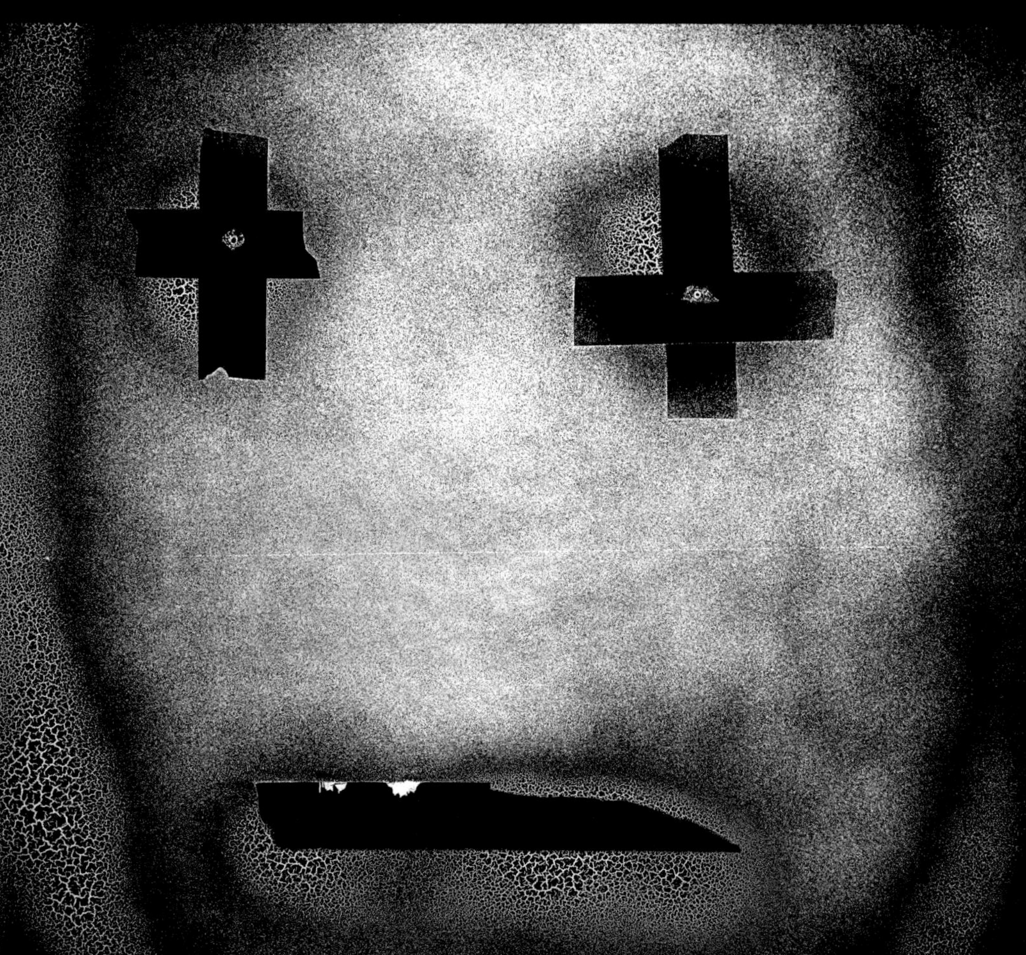

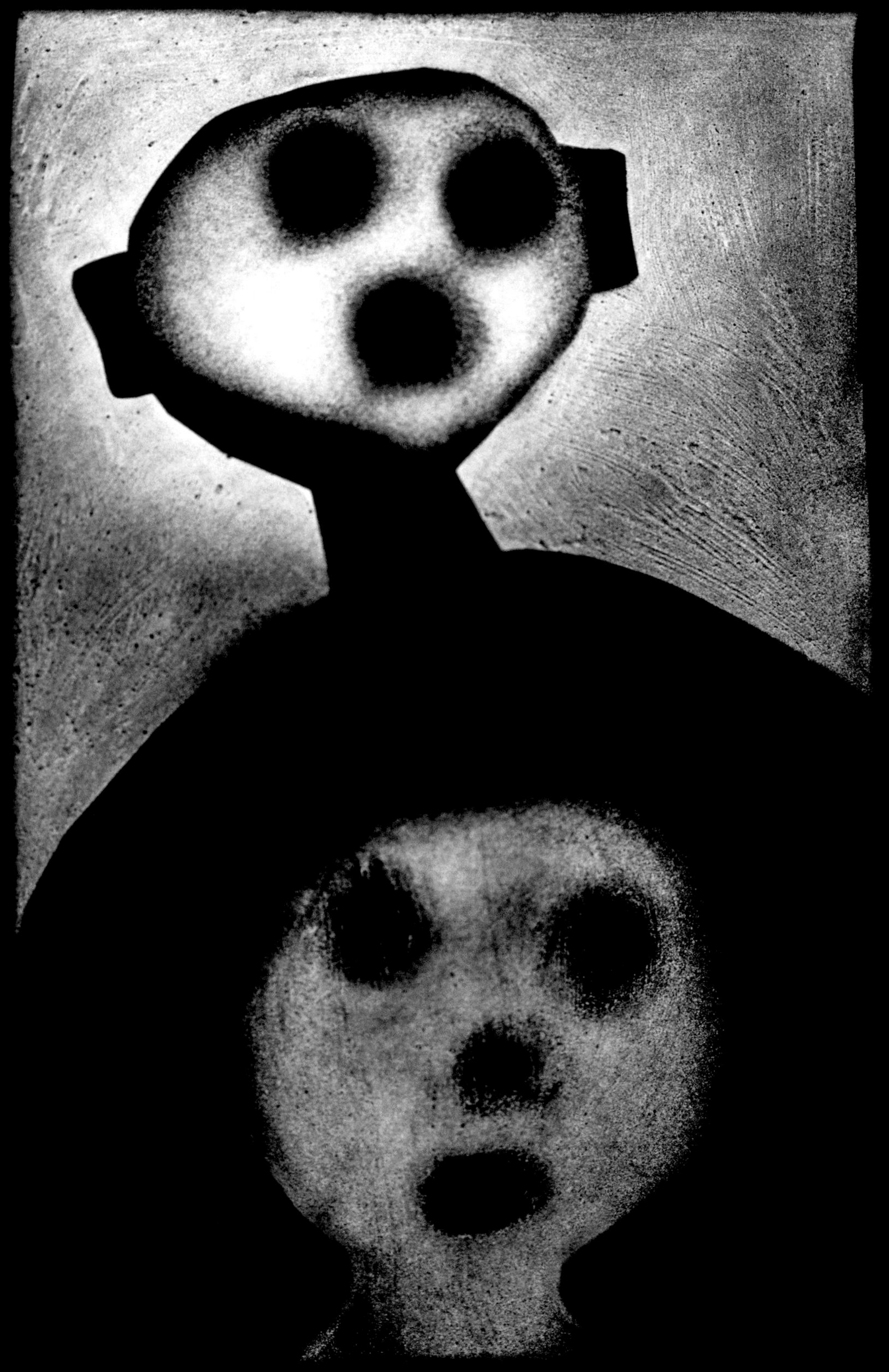

Embryonic, 2009

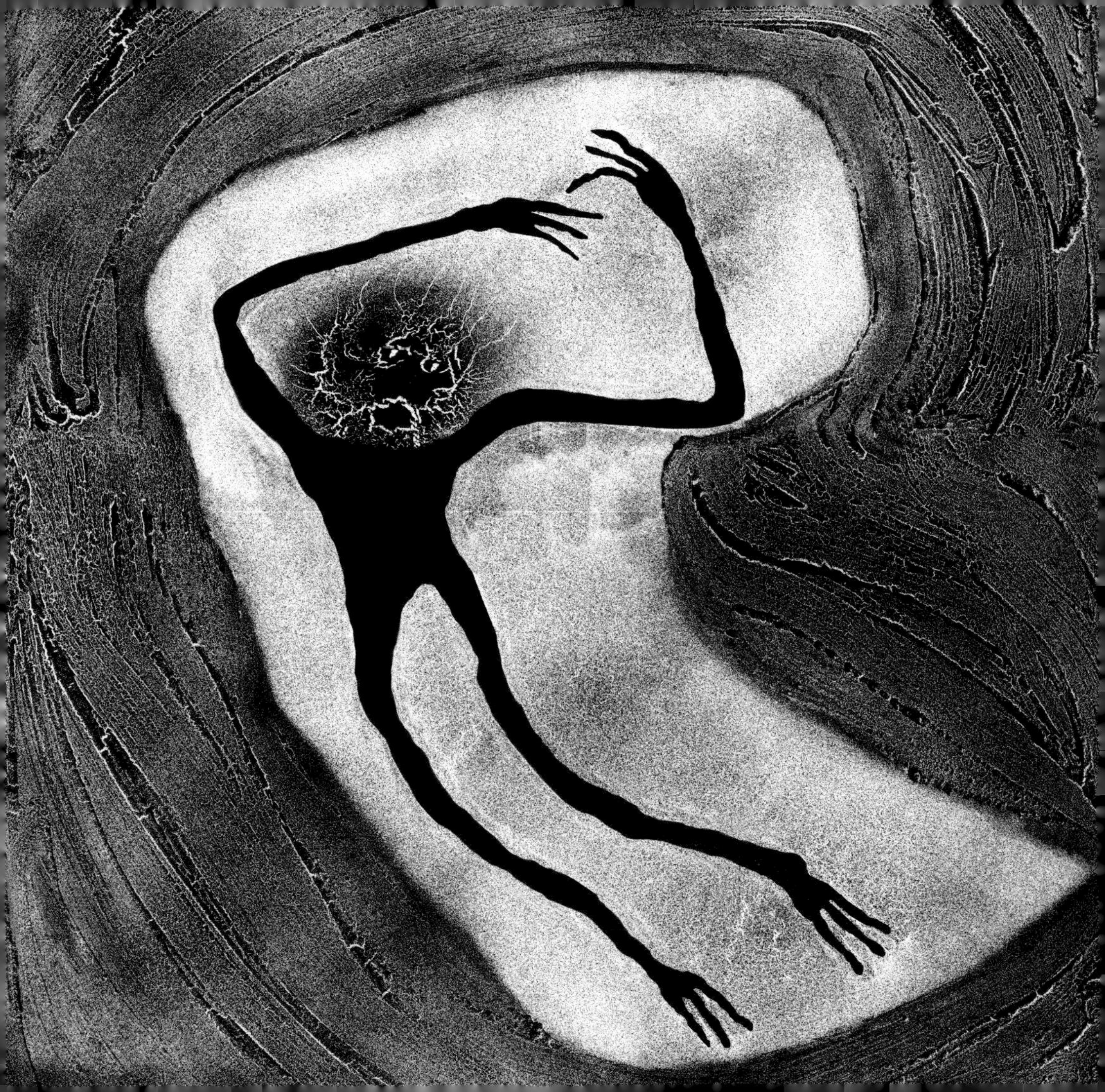

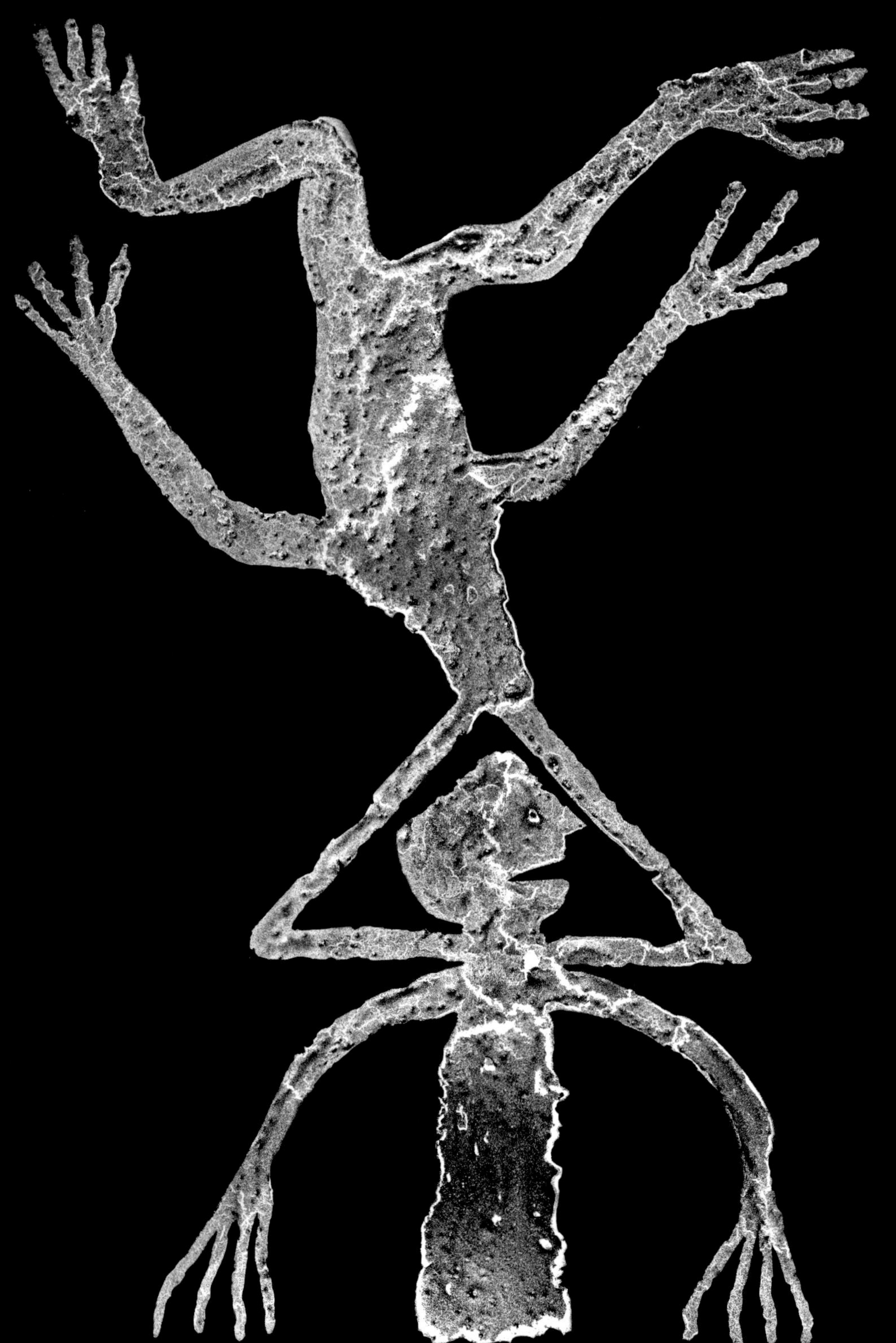

Triangulation, 2012

Down and Out, 2010

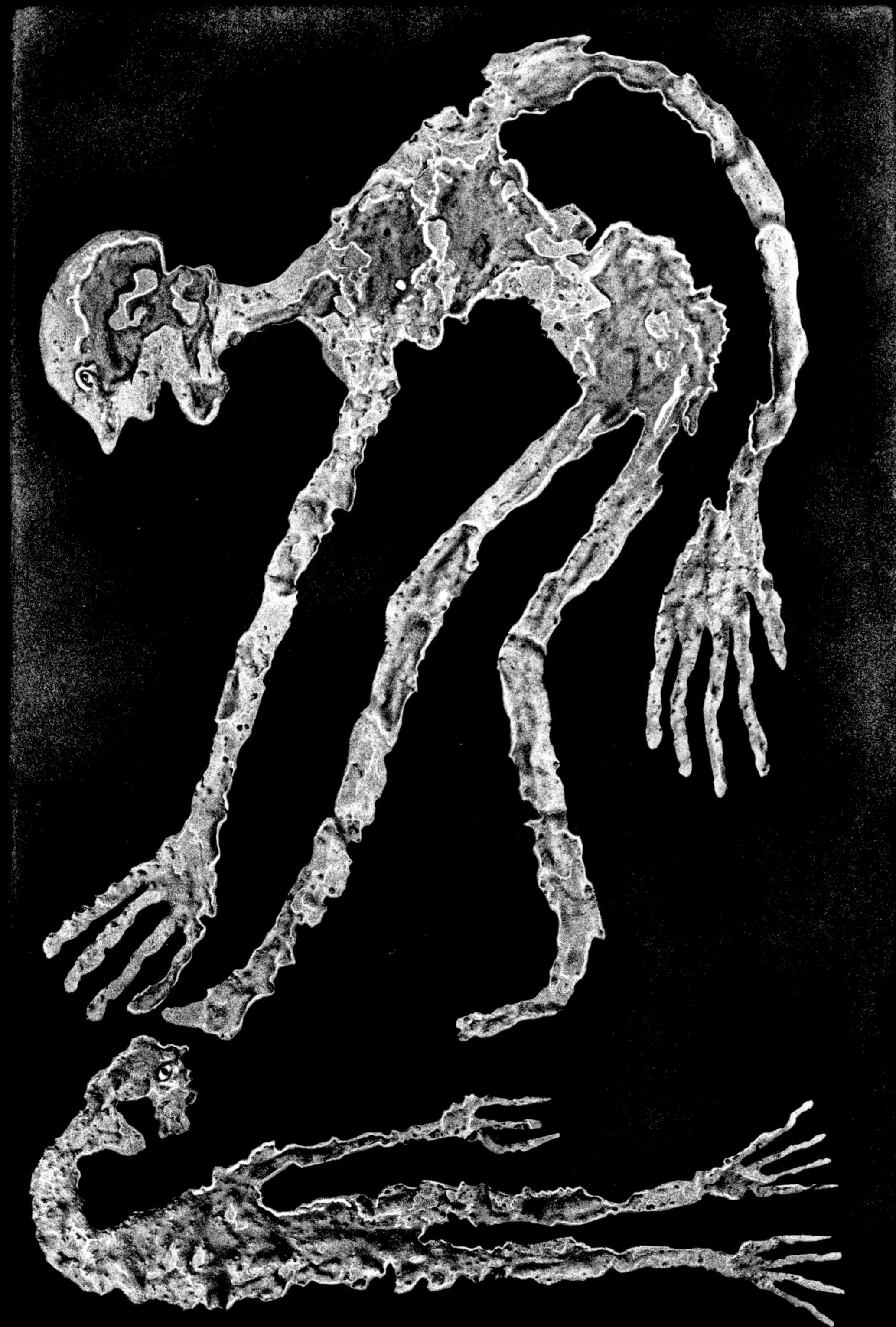

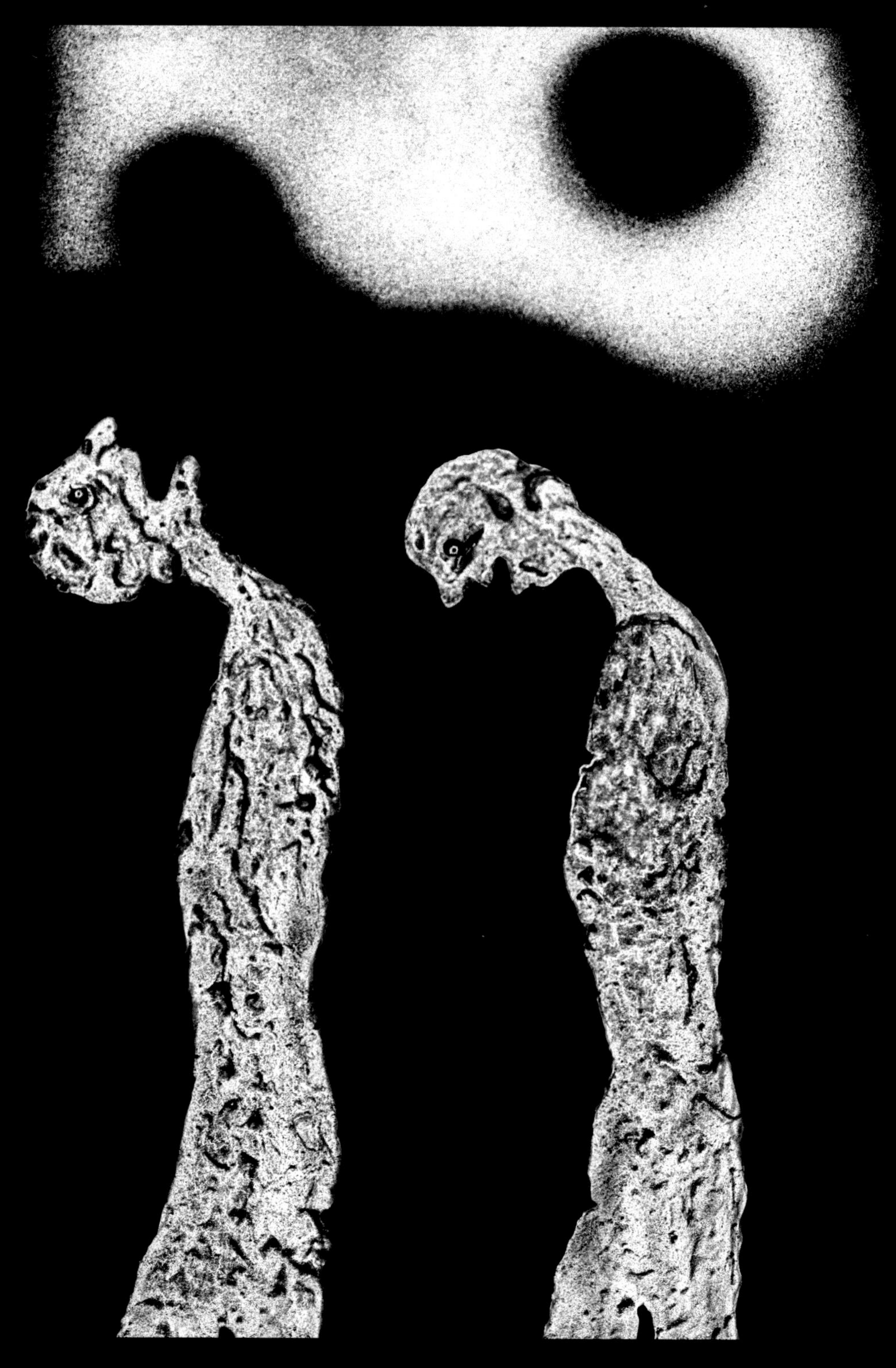

Imploring, 2011

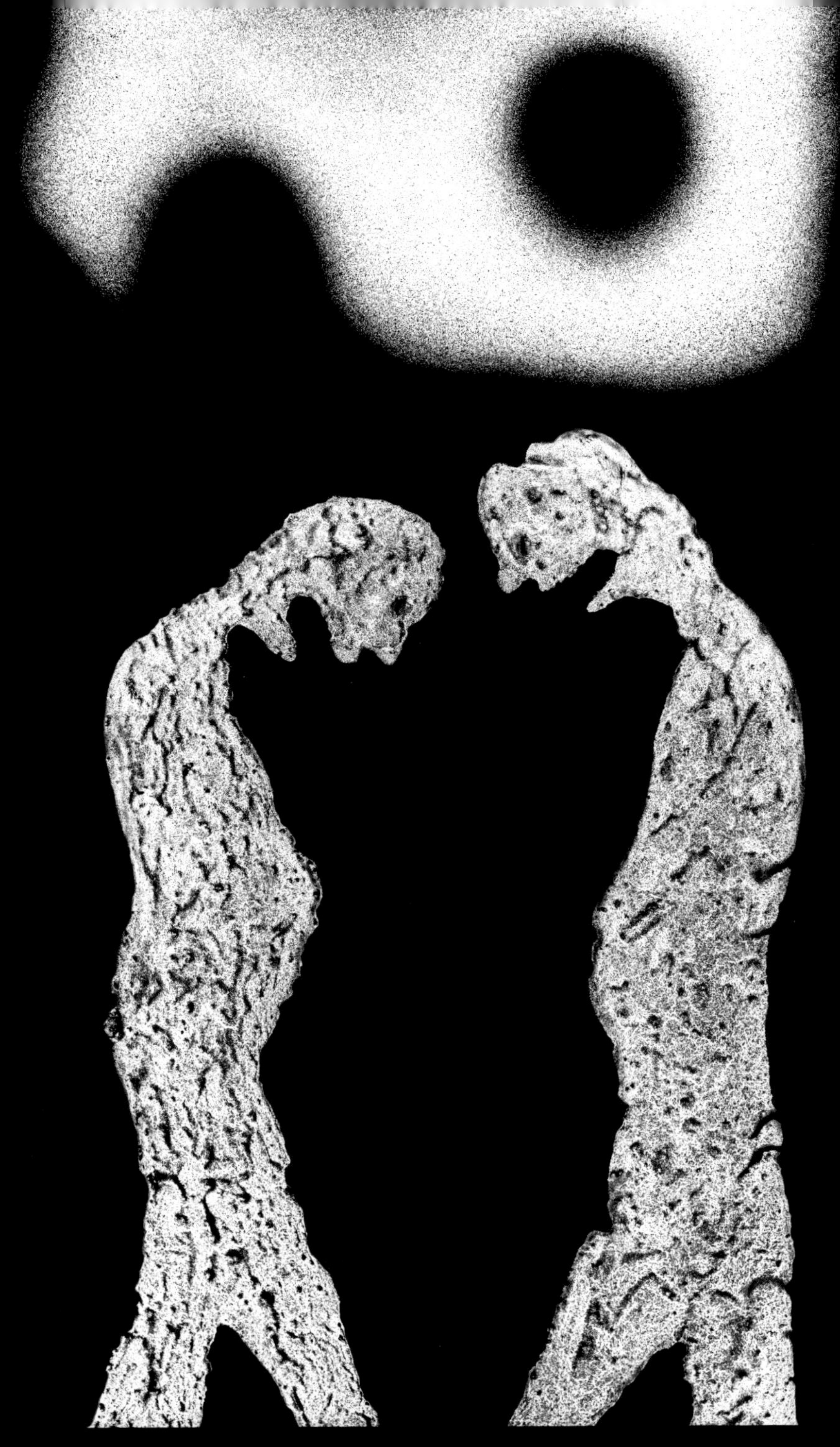

Despondent, 2011

Angst, 2011

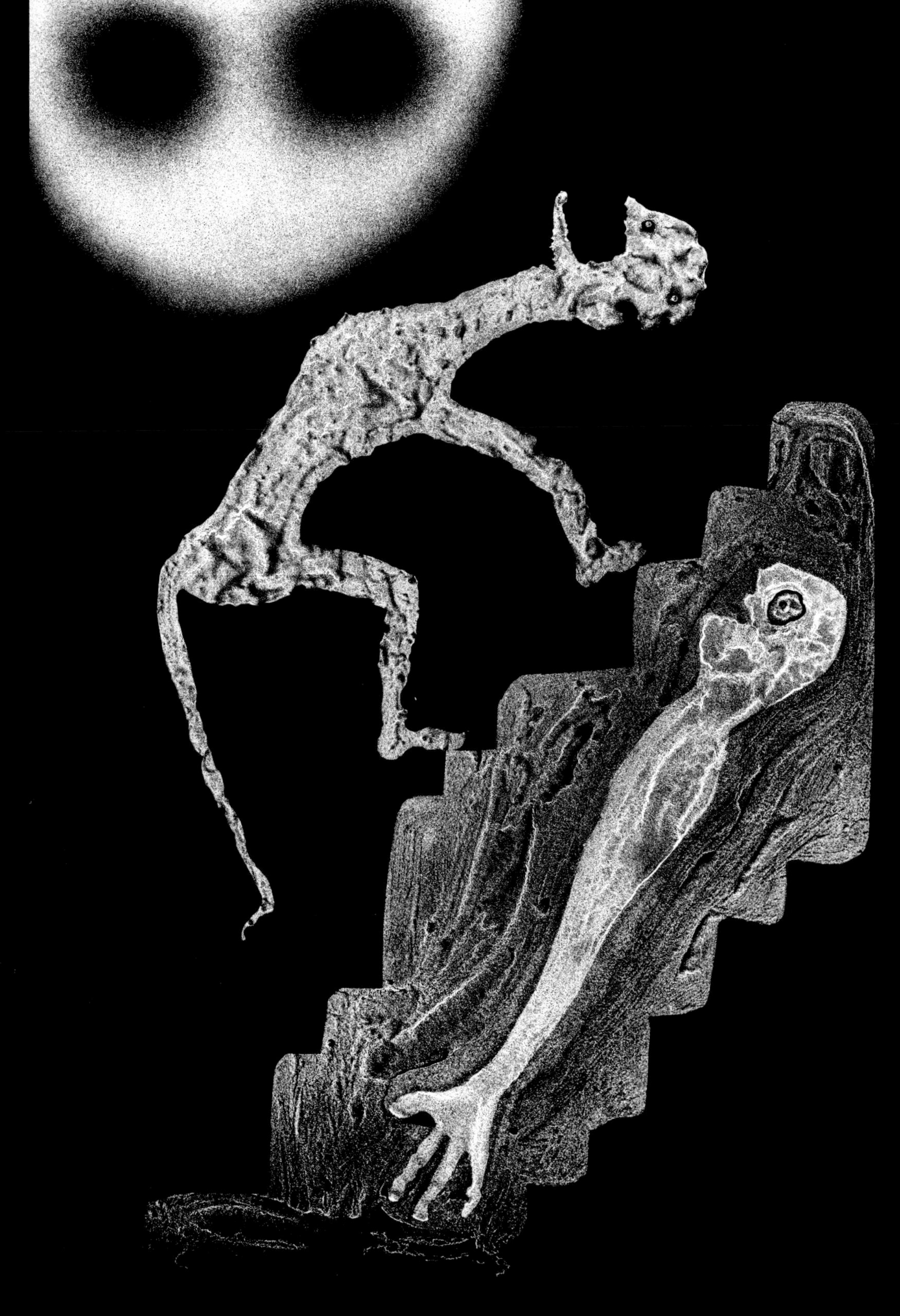

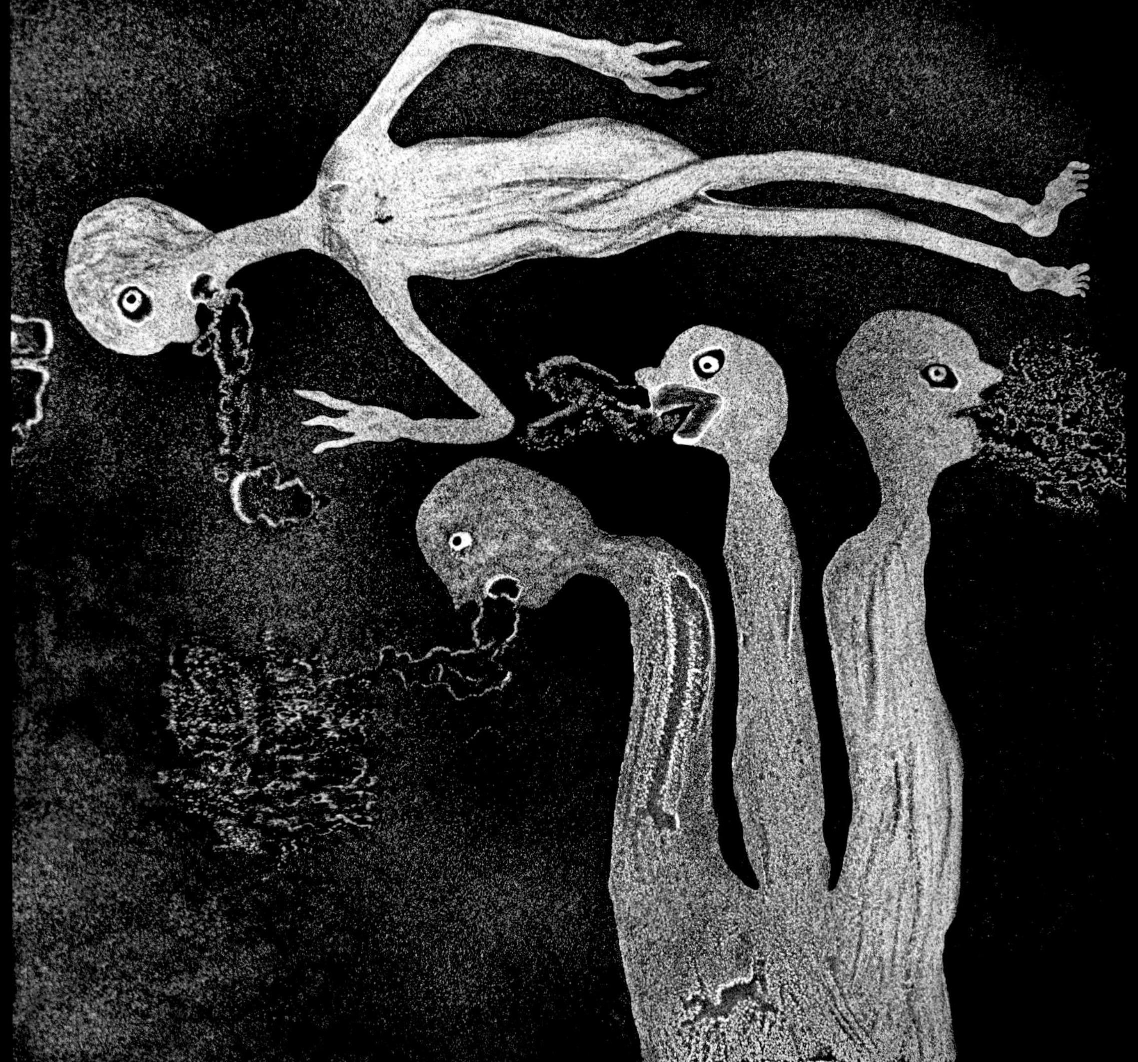

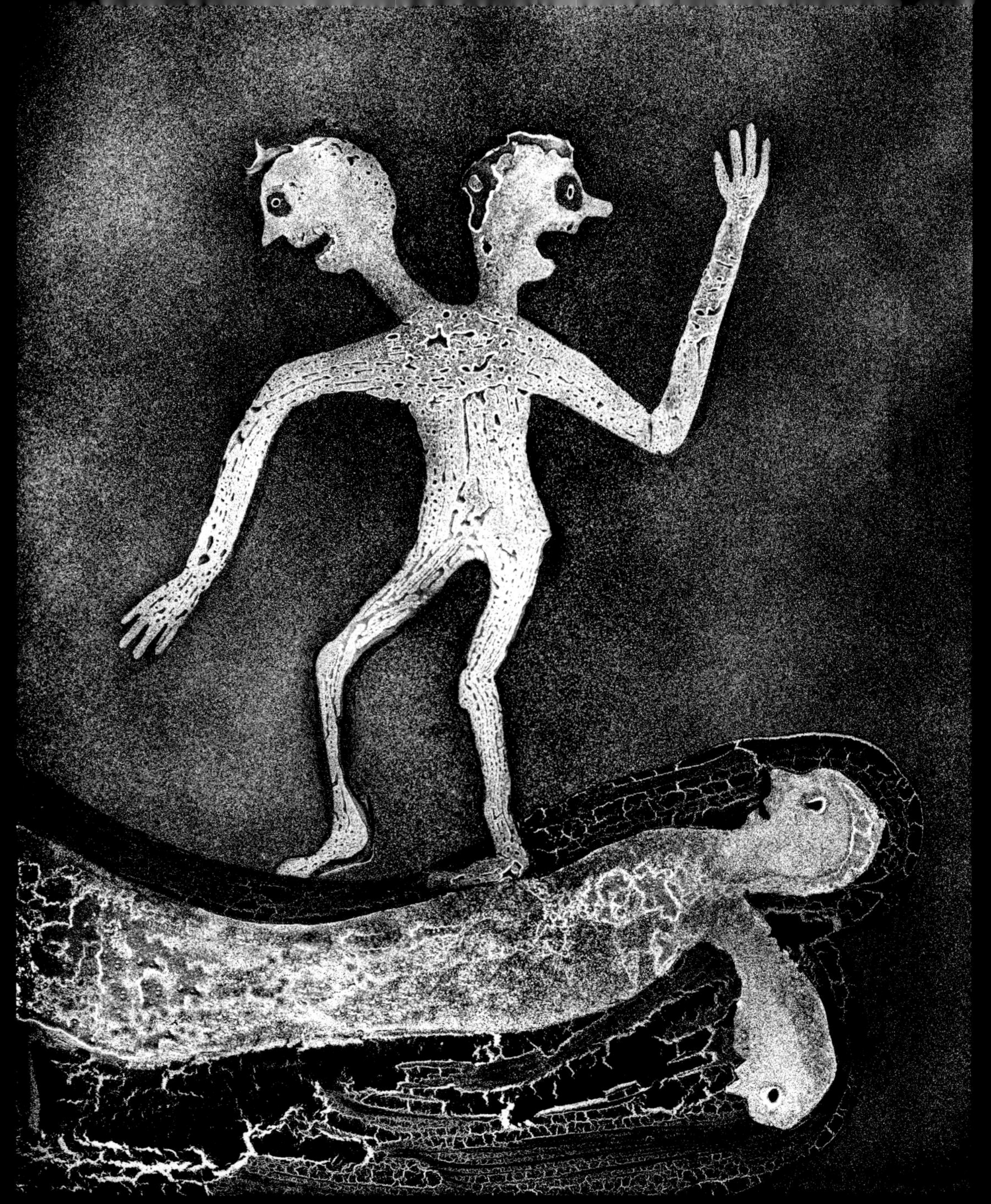

Grave Walkers, 2010

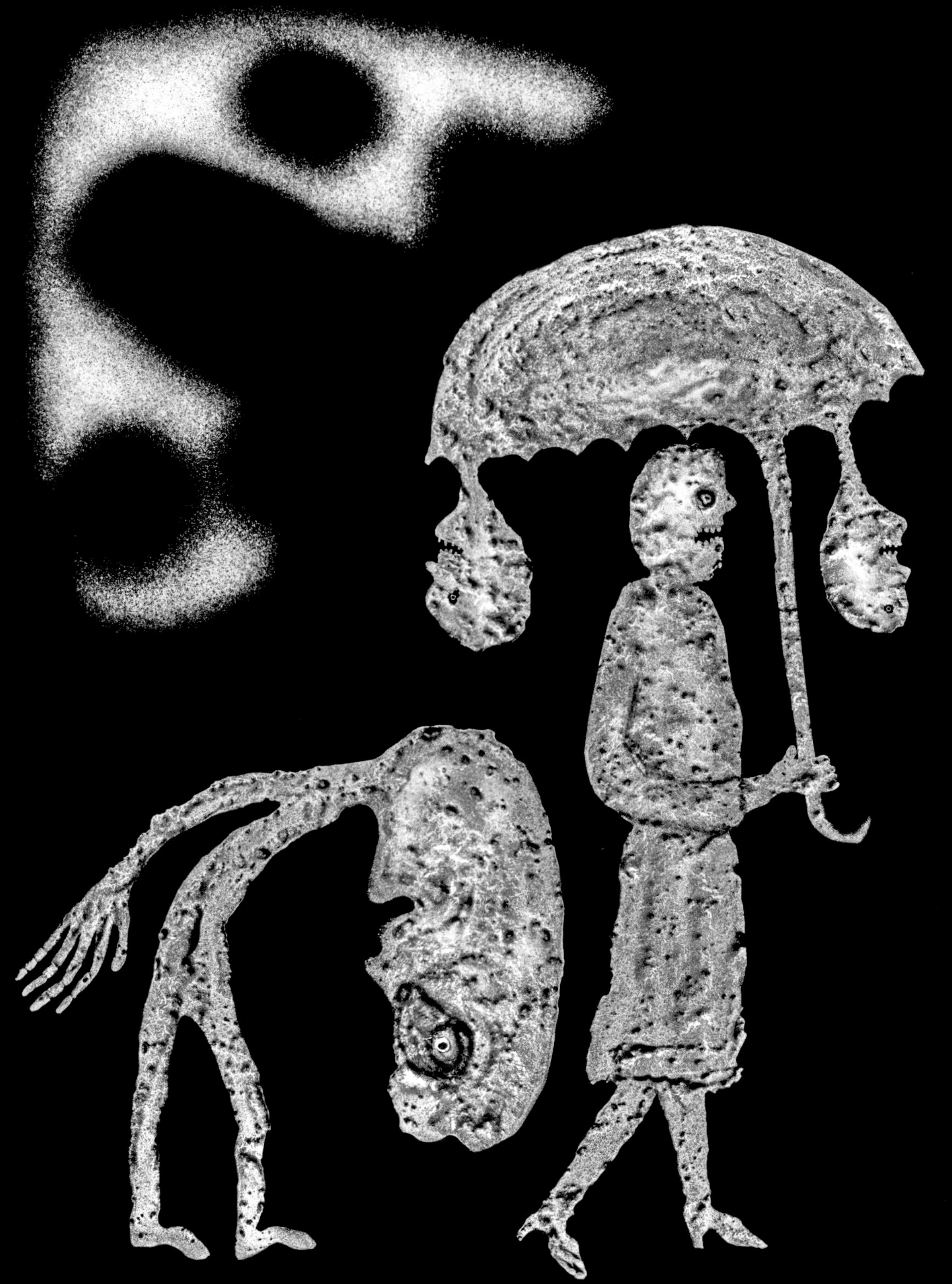

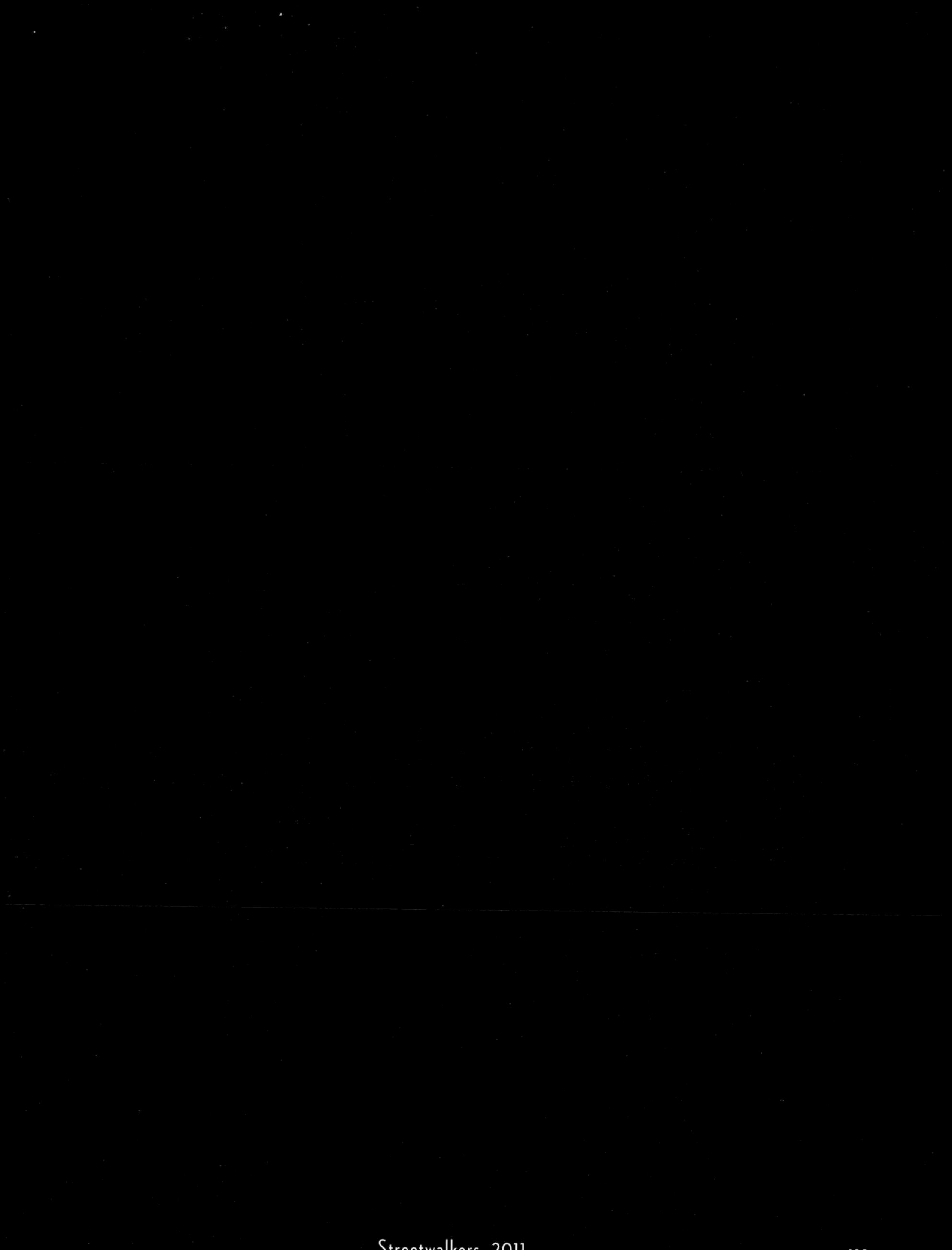

Streetwalkers, 2011

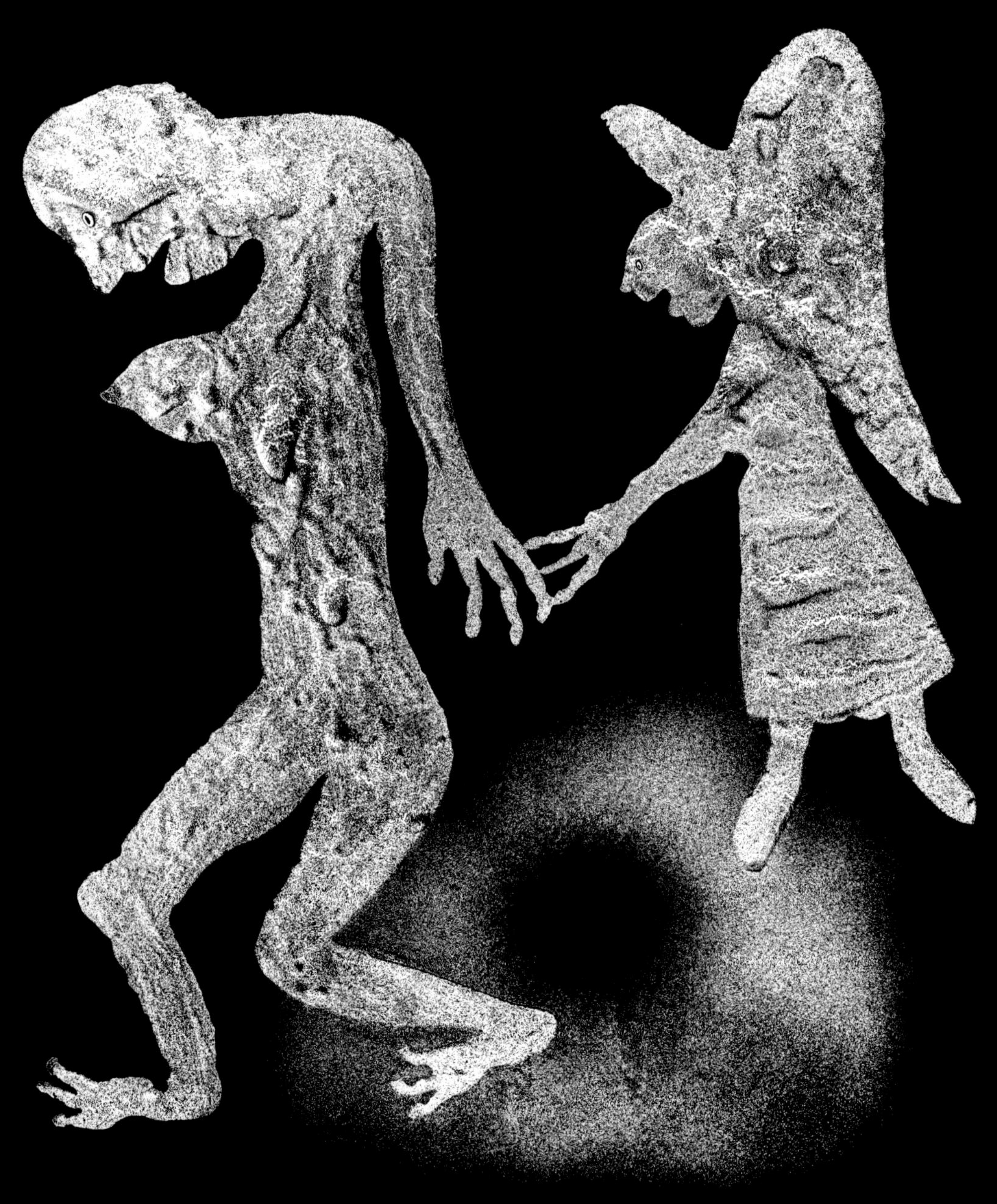

Guardian Angel, 2011

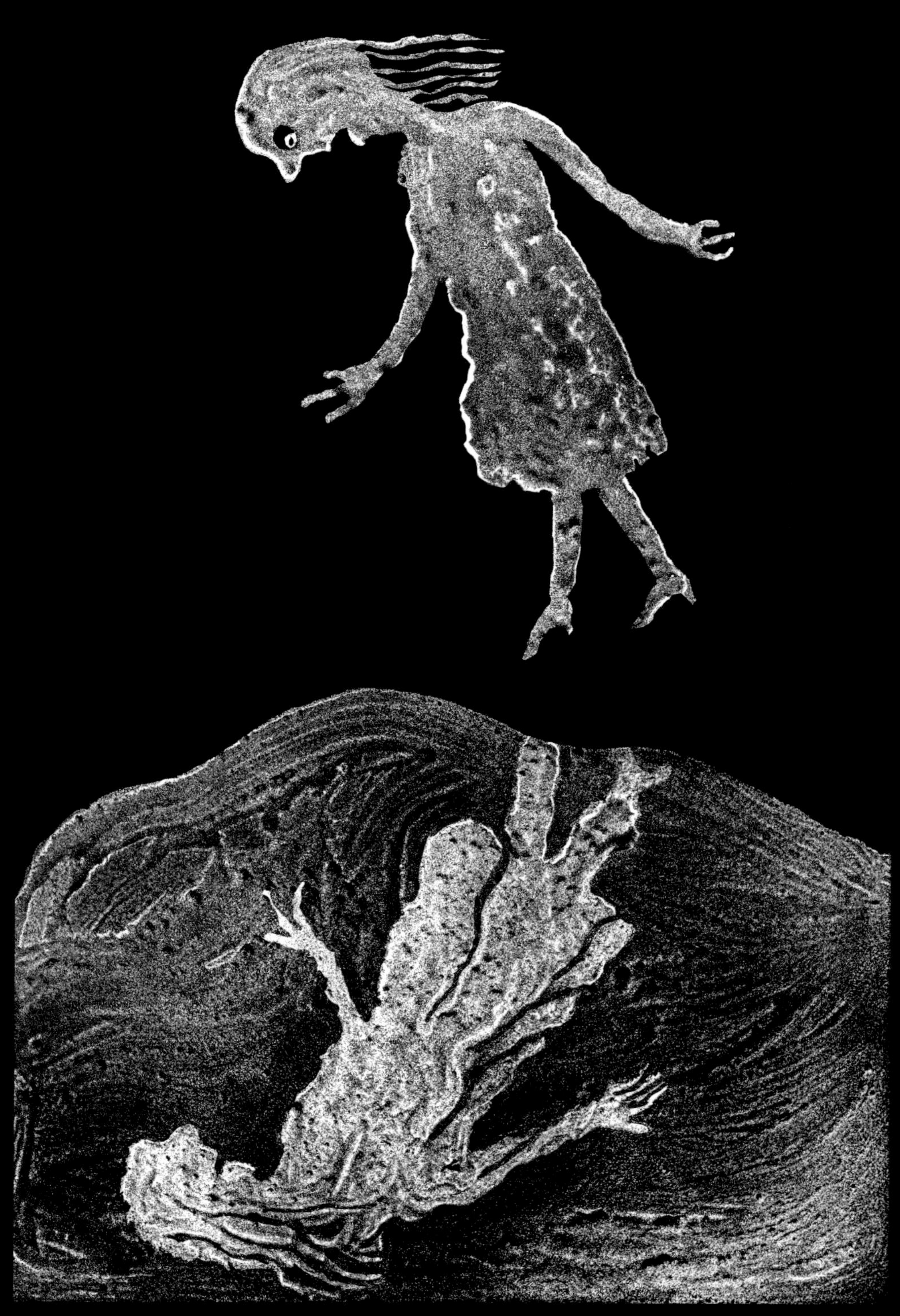

Mirrored, 2011

Shadows and Strangers, 2010

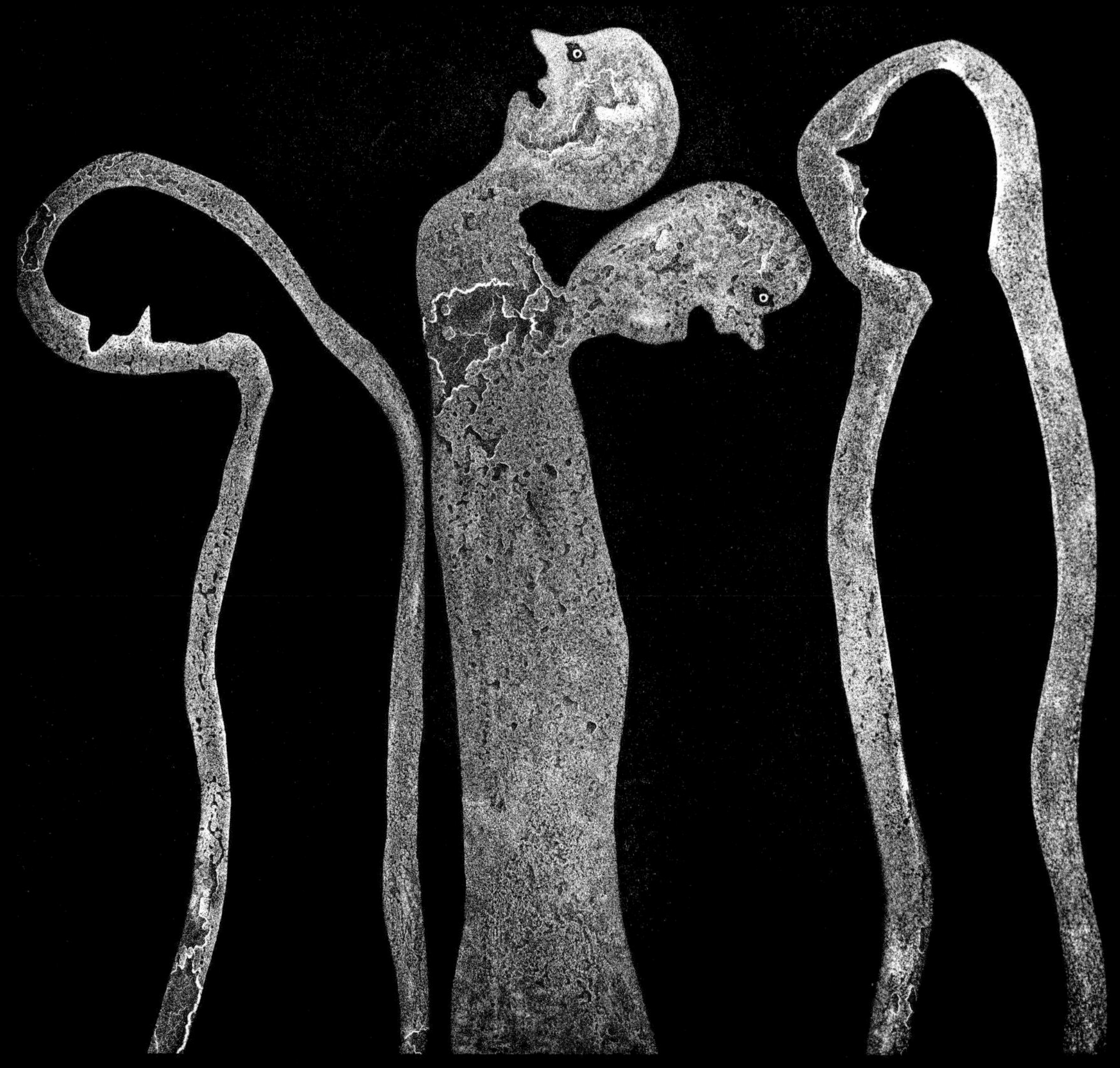

ACT SIX

fragmentation

Giant, 2013

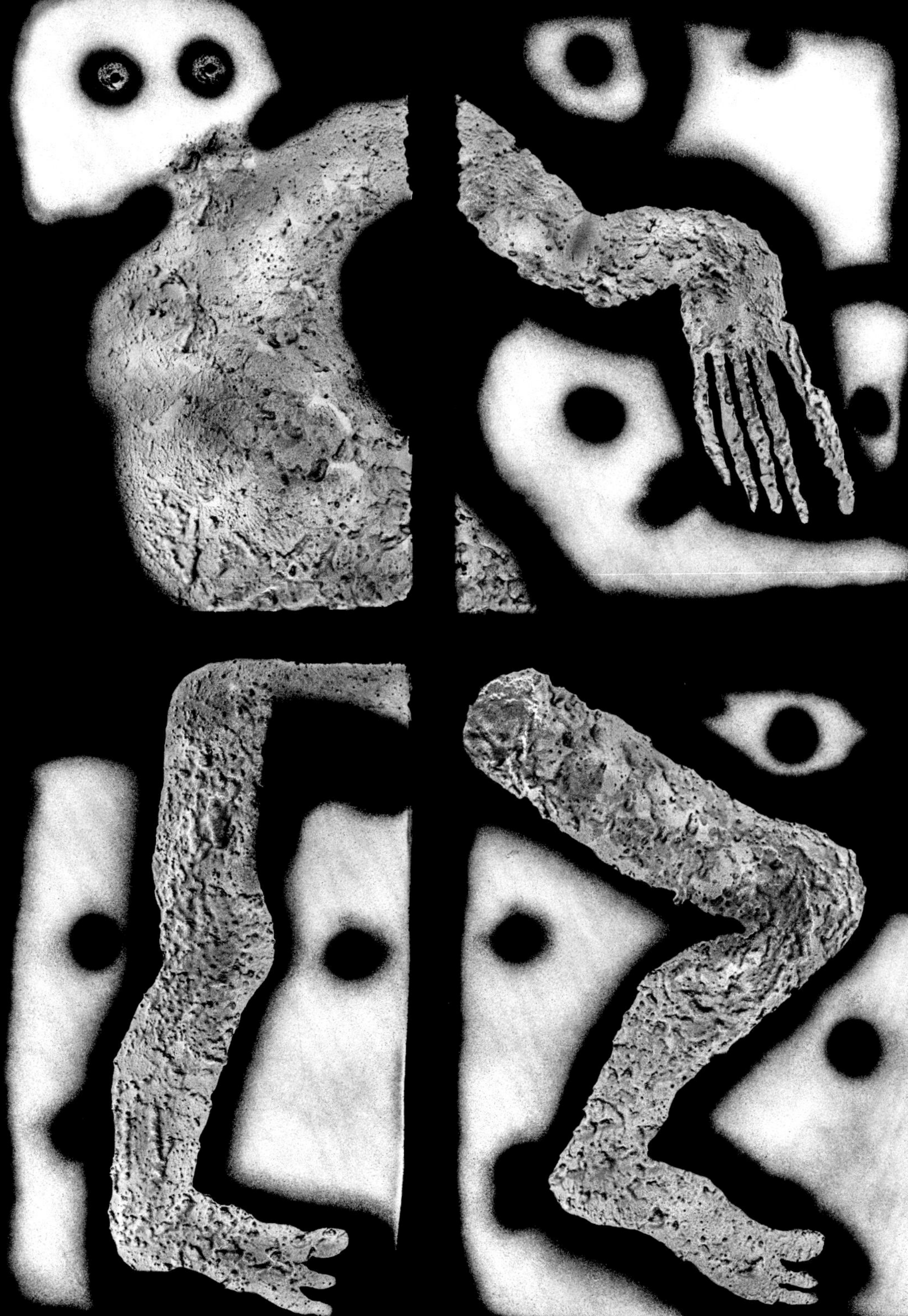

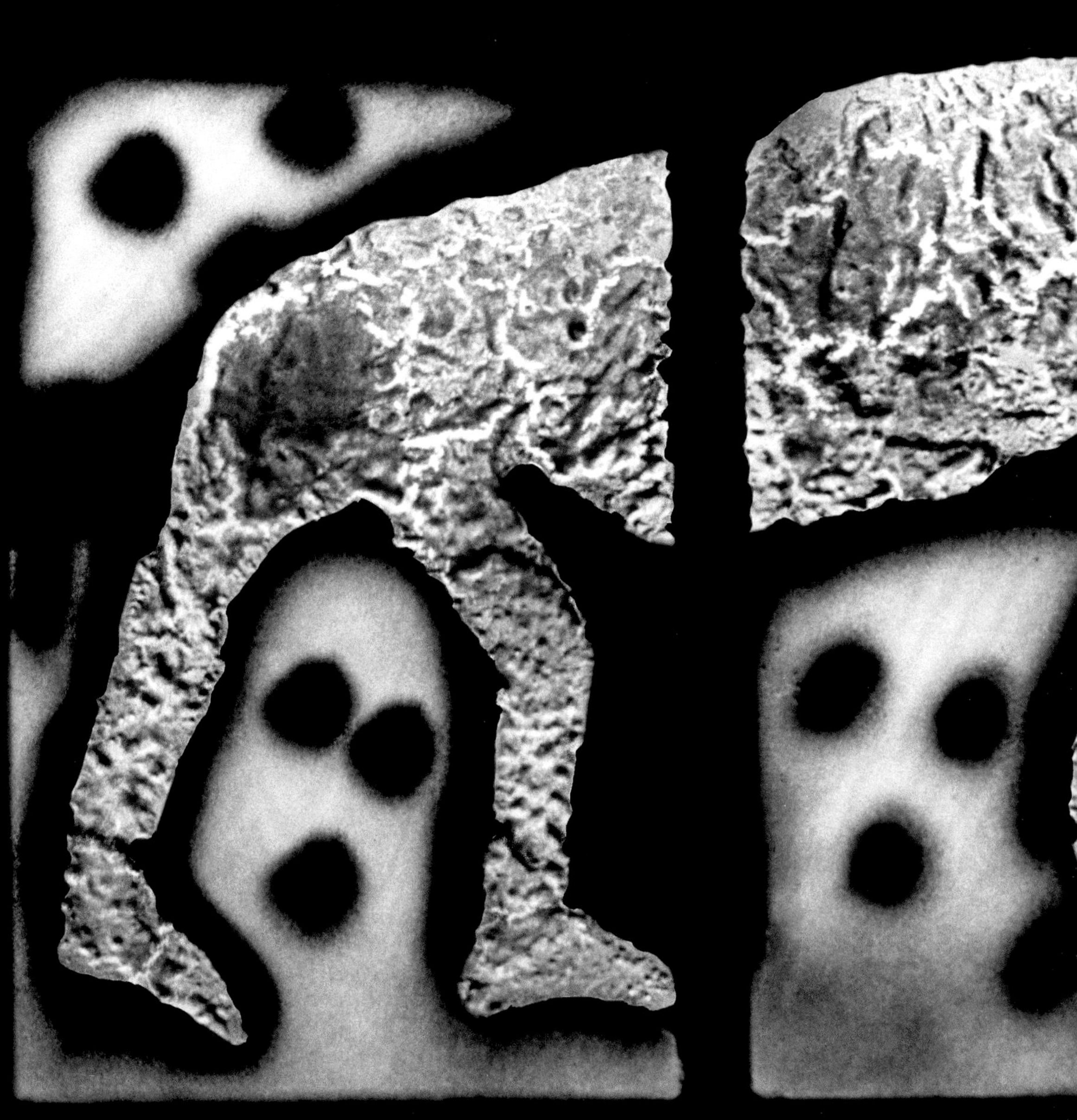

Flipped, 2013

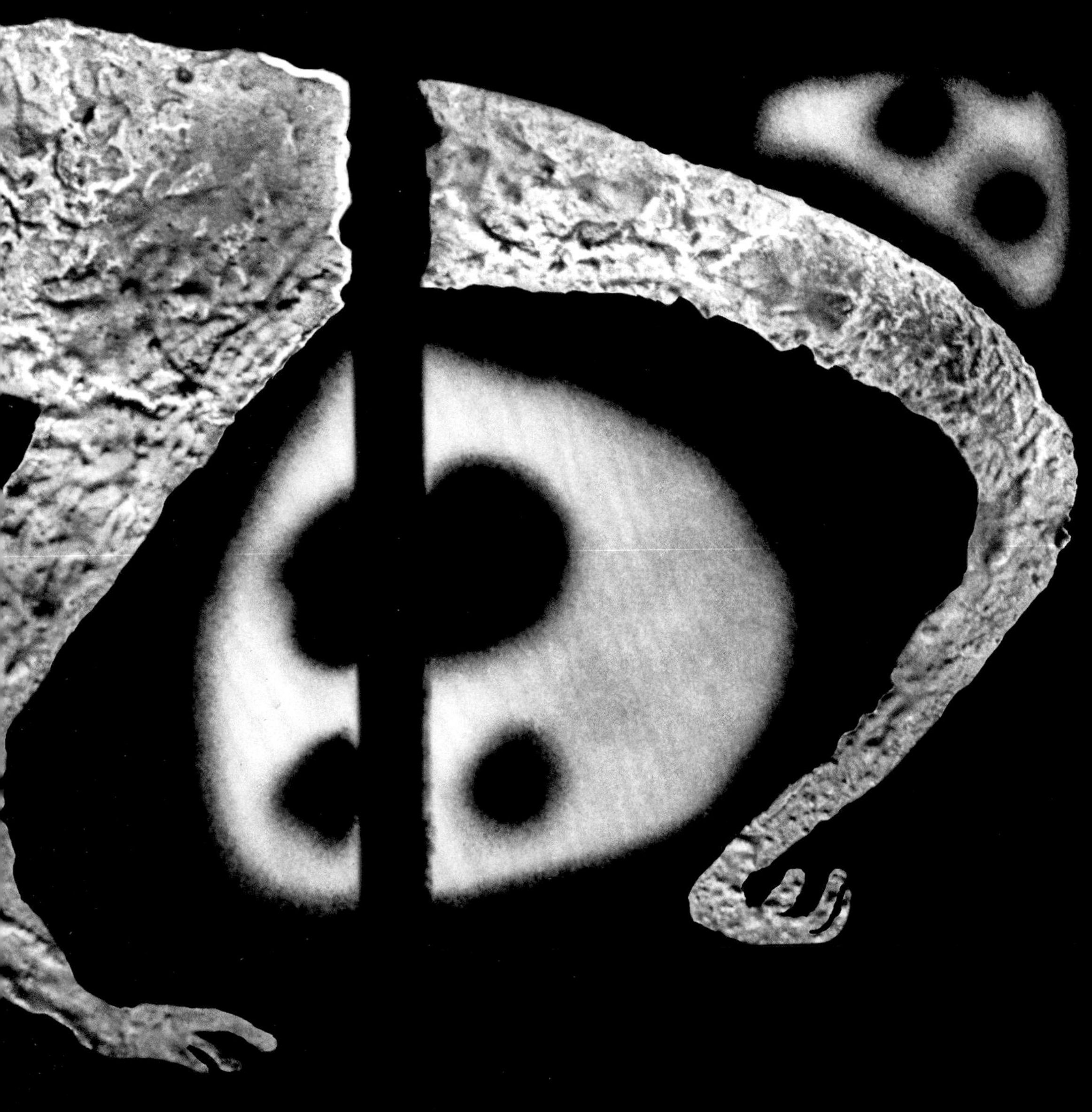

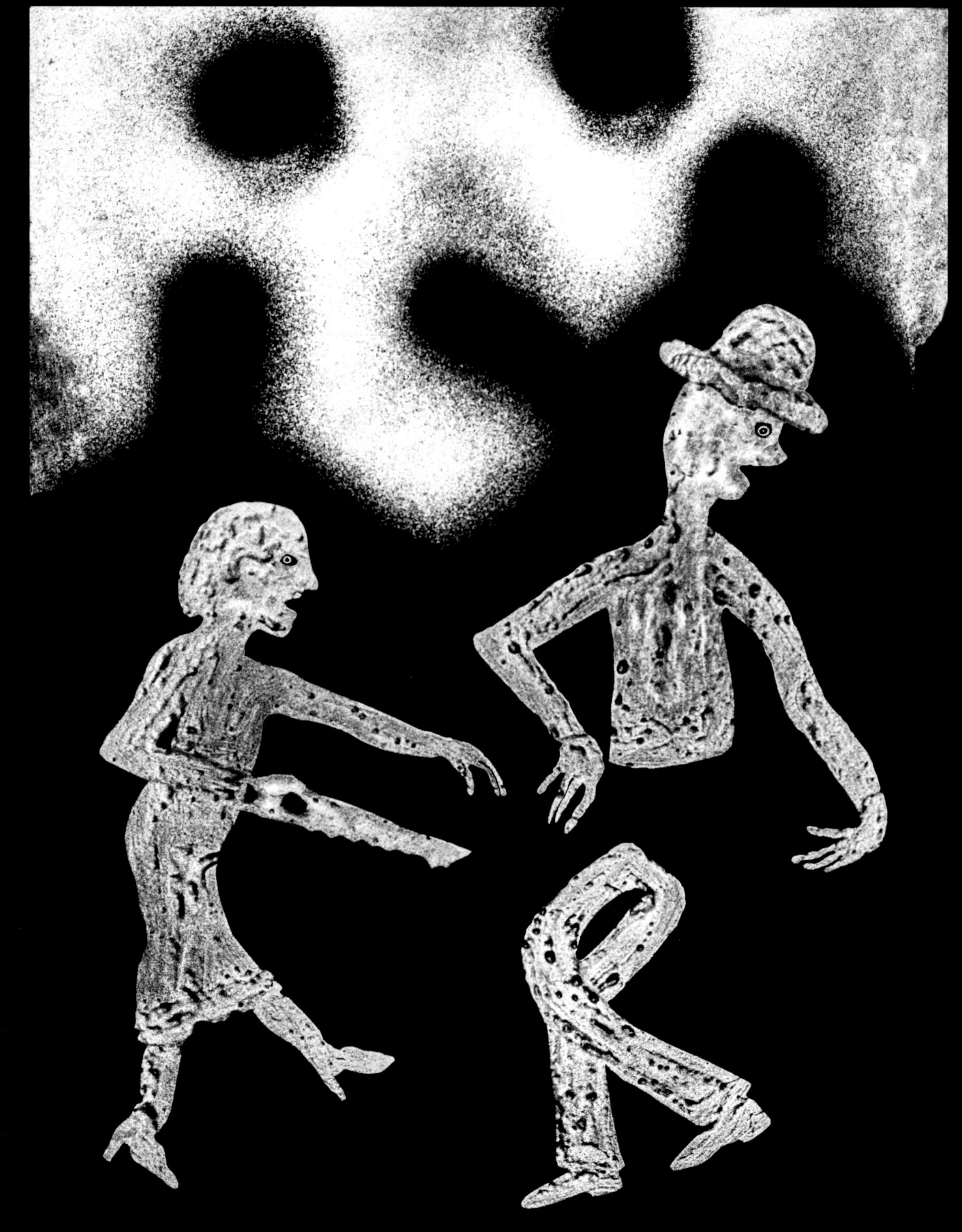

Severed, 2011

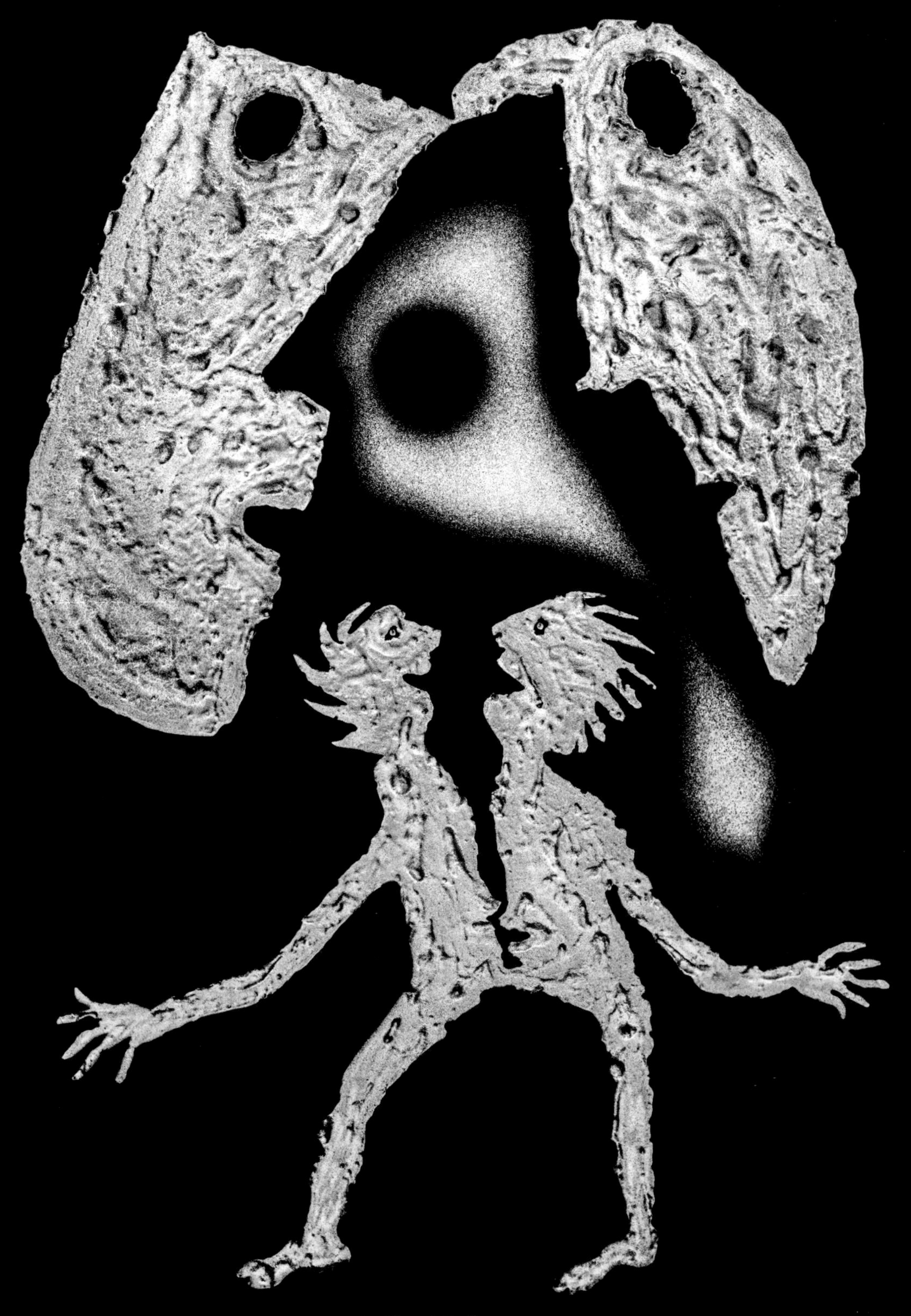

Half and Half, 2012

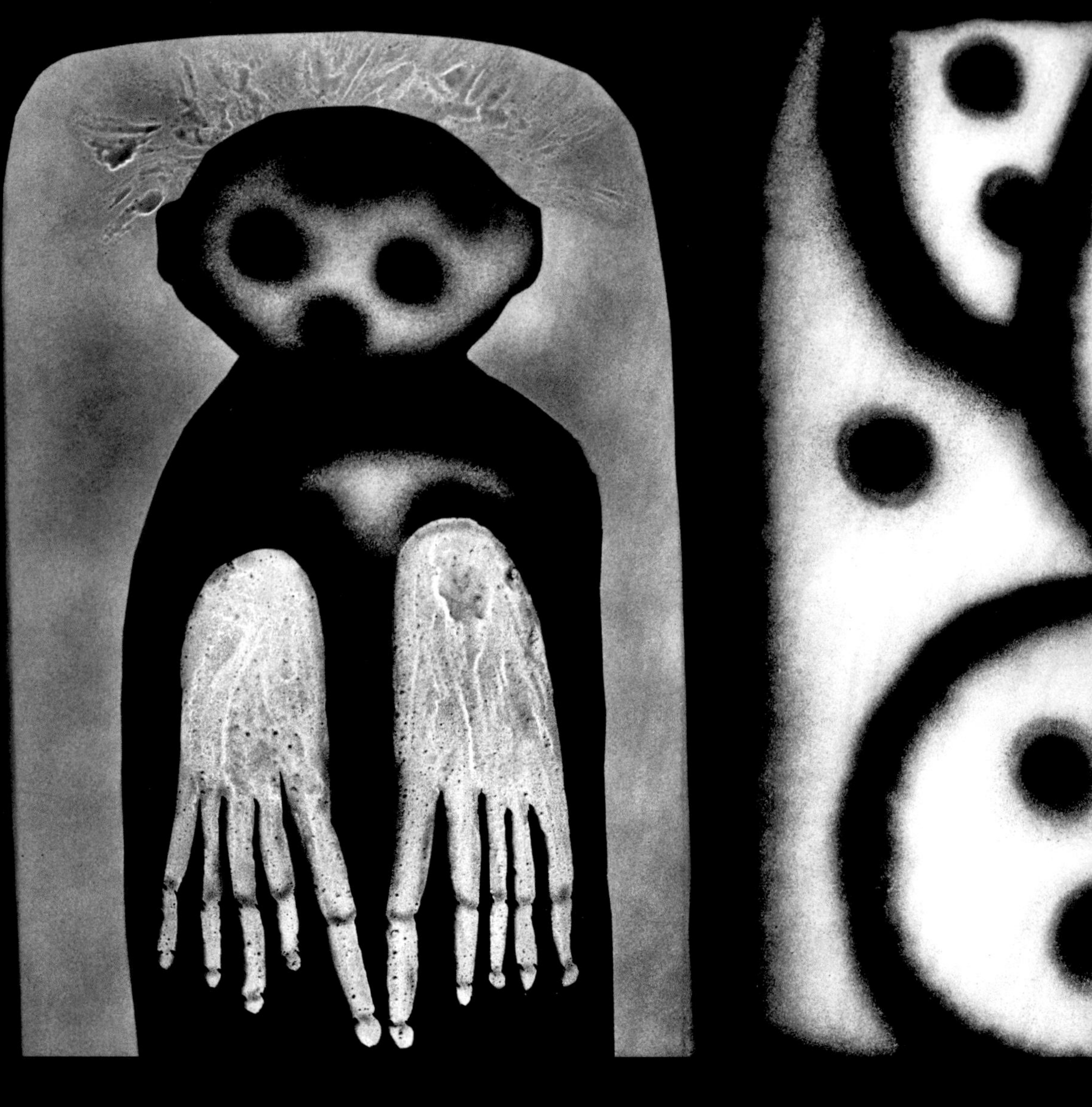

Fingers and Faces, 2012

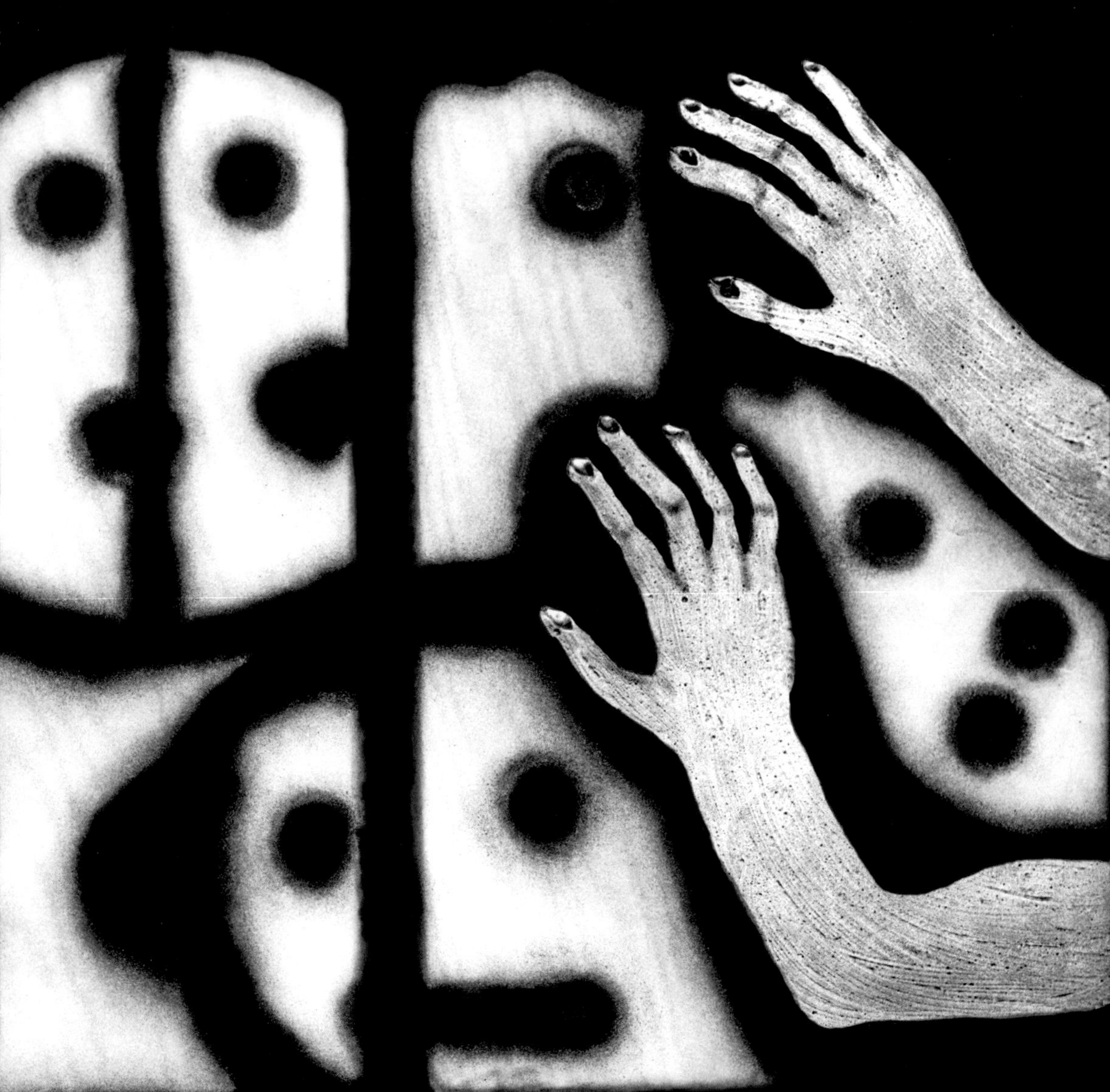

Halved, 2012

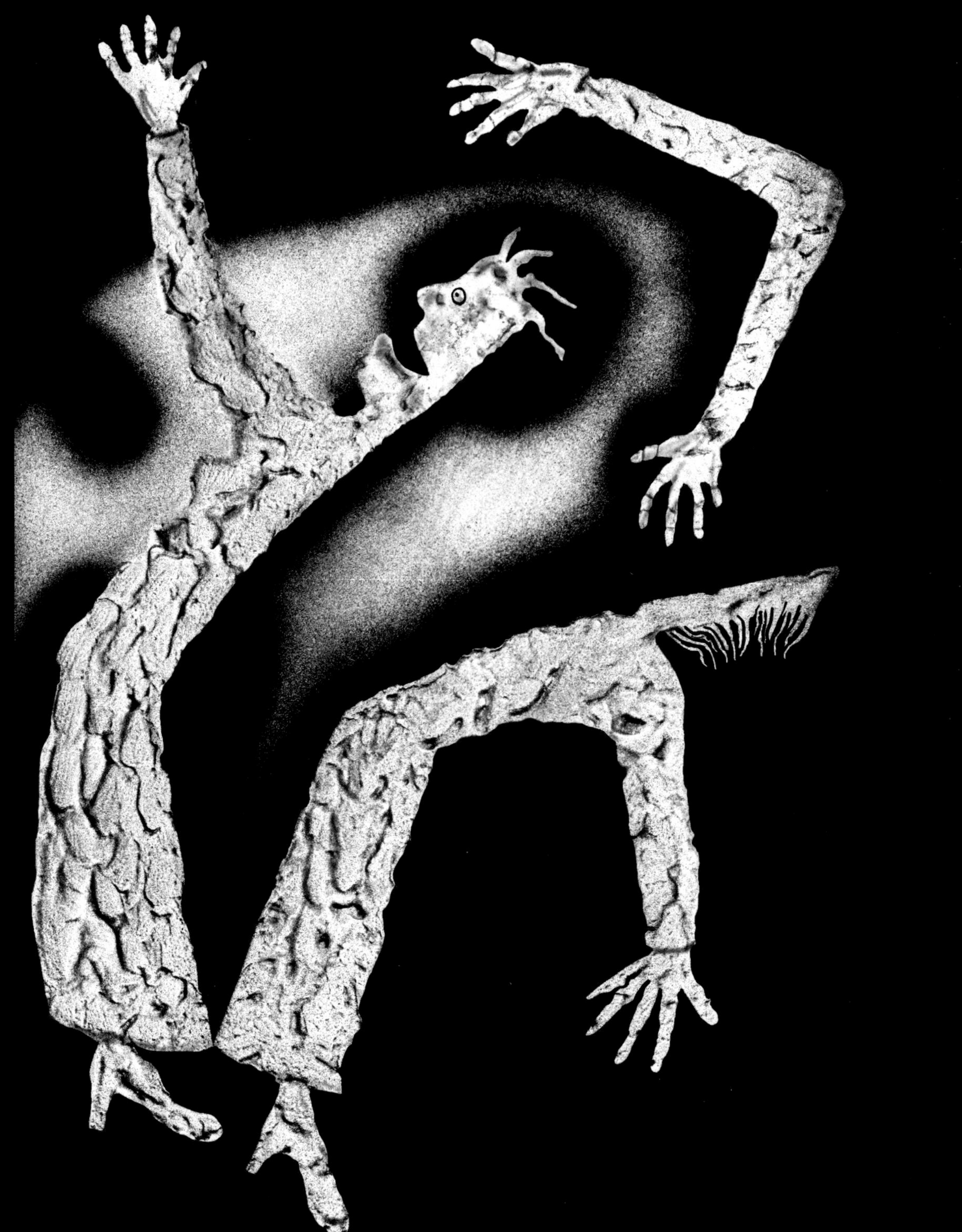

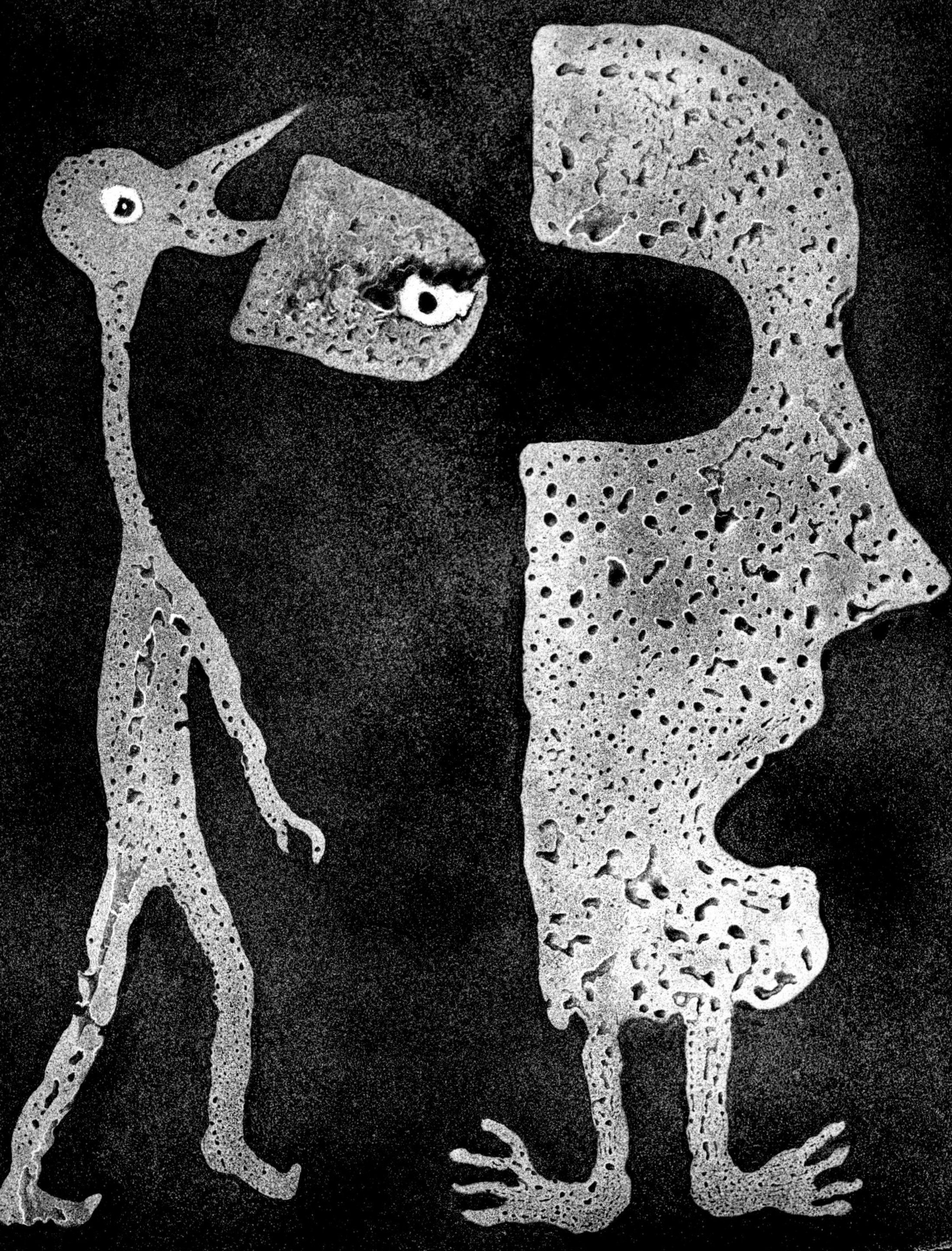

Replacement, 2010

Face Off, 2010

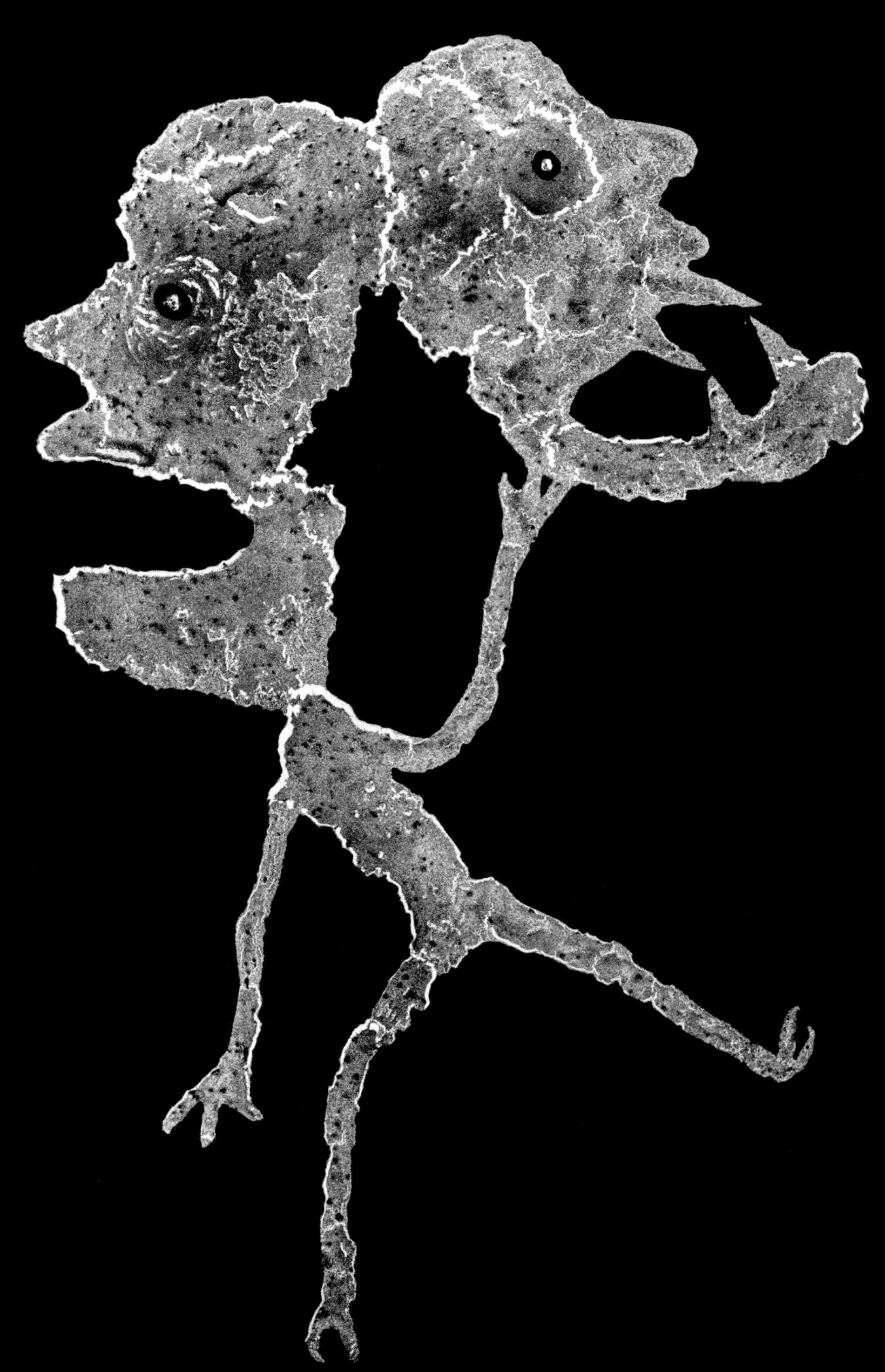

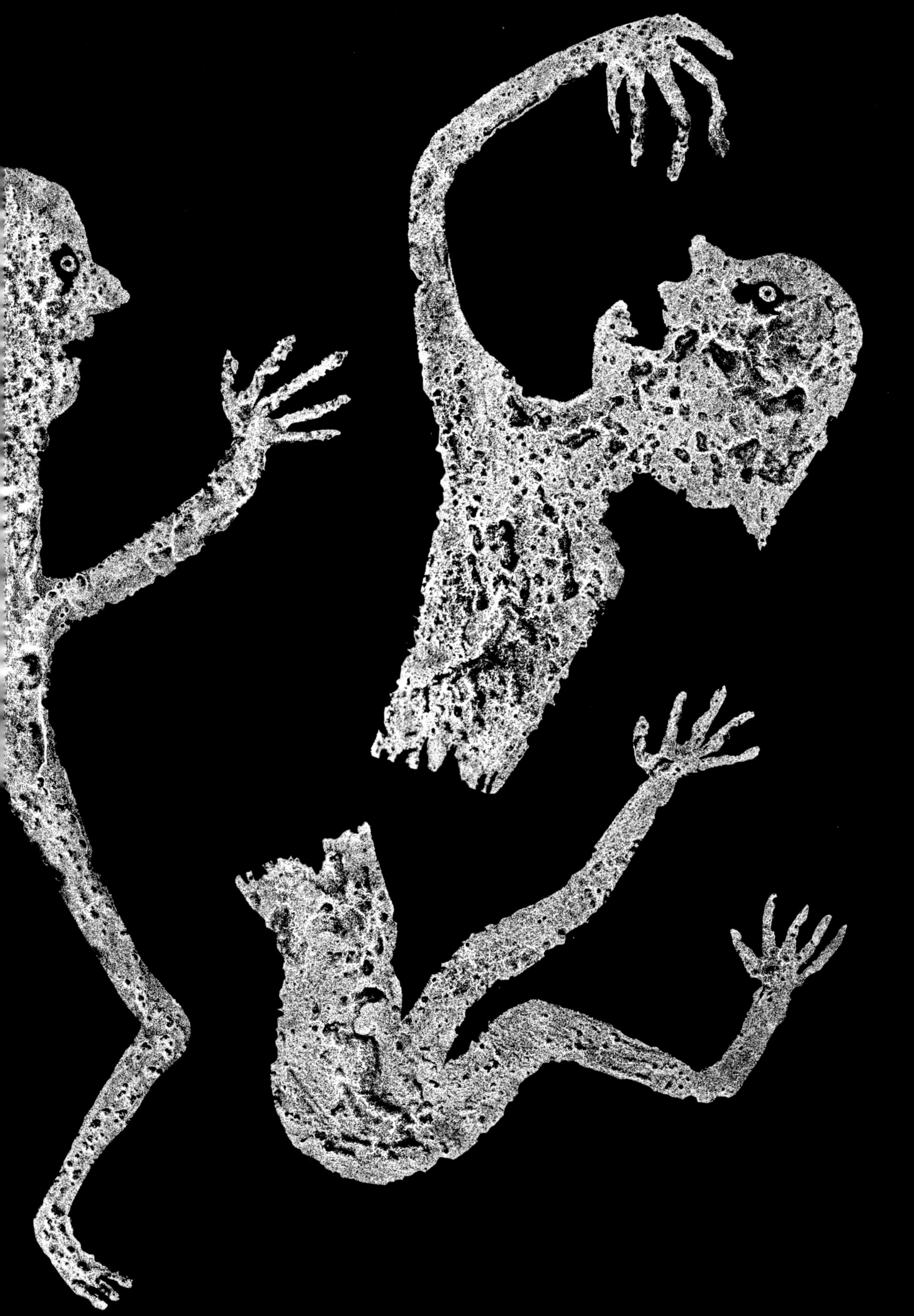

Startled, 2010

ACT SEVEN

ethereal

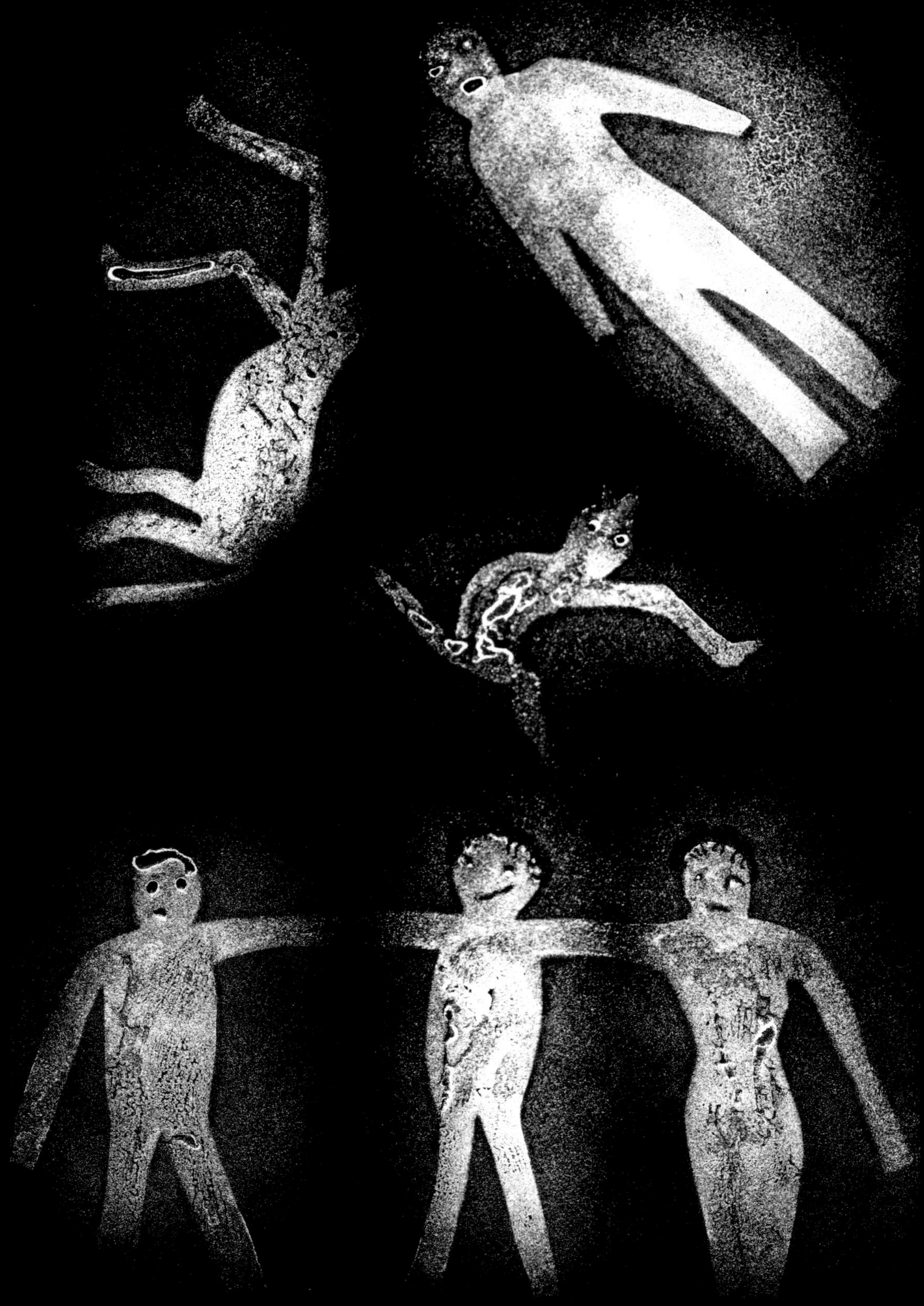

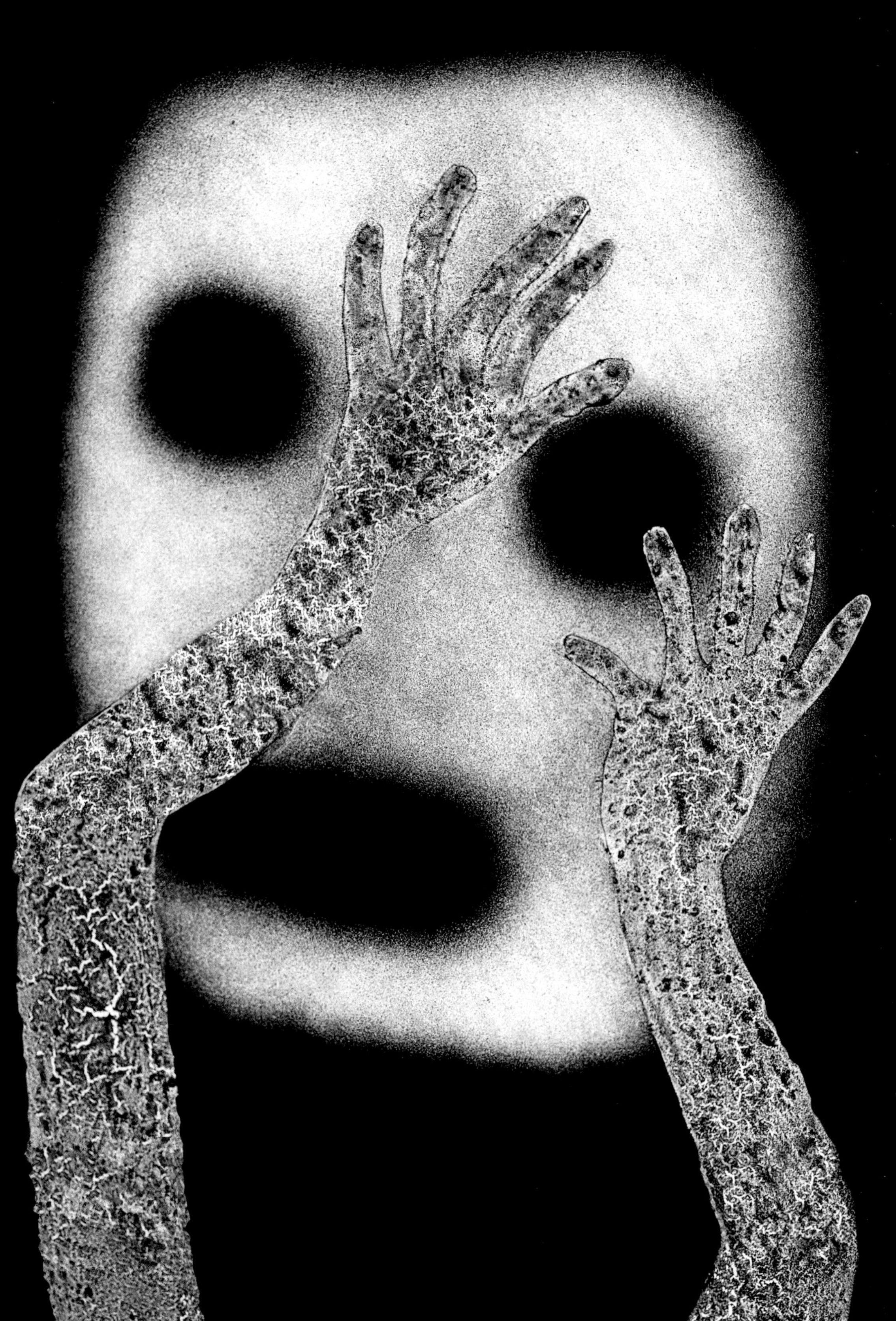

Panic, 2011

Phantom, 2011

Manifestation, 2007

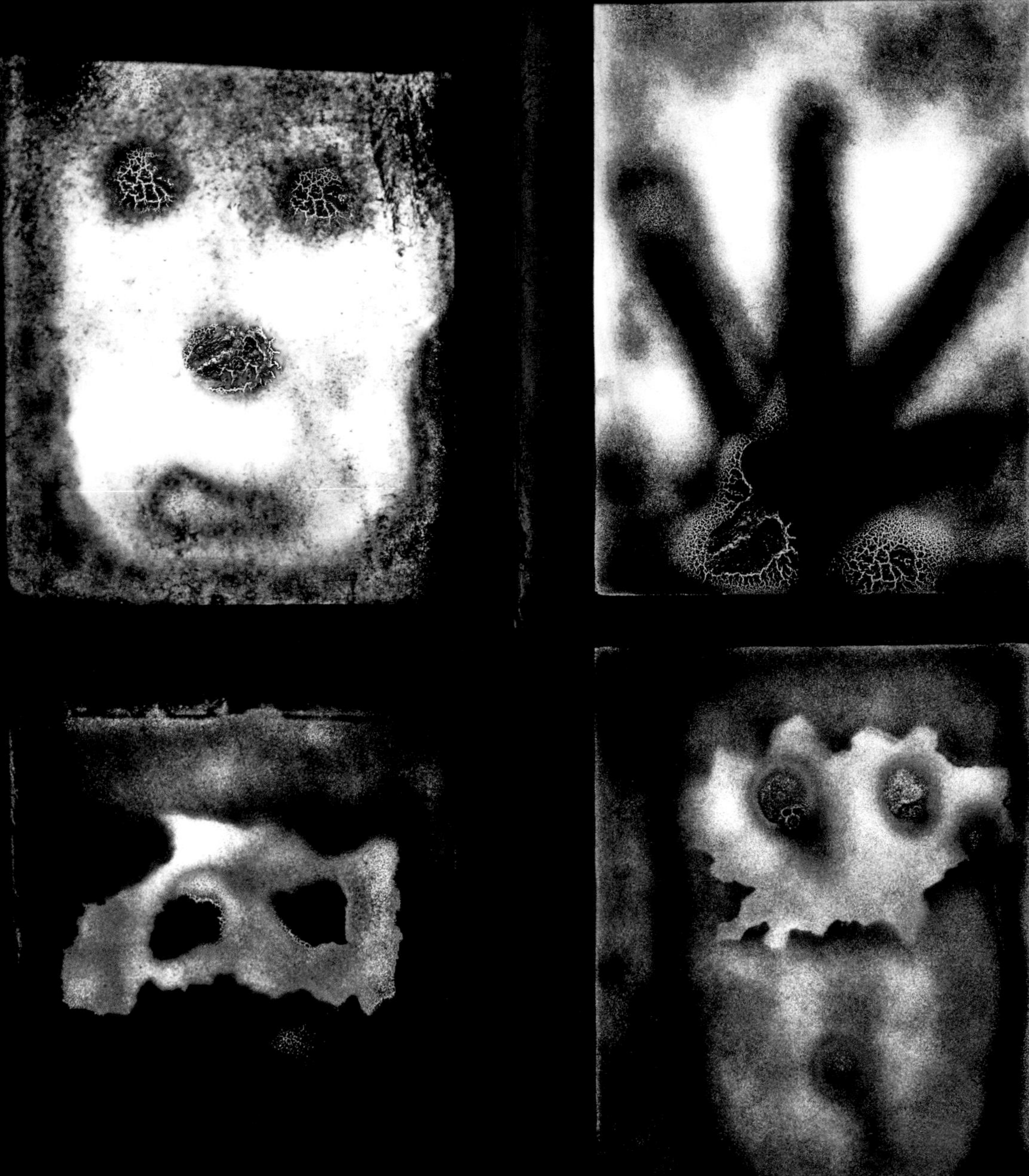

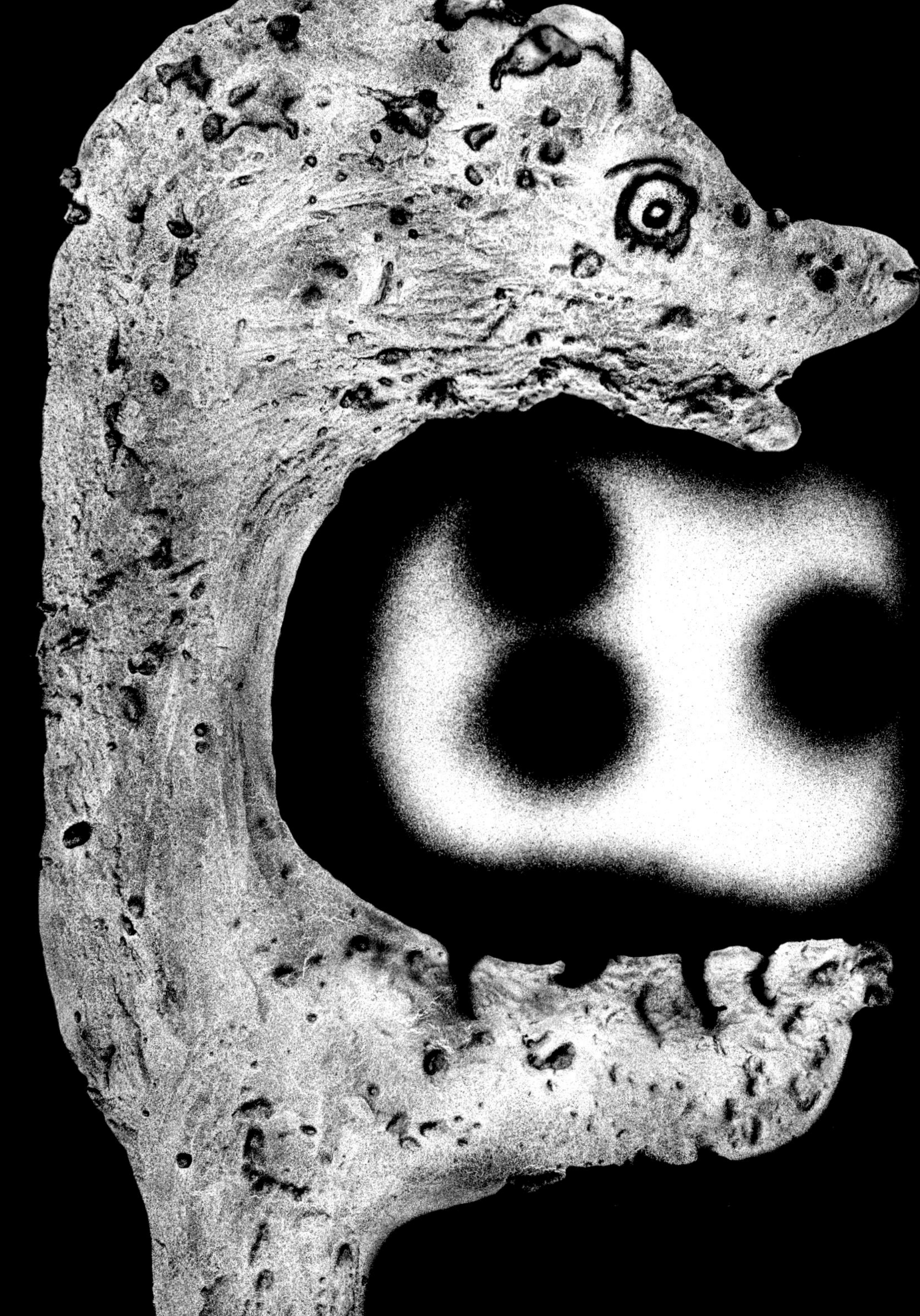

Gulp, 2011

Divided Self, 2007

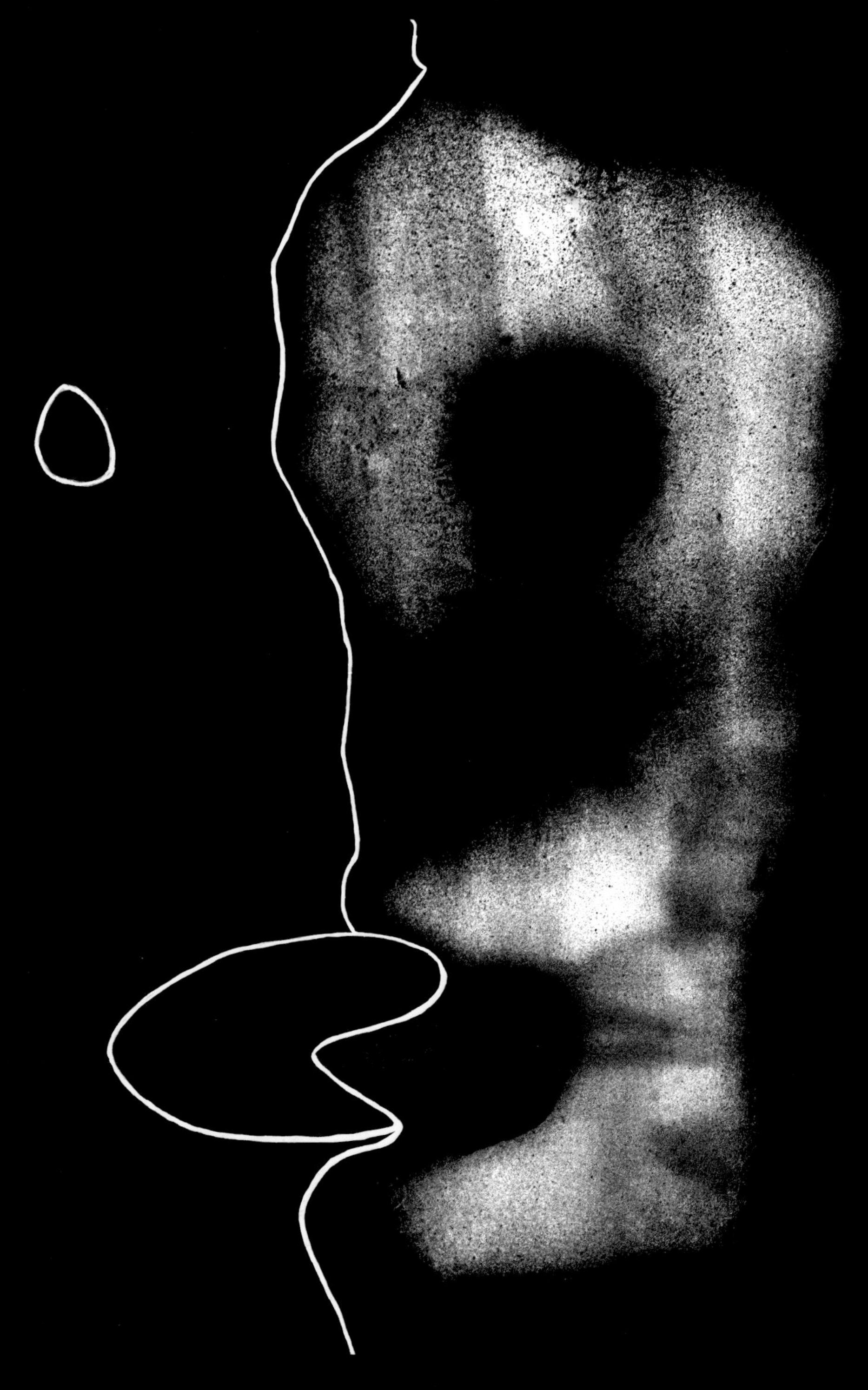

Vaporous, 2011

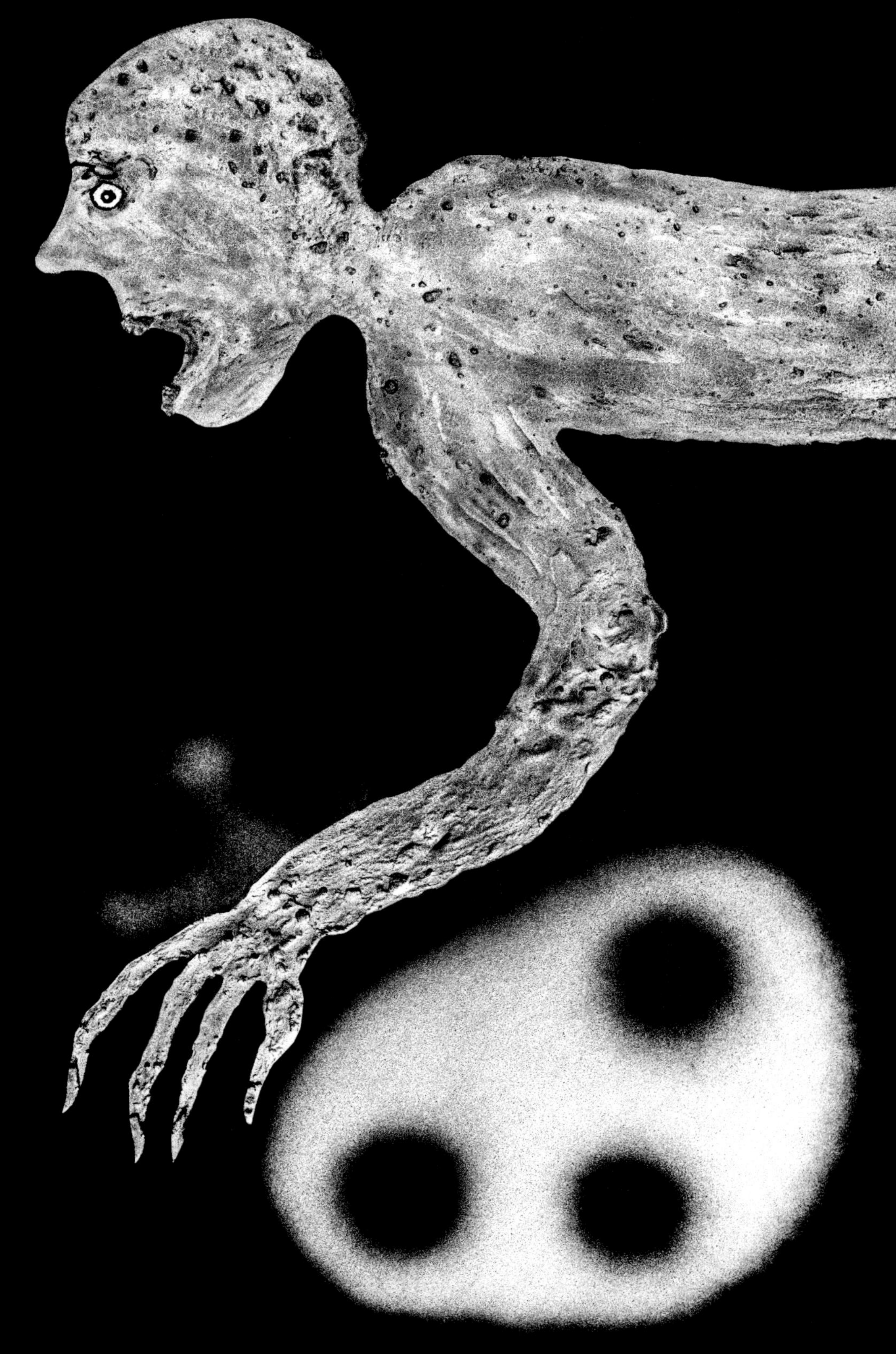

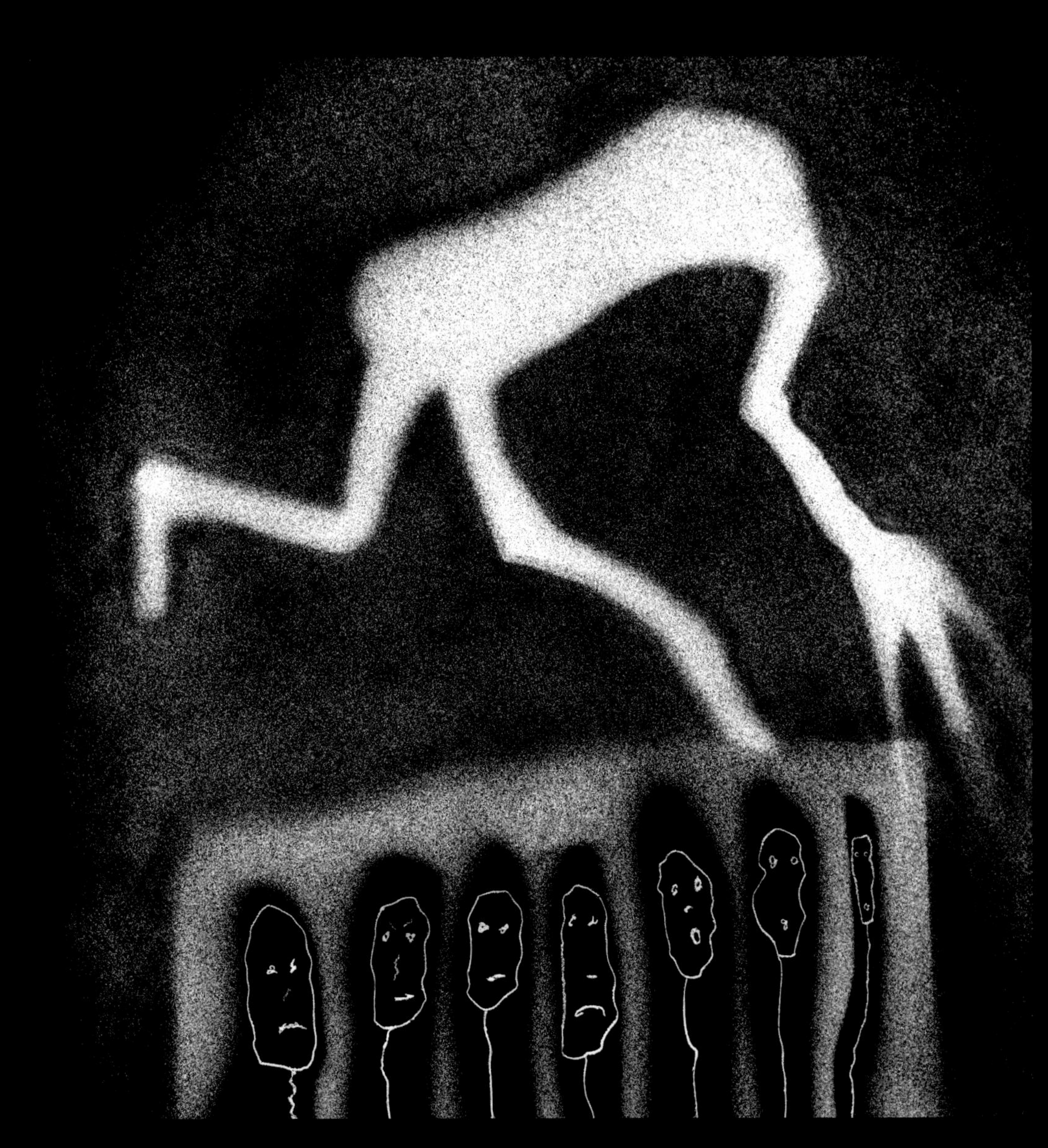

Nightwalker, 2009

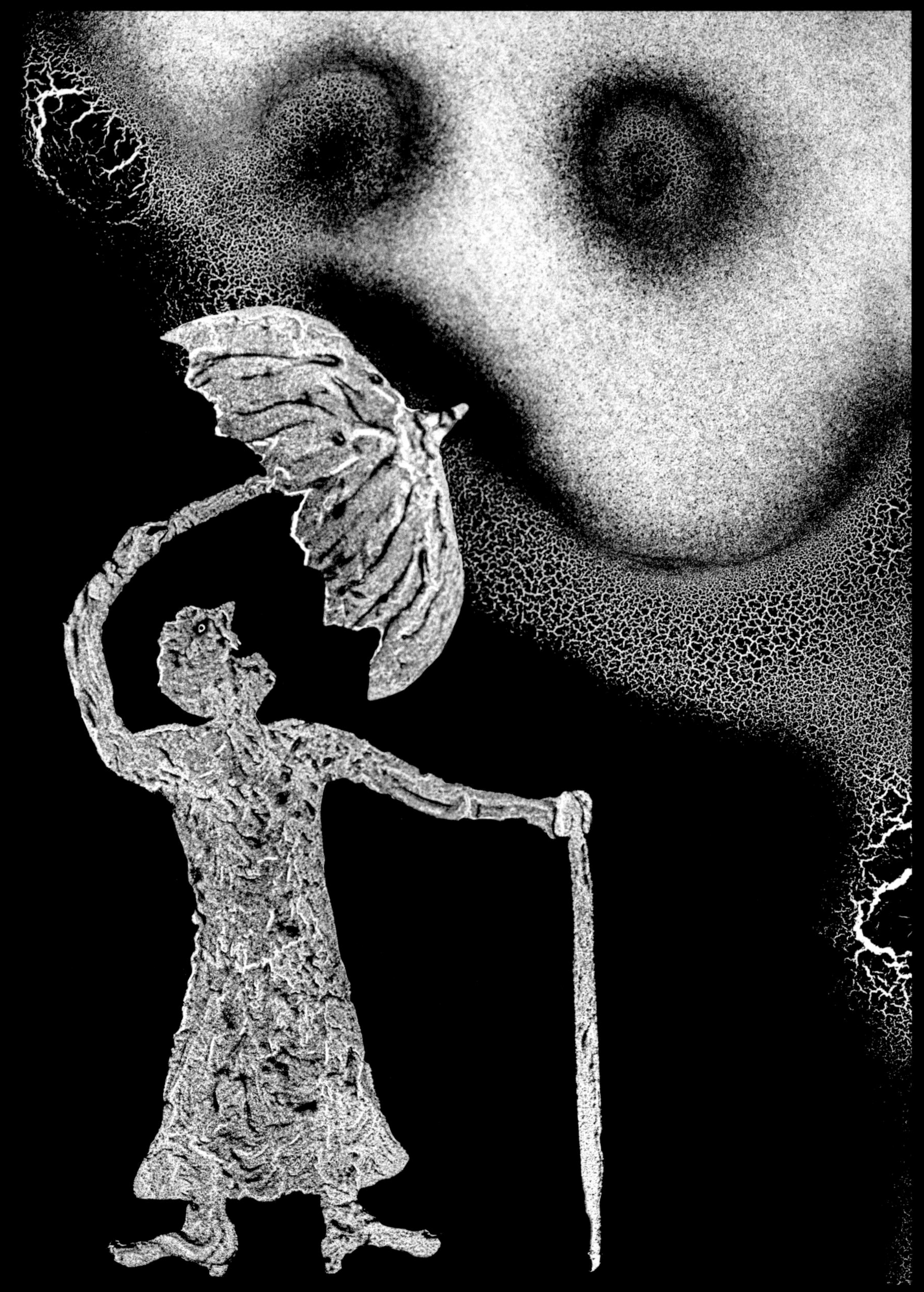

Thunderous, 2011

Muse, 2009

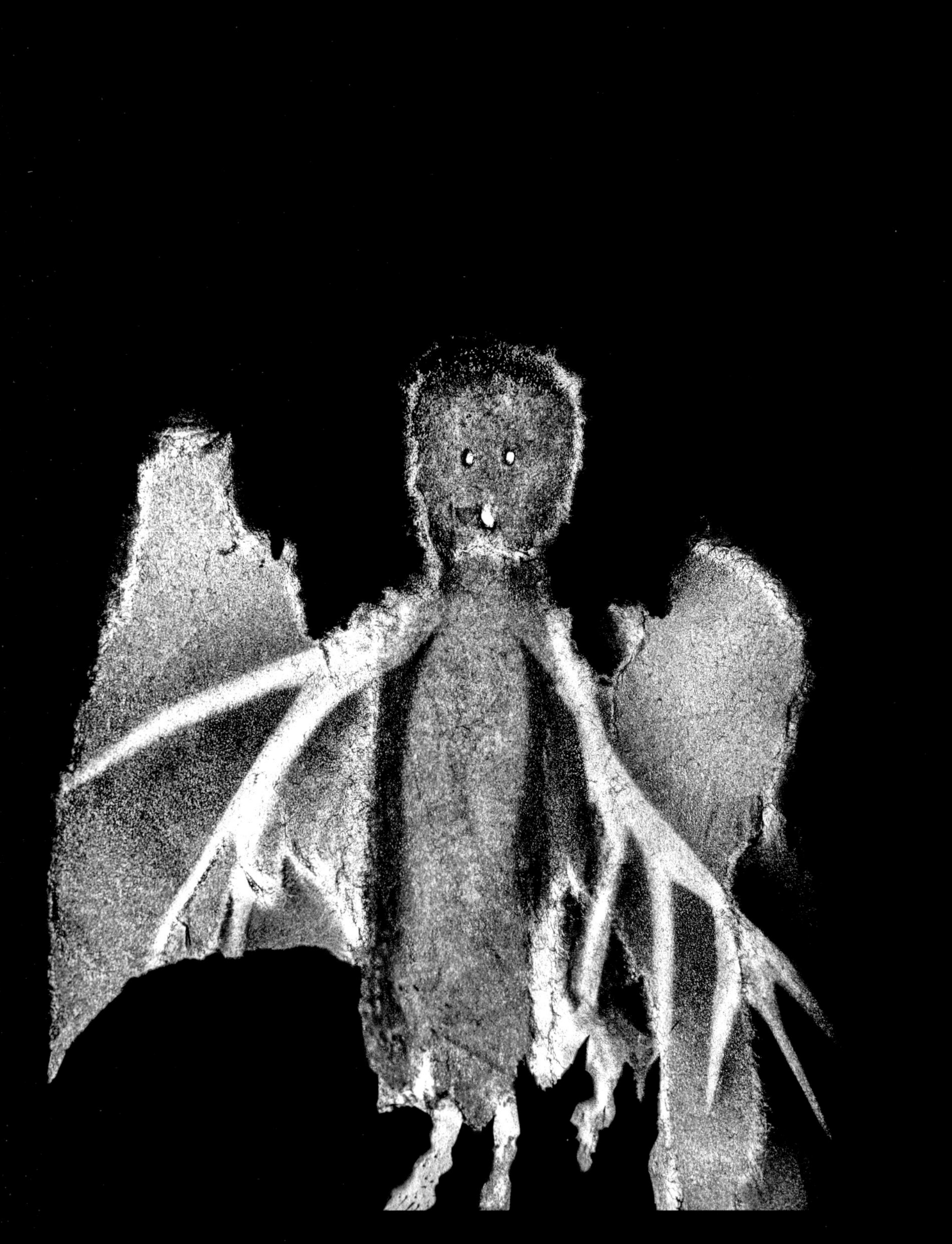

Celestial, 2009

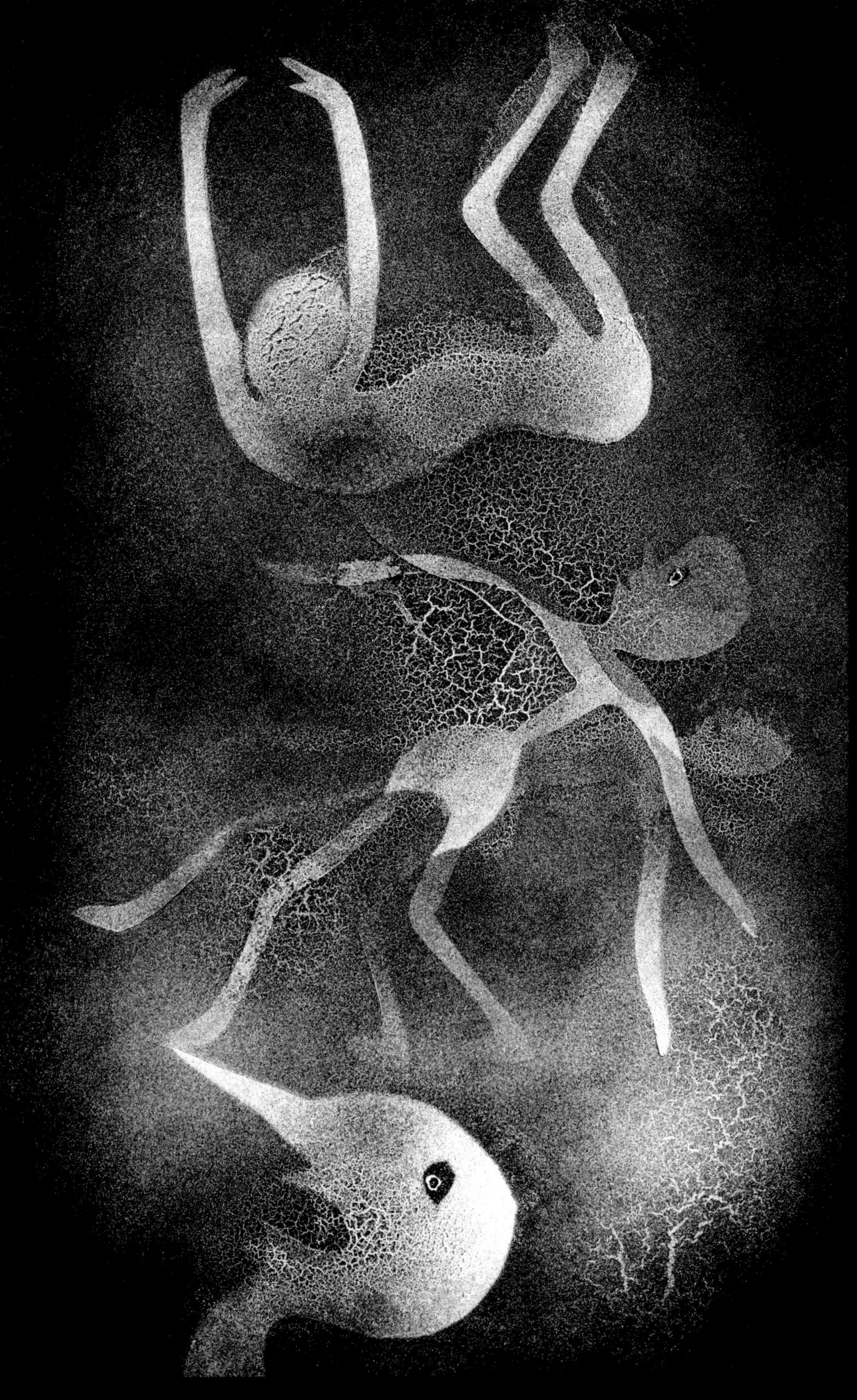

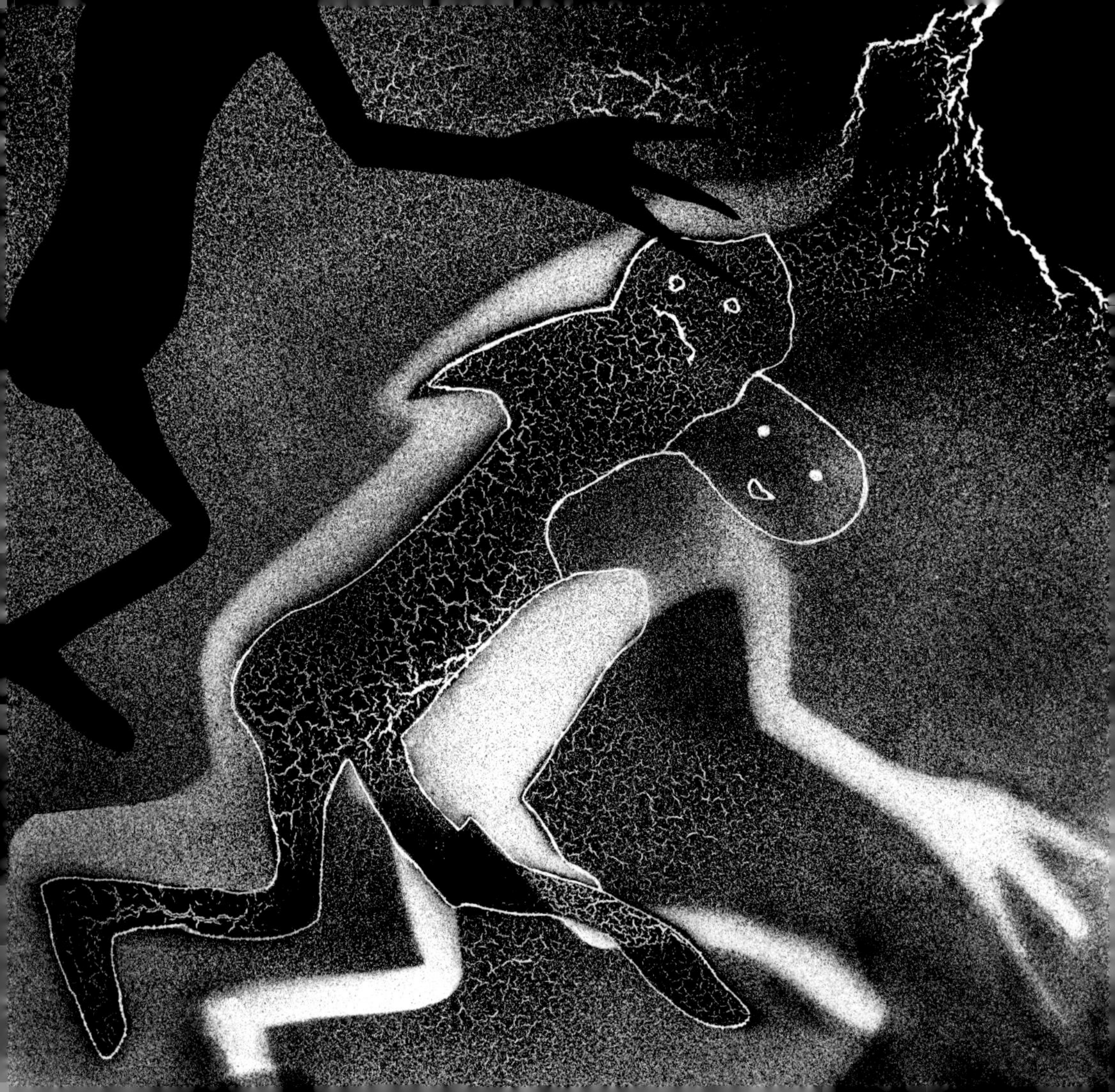

Shivering, 2010
overleaf: Cosmos, 2010

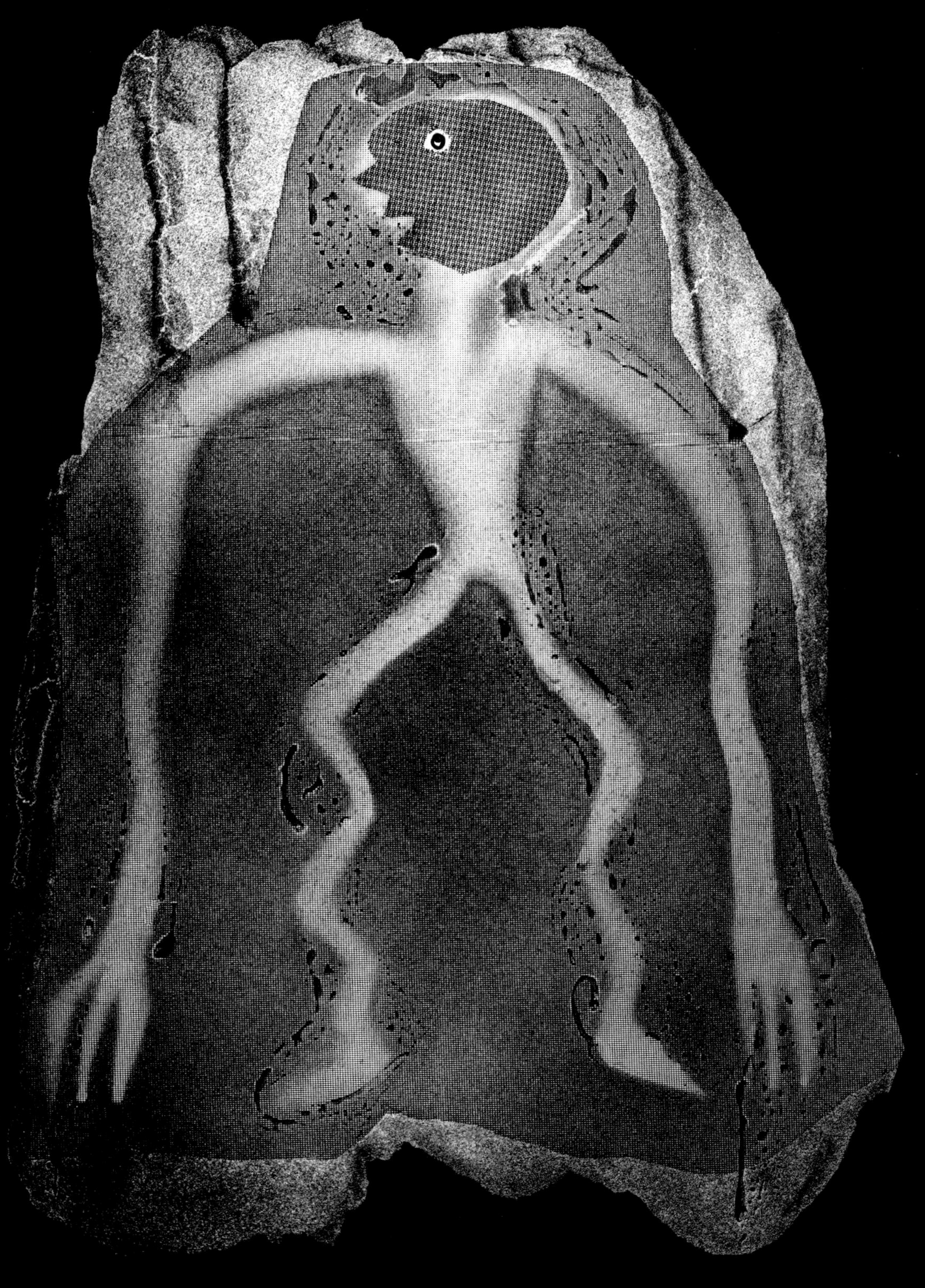

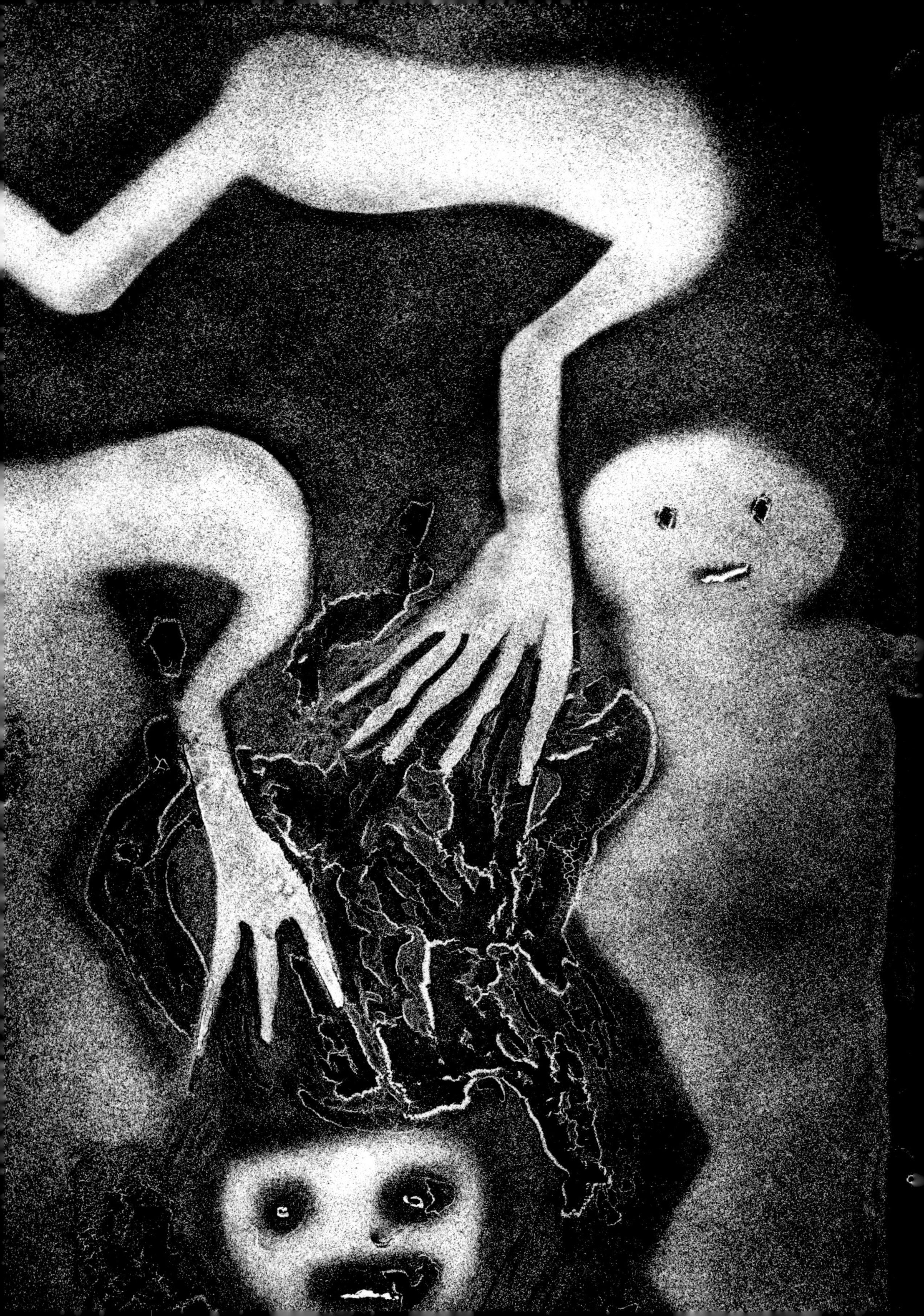

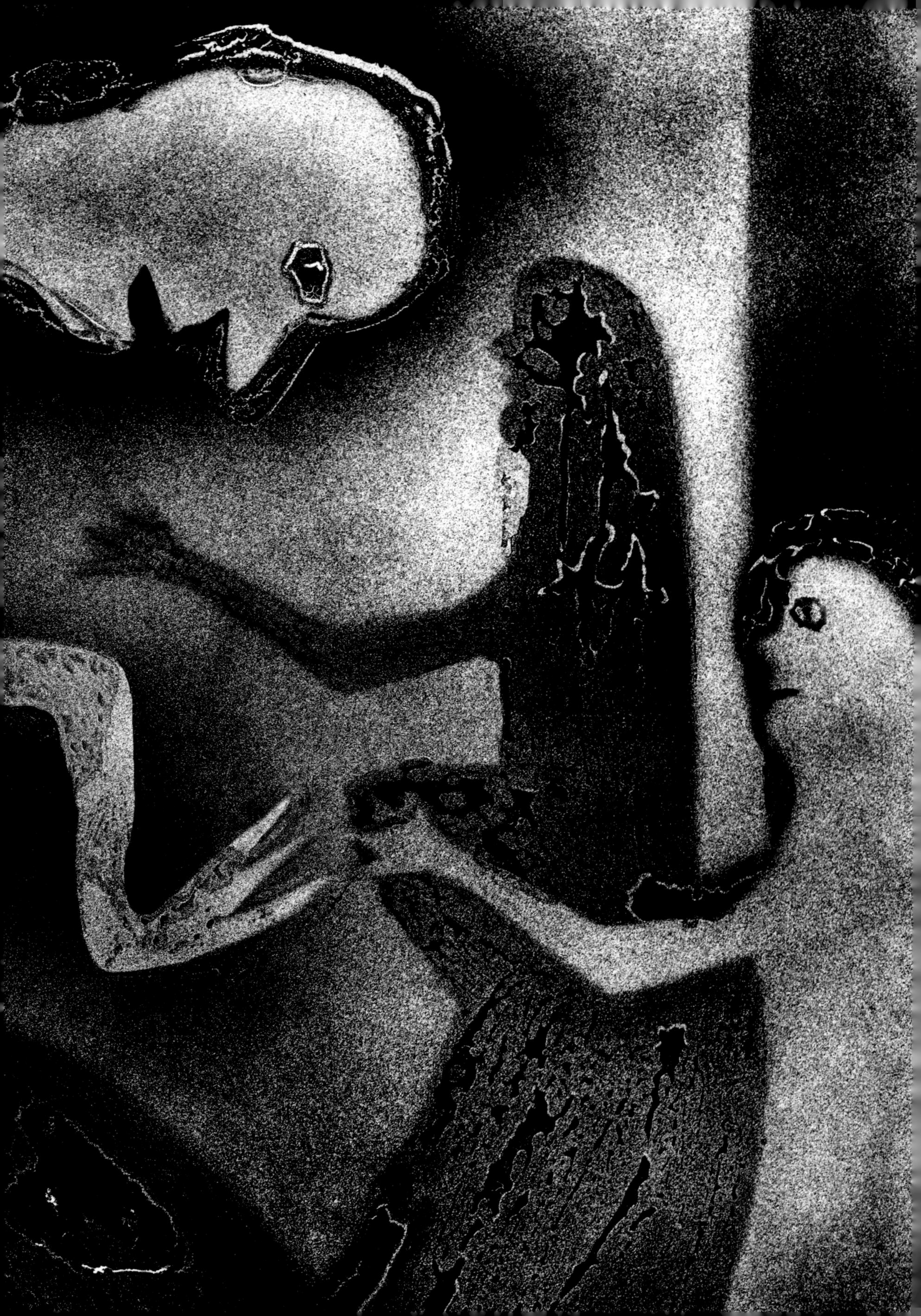

Outing, 2009

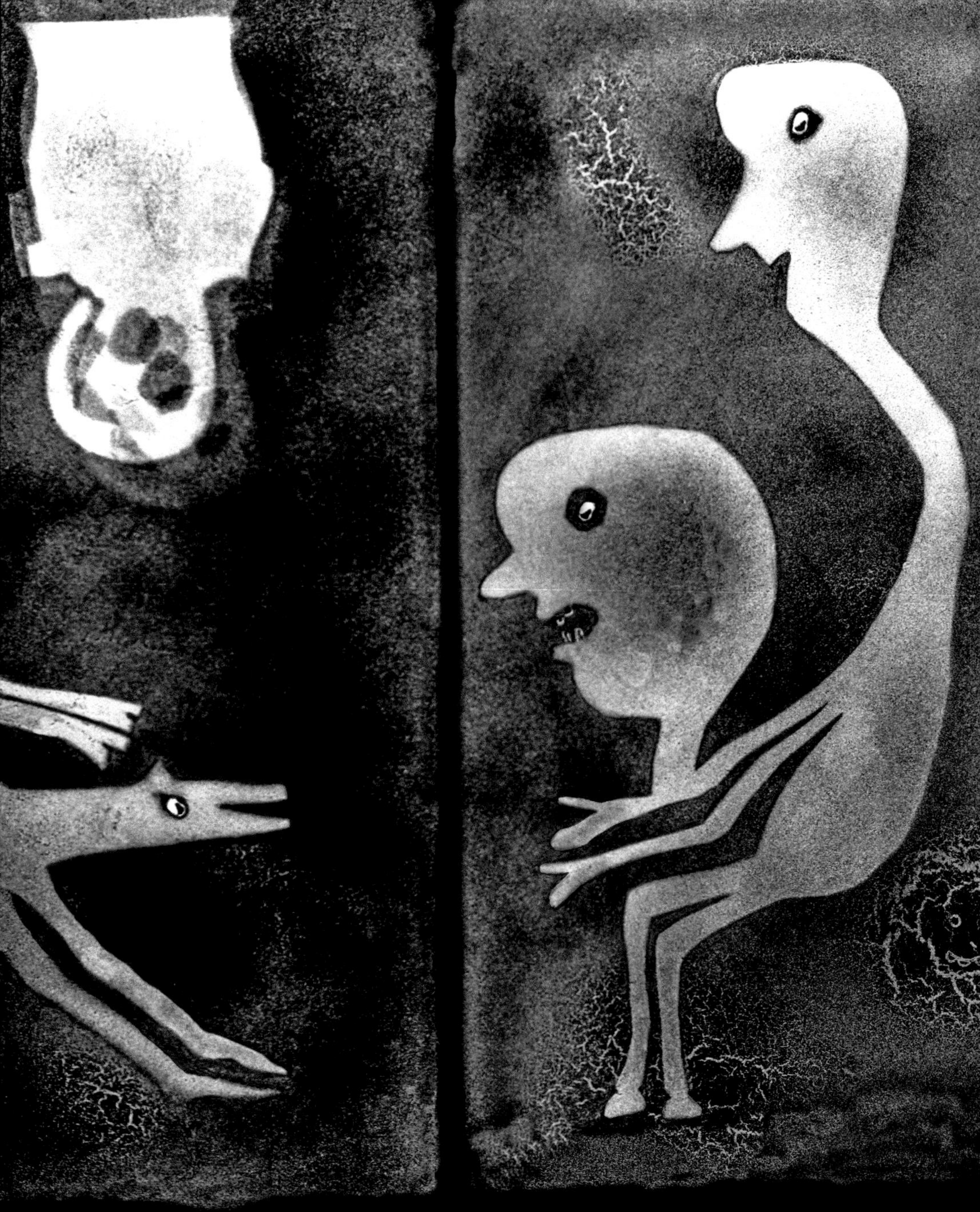

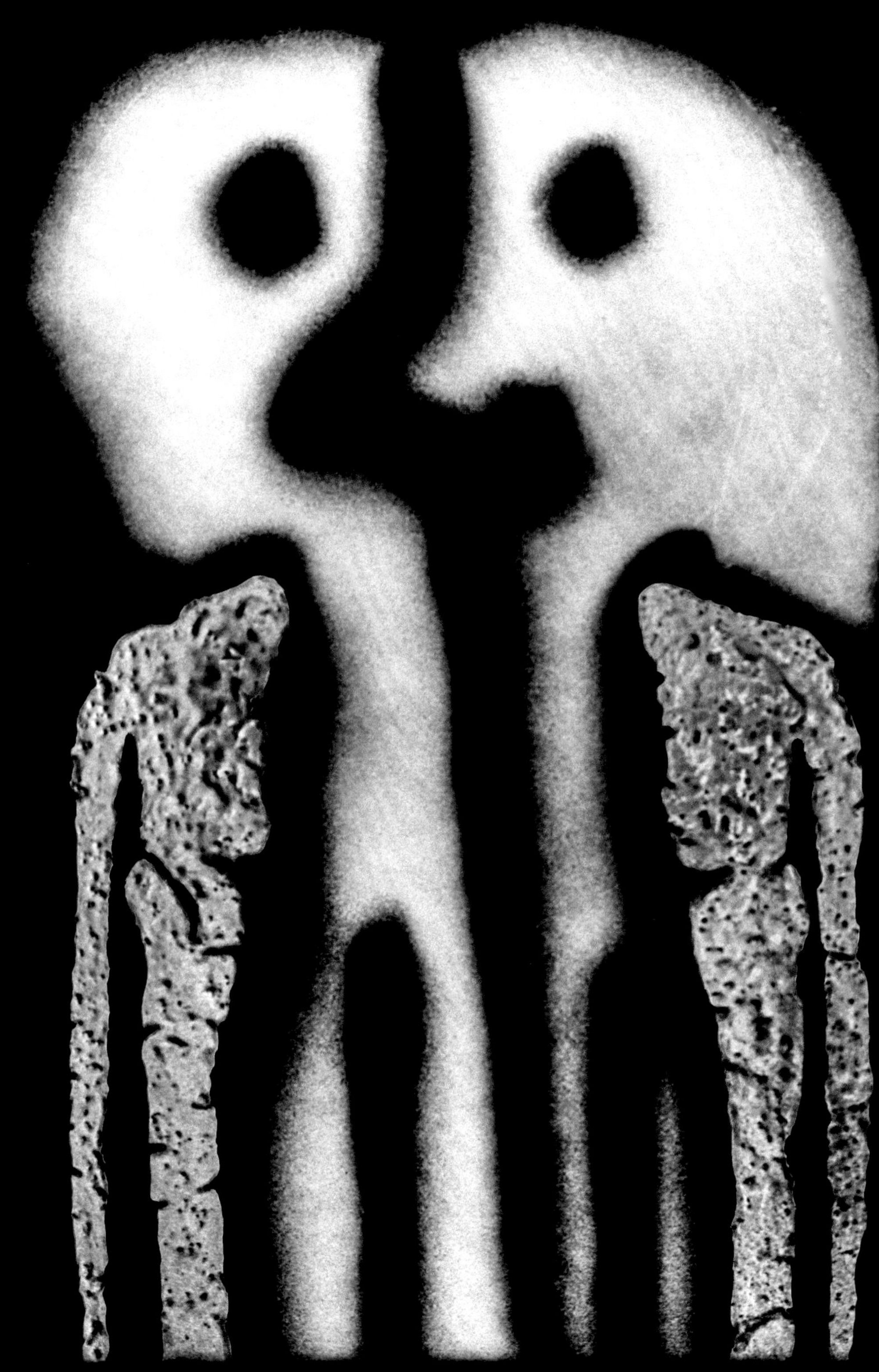

Haunted, 2013

Haunted, 2013

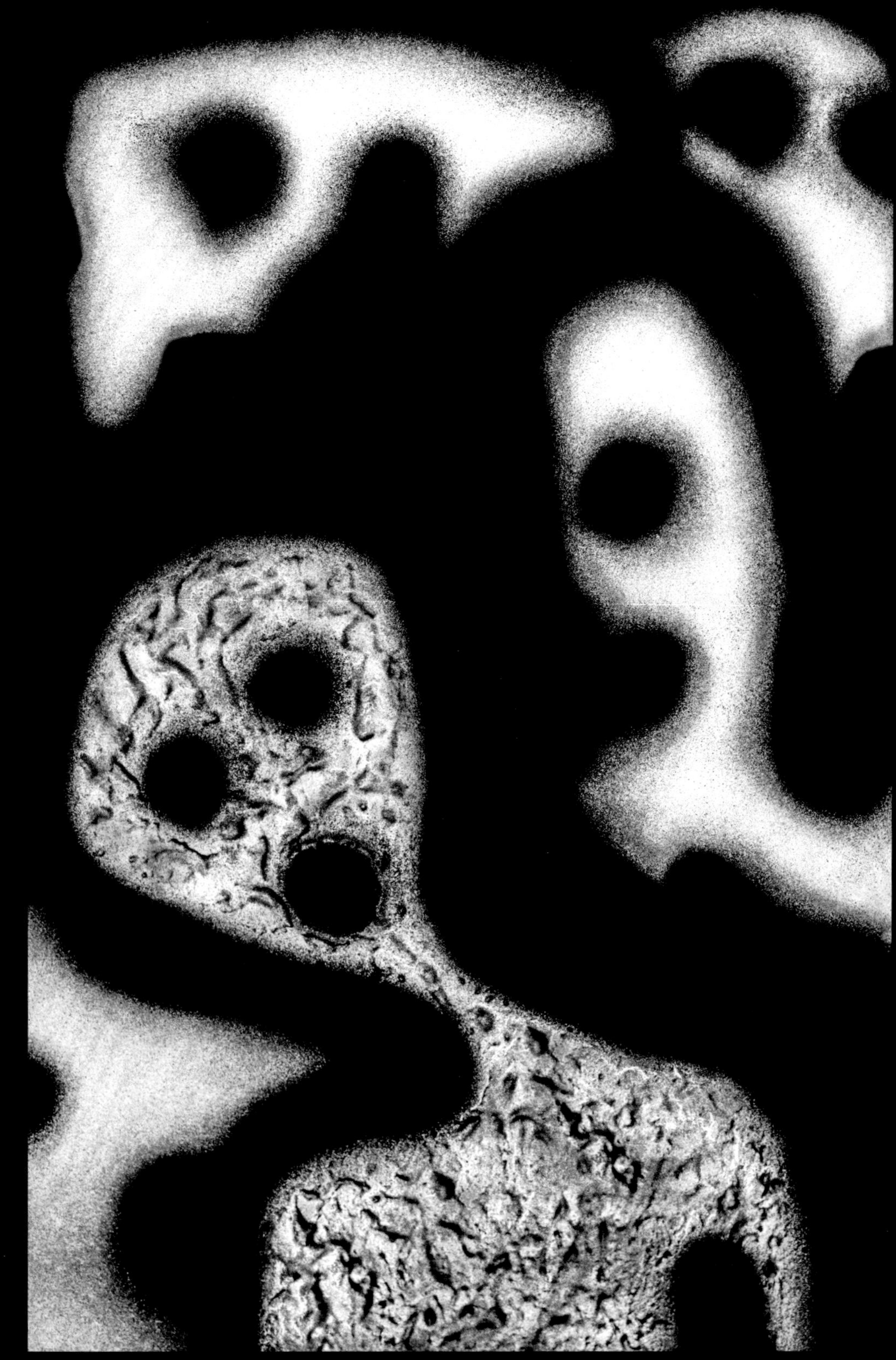

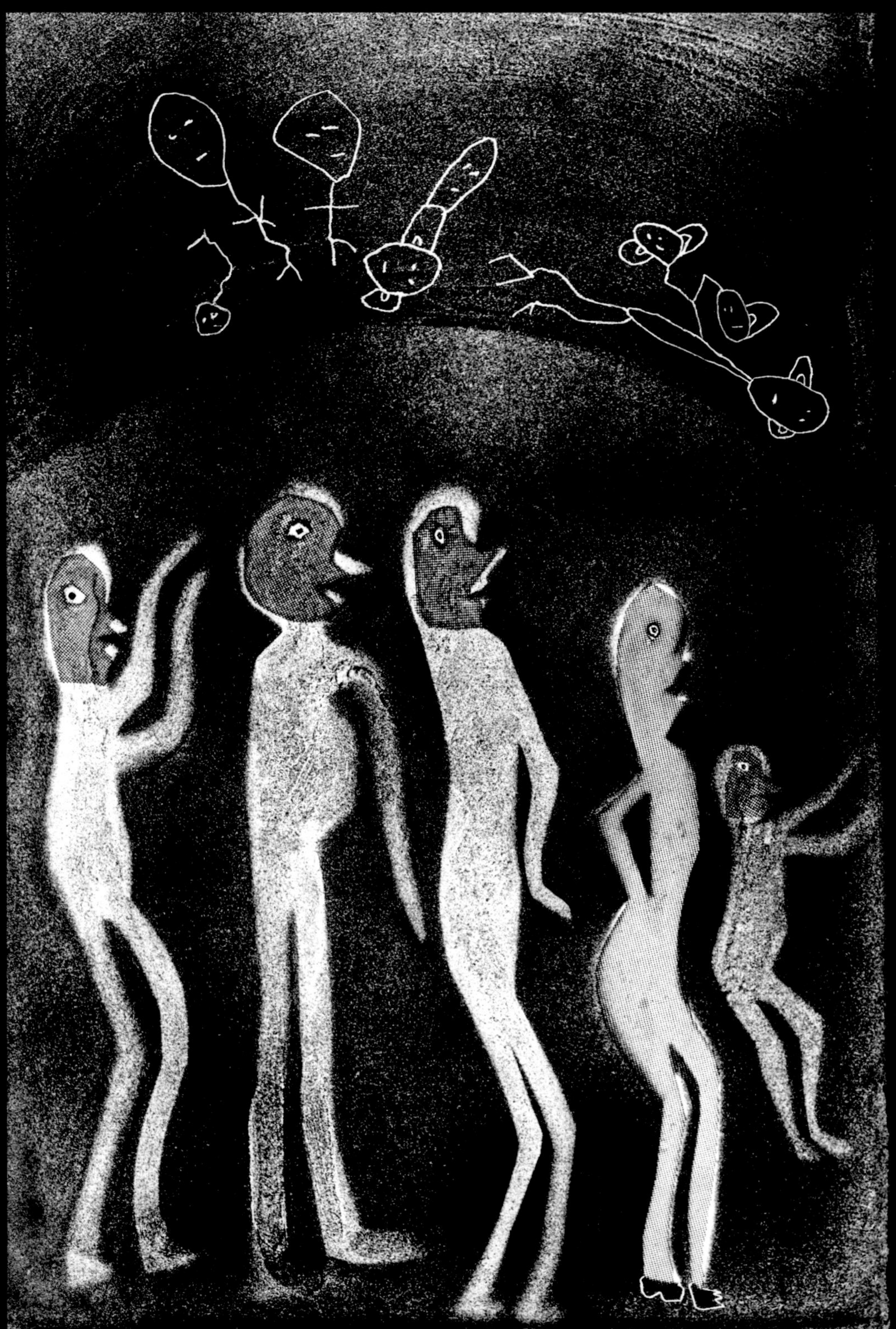

Farewell, 2010

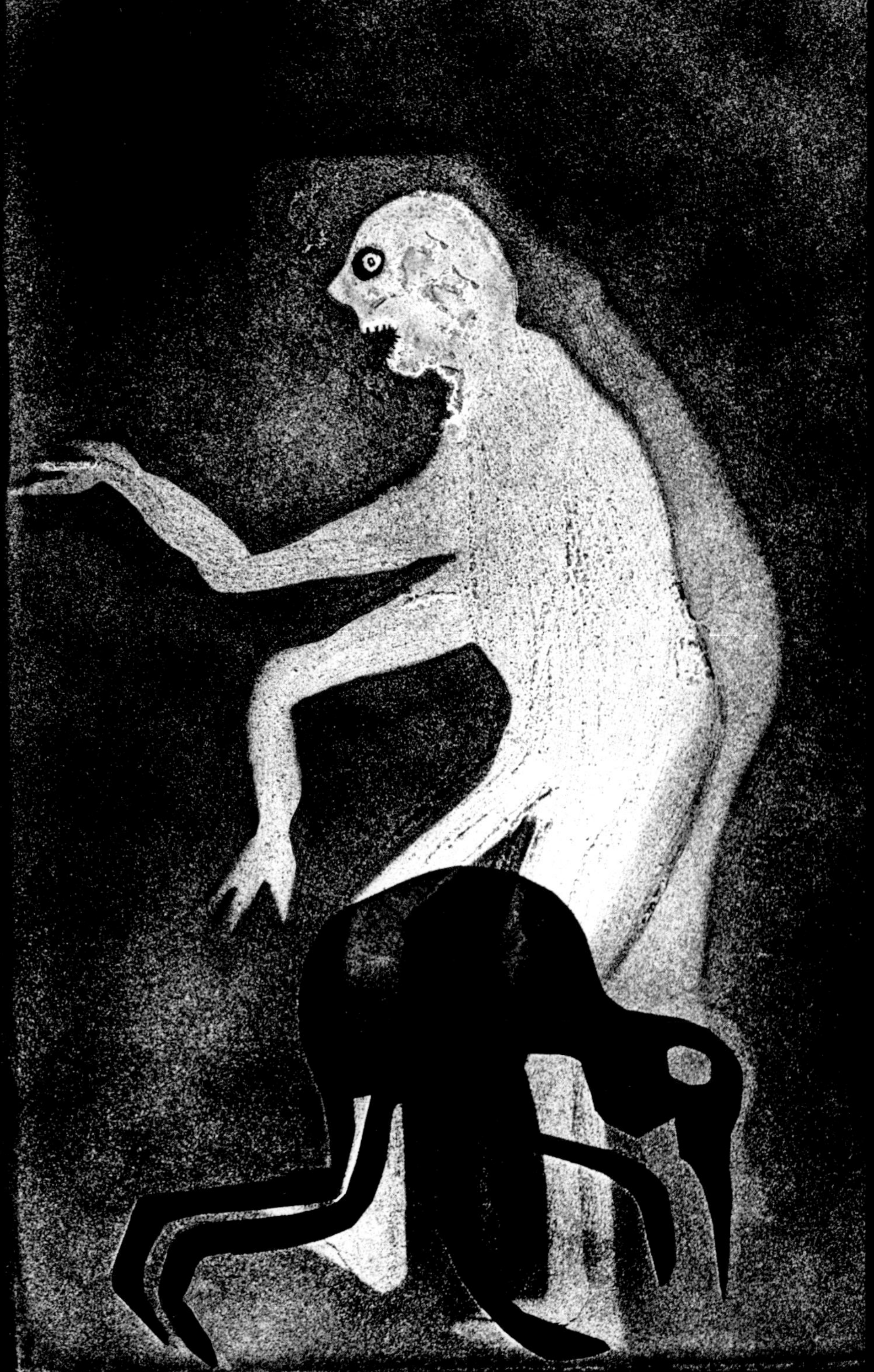

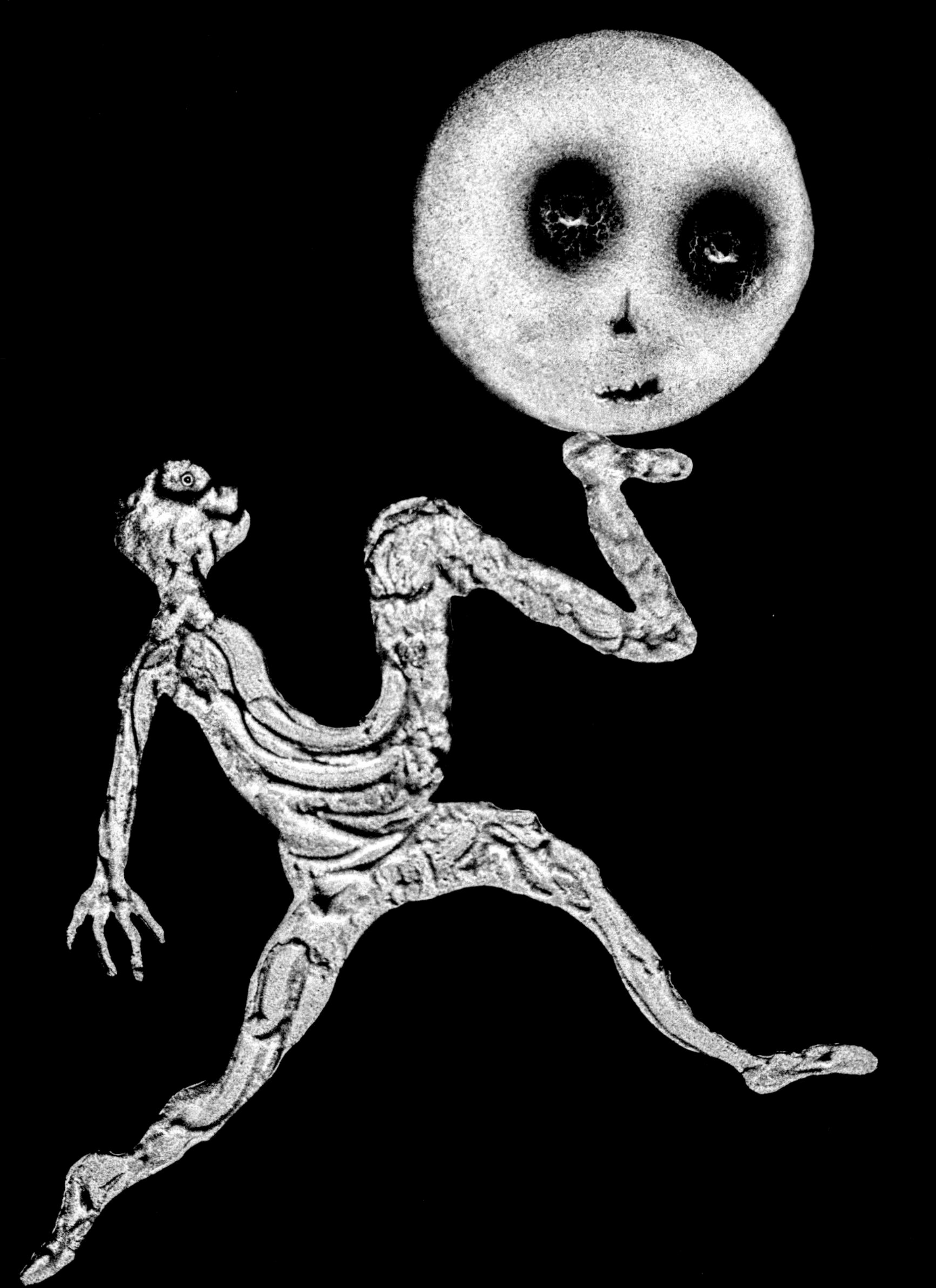

Amulet, 2011

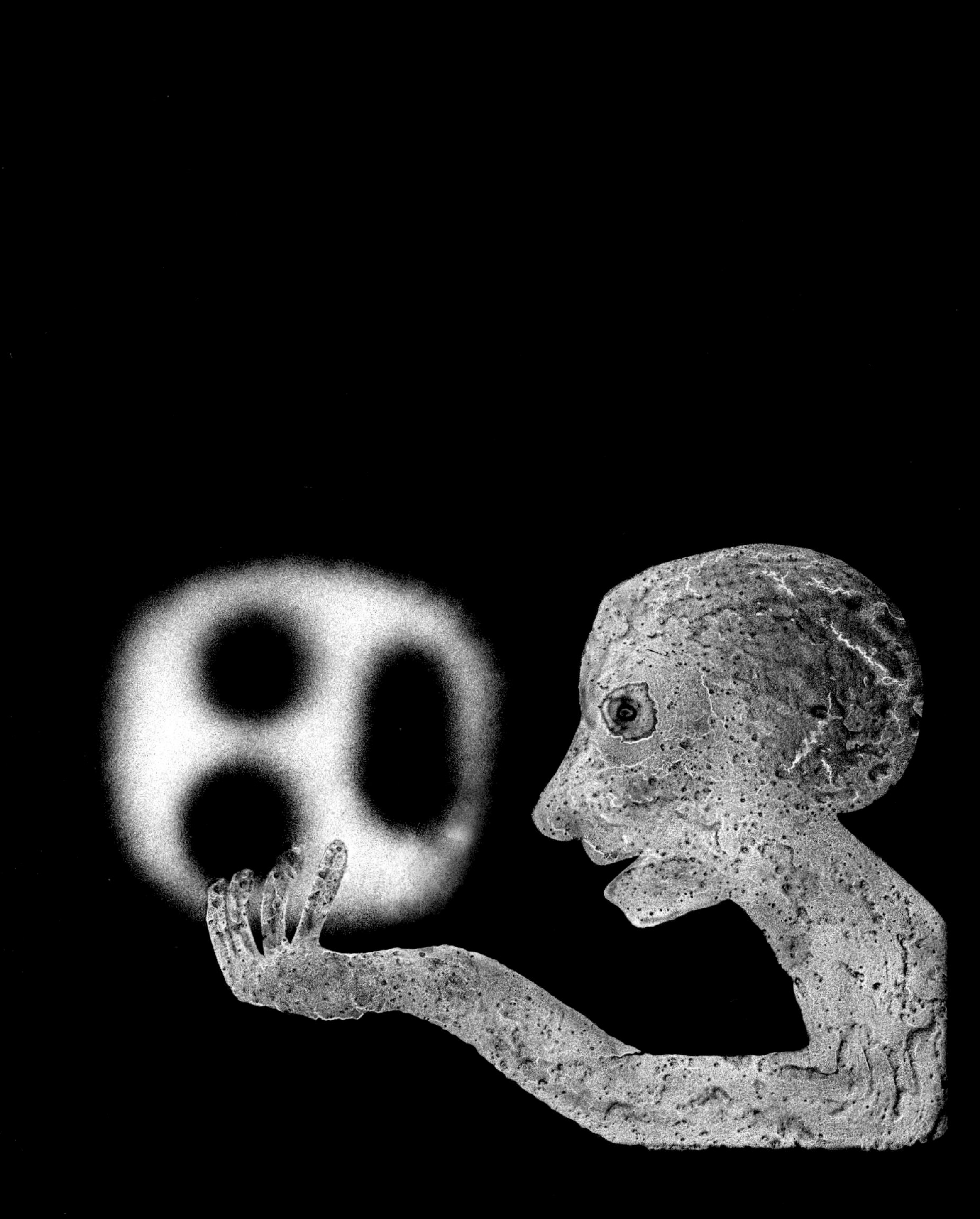

Guardians, 2011

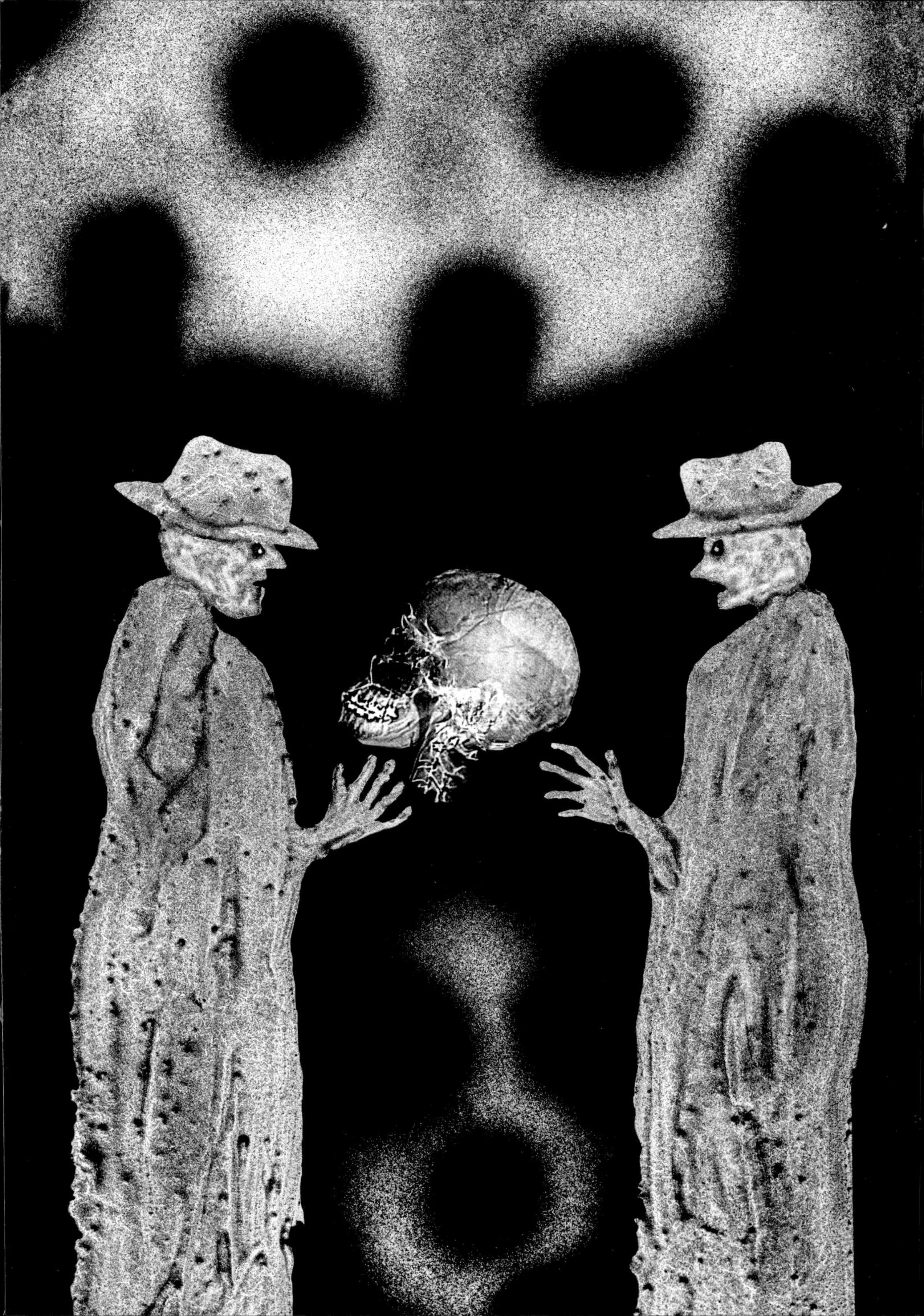

This book is dedicated to Marguerite Rossouw for her unwavering commitment to my photography. These photographs represent a unique collaboration of remarkable vision and purpose. Her psyche is ingrained in these images.

Acknowledgments

Thanks to Andrew Sanigar for his faith in my work and for his steadfast belief in the inherent value of my imagery, which led to this book being published. To Sarah Praill, whose collaboration was crucial to the aesthetic sensibility of this book. Her insightful design input was paramount. She is a true professional in every sense of the word. To Rebecca Sheppard for her valuable editing skills and attention to detail. To Ginny Liggitt, who made certain that the images in this book were reproduced aesthetically.

I am grateful to Colin Rhodes for his friendship and for his illuminating words which will lead to a greater understanding of the complex nature of this book.

Thank you to my daughter Amanda Ballen, whose brilliant mind assisted me in defining the true nature of these images.

Thanks also to Gerald Rossouw, whose scanning and printing skills are of the highest order, and to Sarie Pretorius for her administrative assistance.

My gratitude to Emma Calder and Ged Haney for their creative vision in translating the still image into the moving one.

Thank you to my family – Lynda, Paul and Amanda – for their ongoing companionship and support.

Lastly, I would like to acknowledge those indefinable cosmic forces that have always pervaded my being.

page 2: ROGER BALLEN, Then and Now, 2007

First published in the United Kingdom in 2016
by Thames & Hudson Ltd, 181A High Holborn, London WC1V 7QX

The Theatre of Apparitions © 2016 Roger Ballen

Photographs, captions and preface © 2016 Roger Ballen
Introduction © 2016 Colin Rhodes

British Library Cataloguing-in-Publication Data

A catalogue record for this book is available from the British Library

ISBN 978-0-500-54464-8

Printed and bound in China by Artron

To find out about all our publications, please visit
www.thamesandhudson.com.
There you can subscribe to our e-newsletter, browse or download
our current catalogue, and buy any titles that are in print.